M000206854

Praying the Psalms

A G-Man's Journey
Down the Psalter Trail

One Hundred and Seventy-One Individual Devotions and
Personal Prayers Based on the Book of Psalms

Praying the Psalms: A G-Man's Journey Down the Psalter Trail
Copyright © 2017 Robert A. Blecksmith. All rights reserved
ISBN: 978-0-9997337-0-7 (Kindle)
ISBN: 978-0-9997337-1-4 (Paperback)
ISBN: 978-0-9997337-2-1 (Hardback)
Cover Photo and Design by author
Formatting by Polgarus Studio

Scripture quotations marked "(NASB)" are taken from the New American Standard Bible˚, Copyright © 1960, 1962, 1963, 1968, 1971, 1972, 1973, 1975, 1977, 1995 by The Lockman Foundation. Used by permission. www.Lockman.org

Scripture quotations marked "(ESV)" are from The ESV˚ Bible (The Holy Bible, English Standard Version˚), copyright © 2001 by Crossway, a publishing ministry of Good News Publishers. Used by permission. All rights reserved.

Scripture quotations marked "(CSB)" are taken from the Christian Standard Bible˚, Copyright © 2017 by Holman Bible Publishers. Used by permission. Christian Standard Bible˚ and CSB˚ are federally registered trademarks of Holman Bible Publishers.

Scripture marked "(NKJV)" are taken from the New King James Version˚. Copyright © 1982 by Thomas Nelson. Used by permission. All rights reserved.

Scripture quotations marked "(NLT)" are taken from the Holy Bible, New Living Translation, copyright ©1996, 2004, 2007, 2013, 2015 by Tyndale House Foundation. Used by permission of Tyndale House Publishers, Inc., Carol Stream, Illinois 60188. All rights reserved.

To my parents,
who raised me in a home that taught me the importance of
God's Holy Word and how to value it.

To my high school English teacher, Bill Krapfel,
who through patient perseverance provided perspective on the power of God's
Word and proper practice of the English language (and above all, the alluring
amusement of alliteration).

To my first FBI Supervisor, Joe Hersley,
who demonstrated the importance of striving for excellence in all your work,
and proved it was possible to be an exceptional boss, an ideal leader,
an outstanding teacher, and the consummate G-Man, all at the same time.

Church history has seen several saints named Teresa and most recently a rather
famous "Mother Teresa." But for me, my wife Teresa is both a saint and the
epitome of what every mother should be. This book is dedicated with love and
appreciation to her for the love she daily demonstrates to our LORD, to me, our
four daughters, sons-in-laws, our grandchildren, and the casual stranger she
meets along the way.

Introduction:

There was a time, not too long ago, if you used the phrase "G-Man" everyone knew exactly what you meant. It originally was an abbreviated term for "government man" but by the mid-1930s everyone understood it to be slang for a Special Agent of the Federal Bureau of Investigation (FBI). The origin of that moniker may have been lost in the pages of history, but legend suggests it was pushed into the spotlight in 1933 when the notorious gangster George "Machine Gun" Kelley, just as he was about to be arrested by FBI Agents yelled out, "Don't shoot G-Men, don't shoot." There was even a major motion picture in 1935 starring James Cagney, entitled "G-Men." Although the use of the term has somewhat faded with time, G-Men still exist today...for nearly thirty years, I was one of them.

It is oft said, "you can't judge a book by its cover," and despite the accuracy of that saying don't we all tend to do it? But how about a book's title? How often do we use that as a measuring stick to judge a book? A title should be a preview of the book, not a summary. That can be a challenge, especially if the focus of the book seems at odds with its title. You may have done a bit of a double-take when you looked at the title (and subtitle) of this book and thought, "Huh? How do those dots connect?" Let me explain.

Each one of us is on a journey, on a path we call life. Some are just beginning their journey; others have been making the trek for many years. We all use the experience garnered from previous steps on our journey to help determine our choices for the steps that lie ahead. While we each have some say-so regarding the pace and direction of our journey, none of us have any certainty how many more steps remain. And unlike most journeys, it is not our arrival to a particular destination that determines the trip's conclusion, but rather, it is time itself. Some see life as a race against time. Others see life as a journey in time. I prefer the latter.

Our journey in time is comprised of different stages or phases. This book is a compilation of experiences from one phase of my life that are being incorporated into the transition of the next phase.

In early 2013, I retired as an Assistant Director of the Federal Bureau of Investigation. Soon after retiring, my kids said, "Hey Dad, you need to write a book about it!" As you can imagine, after 28 years as an FBI Special Agent there are many stories I could tell, but the truth is, some of the stories… most of the best stories can never be told…at least not written in a book destined for public consumption. Every individual FBI employee (Special Agent, analyst, professional staff) contributes an important role to form the greatest law enforcement/intelligence organization in the world. From 1985 to 2013, I had the privilege to play a small part by being a member of that team.

Some of those roles and responsibilities included: being a sniper on an FBI SWAT team; arresting white supremacists; being the senior FBI representative at the Pentagon on 9/11; providing "two-a-day" briefings to the FBI Director; overseeing the development and establishment of the nation's domestic response teams to a Weapon of Mass Destruction; and for over five years, leading the FBI division that was responsible for all national tactical, aviation, surveillance and crisis response programs and assets. In all these things and more, I was honored to be a part of that team and yes, I saw a lot. Being an FBI Agent was a childhood dream and lifelong desire and for that honor, I will be forever grateful.

During those nearly three decades, I was also a Christian. While I didn't find it particularly difficult to live my faith while working in the FBI, it was a bit problematic to share it. That challenge only grew as I worked my way up the management ladder. It is similar to the situation when I was a "street agent" and there was no problem bringing in my daughters' sign-up sheets so coworkers could buy Girl Scout cookies. But once I became a Supervisory Special Agent, I could no longer sell their cookies as it would be perceived as coercion… "I better buy those cookies from the boss or else…" Sharing your faith as "a boss" also falls into that category. Certainly, there were times when I was asked about being "religious" and was able to respond in kind, but I wouldn't call it evangelism.

I have no regrets in the work I performed as an Agent. I gave 100% to the job, putting in many long hours. But those efforts came at a cost and the price was paid primarily by my family. I was quick to justify being away from home so much: "I was making the nation a safer place" or "I had no choice, this work has to be done." In hindsight, we can always see alternatives to the choices we have made. I certainly could have done a better job managing my time as an Agent with the responsibilities I had as a husband and father. I was so fortunate to have a wife, Teresa, who truly was the bedrock at home. Through the transfers that uprooted the family to new cities, to the long hours of having to "hold down the fort" by herself, she is my hero. Because of her love and patience, each of our four daughters has grown into beautiful, successful, young women, each married to outstanding young men. If you look at Proverbs 31, I'm sure you will see in the margin of your Bible a picture of my wife.

With retirement came a new phase in life and I was committed to spending more time with my family. Even though you can never "make up" for lost time, you can decide how to better use the time you live each day moving forward. Don't get me wrong, I don't think I was a horrible Dad. I just don't think I was engaged as much as I should have been. I think I'm a much better Dad now and if I may say so, I think I'm a pretty good grandfather.

Speaking of which, I love being a grandpa. I like to jokingly say I've gone from being a "G-man" to a "G-pa" (as they now call me). It is particularly nice being one at a fairly young age, having our first grandson in my 40s and having six grandchildren while still in my 50s.

Retirement also provided me an opportunity to focus more on my relationship with the Lord. From my earliest days of childhood, I regularly attended Sunday School classes where I read and memorized Bible verses. Because of that, as well as four years at a Christian high school and my first two years of college at a Christian university, I was saturated with God's Word. I have always loved the Bible but I really wanted to take it a step further. The best way to make sure scripture has an effect on your life is to make it a part of who you are.

I also wanted to improve my prayer life. Although I prayed daily, my prayers did not always consist of the deep heartfelt dialogue I longed for or that God desires. I wanted to go beyond whispered words wandering aimlessly heavenward and rather, have them become part of a more vibrant discussion with God. It was with this background and desire that I decided I would read one Psalm a day and convert each one into a personal prayer. Once I accomplished writing each prayer, I went back and created a daily devotional to correspond to each Psalm.

What follows are simple prayers and devotional thoughts I composed based on my daily readings of the Psalms over a two-year period. Many of the Psalms in our Bible are already written in the form of a prayer, while others are not. That said, by merely taking what the Psalmist wrote and personalizing it, you can make each one your own private prayer. These are mine.

While each prayer contained in this book is based on a specific Psalm, it is important to remember these are personal prayers and not scripture itself. Only God's Word is holy and wholly infallible. Nevertheless, I have done my very best to capture what I believe the Psalmist was trying to convey and retain its scriptural accuracy and integrity. I pray nothing I have written is contrary to the Holy Spirit's intent.

The process I used to compile these prayers is set forth below. I call it my "Cycle of Seven" system and you can easily use it yourself:

- ***PRAY*** – Before you begin, ask God to show you what He wants you to hear
- ***PASSAGE*** – Read it; slowly and in different translations.
- ***PONDER*** – Meditate upon it. What is God saying?
- ***PRACTICALIZE*** – What does it mean in the context of today's world?
- ***PERSONALIZE*** – How does it apply to YOU in your current life?
- ***PRESERVE*** – Write it into a journal for future reference and worship.
- ***PRAY*** – Convey those captured thoughts into a prayer, a conversation with God.

So often when we pray, it is our tendency to ask God for things, not the least of which is: "LORD, please bless me." The beauty of the Psalms is when we pray them we are actually blessing God, not just ourselves. Think about it – the LORD God Almighty, Creator of heaven and earth is blessed by something we do! And why shouldn't He be blessed? For in the Psalms, He has provided for us the perfect script of the words He most wants to hear from us. They truly are the spiritual seasoning for our souls; they are the leaven to lift up our lives.

The Psalms are often referred to as the Prayer Book of the Bible. Many of the "Giants of the Faith" have written books and commentaries specifically on the Psalms including those by Thomas Aquinas, Saint Augustine, Dietrich Bonhoeffer, John Calvin, Timothy Keller, C. S. Lewis, Martin Luther, Eugene H. Peterson, Charles H. Spurgeon, Chuck Swindoll, and N. T. Wright, just to name a few. In fact, in 1827, Charles Bridges, a 33-year-old evangelical writer in the Church of England wrote an entire book on just a single Psalm (119).

With such a host of great biblical scholars and teachers who have delved deeply into the Psalms and produced such wondrous works, what more can be said about them and certainly, what could I possibly add? What makes a retired FBI Agent qualified to write a book on the Psalms? Those are good questions. This was never intended to be a book but rather, started out only as a handwritten personal prayer journal. It was only later, at the urging of others, that I began to incorporate the experiences and observations of almost six decades of life (half of which were spent as an FBI Agent) into individual devotions to accompany each prayer. My comments are also based, in large part, on the lessons learned in sharing nearly two-thirds of my life with my wife, coupled with being the father of four daughters and a grandfather of six. It is also based on the results of the teaching, training, and tutelage (in person or podcast) by some amazing men of God. The truth is, it was not my potential ability that prompted me to write this short essay, nor my obvious limitations that stopped me from proceeding with it. Rather, it is about God's Word which continues to give abundantly to those who will read it, from one generation to the next. It has an innate capacity to overshadow any individual ability and overcome any such shortcoming.

Martin Luther may have summed it up best in his preface to the Psalms when he said, "It is therefore easy to understand why the Book of Psalms is the favorite book of all the saints. For every man on every occasion can find in it Psalms which fit his needs, which he feels to be as appropriate as if they had been set there just for his sake. In no other book can he find words to equal them, nor better words."

A Note on Psalm 119

Because Psalm 119 is so lengthy (176 verses and by far the longest chapter in the Bible), I have divided it into twenty-two individual devotions and prayers instead of a single one. They are formatted along the same lines as the twenty-two stanzas that separate the chapter into eight-verse sections. Each stanza corresponds to one letter of the Hebrew alphabet forming what is known as an acrostic. Moreover, each verse contains one of the seven different words referring to God's Word throughout (those being word, law, ordinances, commandments, statutes, decrees, and precepts).

A Note on Translation, Style, and Format

The primary translation I used for composing my prayers was the New American Standard Bible (NASB) utilizing the Spiros Zodhiates Hebrew-Greek Key-Word study format. It offers exceptional clarification in word studies even if you don't speak Hebrew or Greek. I was also fortunate to find a copy of the "Twenty-Six Translations of the Holy Bible" which provides every verse in the Bible in the King James Version with supplemental translations for additional perspective. For the composition of the devotions, I mainly used the English Standard Version (ESV) and the New King James Version (NKJV). When quoting the actual verses from the book of Psalms, I used the NASB, ESV, NKJV as well as the New Living Translation (NLT) and the Christian Standard Bible (CSB).

Throughout this book, you will notice that certain words are capitalized that normally might not otherwise be. The foremost examples of this are pronouns referring to God (e.g., You, Your). Since each Psalm is offered as a prayer, I felt it somewhat difficult at times to address the LORD directly without using "Thee" or "Thy" so at the very least a capitalization of the pronoun is merited. It is another way to remember with Whom we are in dialogue!

You will also see the word "Word" often capitalized. I do so out of respect for God's holy Word. Through the Holy Spirit, it is His inspired Word – a divine revelation and message to us on earth. It was also the Apostle John who told us that in the beginning was the Word, and the Word was with God and the Word was God. We have both the Living Word and the written Word to call upon.

Finally, if we remember that our prayer is a conversation with God, directly to Him, such capitalization should act as a gentle reminder that we, the created, are ever so blessed to be granted an audience with He, the Creator. It is only through His grace and lovingkindness that such a thing could ever happen.

Names of God

Contained within the Bible are dozens of descriptive compound names for God, many of which are contained within the book of Psalms. Sprinkled throughout these prayers you will find examples which nearly always begin with "Jehovah" followed by the Hebrew word(s) that describe a redemptive or powerful attribute of our LORD God.

Poems

Interspersed within these Psalms are also ten poems that I have written over the past few years. Some are based on New Testament passages and others on the Old Testament. And yet, I believe they are all connected to the Psalms. My hope is you enjoy reading them as much as I did writing them.

"Let the words of my mouth and the meditation of my heart be acceptable in Your sight, O LORD, my rock and my Redeemer." Psalm 19:14 (NASB)

O LORD,
Let my life be a conscious, continuous confession of faith. Make it of deepest
devotion and not some half-hearted ritual of no accord.
May my life's longing be to daily dwell in Your presence
with a patient and listening heart
so that Your love severely saturates my soul and Your Word intensely infuses my
mind to think only Your thoughts; to whisper only
Your words; to do only Your deeds.
Give me a spirit of gratitude for the gift of Your salvation that I might reflect
Your light and demonstrate Your love to all I encounter this day. Amen

Psalm 1

1 How blessed is the man who does not walk in the counsel of the wicked, Nor stand in the path of sinners, Nor sit in the seat of scoffers! 2 But his delight is in the law of the LORD, And in His law he meditates day and night. 3 He will be like a tree firmly planted by streams of water, Which yields its fruit in its season And its leaf does not wither; And in whatever he does, he prospers. 4 The wicked are not so, But they are like chaff which the wind drives away. 5 Therefore the wicked will not stand in the judgment, Nor sinners in the assembly of the righteous. 6 For the LORD knows the way of the righteous, But the way of the wicked will perish. (NASB)

Upon arriving at the FBI Academy as a new Agent trainee, I was issued a set of huge three-ring binders with the ominous titles: the "Manual of Administrative Operations and Procedures" and the "Manual of Investigative Operations and Guidelines." They became part of our daily required reading and were veritable "how to" books designed to help us grow in our knowledge of how to survive life in the Bureau and properly conduct investigations. This first Psalm is also a manual – the manual of life. It is a perfect portal to better understand the rest of the book of Psalms; a definitive introduction and summation. It describes the progression of two very different lives: one who ignores God's Word and one who makes it an integral part of his life. Those who delight in God's Word flourish and are fruitful. The Bible uses many botanical analogies because God wants us to grow. In the New Testament, Jesus said He is the Vine and we are the branches. We are told the Word of God is like a seed, scattered in different soil. Finally, we are told how we should live as Christians by displaying the "fruit of the Spirit." We are not only to read God's Word but to deeply desire it and to passionately pursue its innermost meanings through meditation. If we ponder it, we will grow in the way God desires and walk the path to know His true peace.

O God, I pray that You give me the will and desire to meditate on Your Word, day and night, for through it I am blessed and whatever I do in response to it will not be in vain. Remind me that the works of the wicked will perish, driven away like worthless weeds in the wind on a blustery day. Keep my heart intensely ingrained and my feet roundly rooted in Your Word, like a tree purposely planted by the water's edge, stable and strong to do the work You have given me to do at the time and place You want me to do it. Amen

Psalm 2

1 Why do the nations rage and the peoples plot in vain? 2 The kings of the earth take their stand, and the rulers conspire together against the Lord and his Anointed One: 3 "Let's tear off their chains and throw their ropes off of us." 4 The one enthroned in heaven laughs; the Lord ridicules them. 5 Then he speaks to them in his anger and terrifies them in his wrath: 6 "I have installed my king on Zion, my holy mountain." 7 I will declare the Lord's decree. He said to me, "You are my Son; today I have become your Father. 8 Ask of me, and I will make the nations your inheritance and the ends of the earth your possession. 9 You will break them with an iron scepter; you will shatter them like pottery." 10 So now, kings, be wise; receive instruction, you judges of the earth. 11 Serve the Lord with reverential awe and rejoice with trembling. 12 Pay homage to the Son or he will be angry and you will perish in your rebellion, for his anger may ignite at any moment. All who take refuge in him are happy. (CSB)

How often do you stop and ask yourself, "What in the world in going on?" It is likely that every generation of human history has probably paused to ponder that thought, but I dare say today's world has really pushed the envelope as things appear to get more chaotic. Working in the law enforcement profession for almost 35 years I saw my fair share of human depravity and destruction. How reassuring is it to realize that God doesn't need to ask what's happening? He not only has the infinite knowledge to know *what* is going to happen, but He has the boundless power and limitless time to keep things in order, according to His perfect plan. The good news is He does have a plan! I've heard the saying that "God always has a plan B" but the truth is, He always sticks to plan A because He is in total and complete control. He isn't scrambling to correct course, mend mistakes, or overcome obstacles. Because of this, we should find comfort to rest in His perfect peace.

O God, I live in a crazy, maniacally messed up world, where nations not only take a stand against each other but against You and Your Anointed One. How foolhardy can they be? I worship You with reverence and rejoice with trembling because of Your holiness and majesty. To You, I give homage and embrace, accept, and attach myself to Your Son, whom You have begotten. I am blessed when my trust is in You Jehovah Machsi, the LORD My Refuge. Amen

Psalm 3

A Psalm of David when he fled from Absalom his son. **1** Lord, how they have increased who trouble me! Many are they who rise up against me. **2** Many are they who say of me, "There is no help for him in God." Selah **3** But You, O Lord, are a shield for me, My glory and the One who lifts up my head. **4** I cried to the Lord with my voice, And He heard me from His holy hill. Selah **5** I lay down and slept; I awoke, for the Lord sustained me. **6** I will not be afraid of ten thousands of people Who have set themselves against me all around. **7** Arise, O Lord; Save me, O my God! For You have struck all my enemies on the cheekbone; You have broken the teeth of the ungodly. **8** Salvation belongs to the Lord. Your blessing is upon Your people. Selah (NKJV)

Do you occasionally find it too easy and sometimes despair and worry about the situation in which you find yourself? David knew what it was like to be surrounded by foes throughout his entire life. When he alone faced Goliath, he put his faith in God alone – no one else really thought he had a chance of victory (to include his king, countrymen and even his own brothers). When that same king (Saul) turned on him in jealousy and wanted to kill him, his hope was in the Lord. And when even his own son became rebellious to the point of seeking his father's death, David knew he was in the palm of God's hand. He consistently practiced a life of dependency upon the Lord, knowing God would hear his cry and come to the rescue, according to His will. We can have that same assurance that God is there to hear our pleas for help if we only trust in Him and obey.

O God, do not let me become distracted, discouraged or disheartened by those around me who want to do me harm. I know when I cry out, You will hear and answer me. You are the sustainer of my life and my salvation. For You are Jehovah Magen, the LORD My Shield and are all around me; You are my glory and the One who lifts my head. As You gently cradle my chin and my head rises up, let my eyes seek Your face. As I lay my head down on the pillow each night, let my final thought be that it is You who sustains me to begin the day anew. No matter what trials I face each day, I will remember that You, O LORD, are my salvation! Amen

Psalm 4

To the choirmaster: with stringed instruments. A Psalm of David. **1** Answer me when I call, O God of my righteousness! You have given me relief when I was in distress. Be gracious to me and hear my prayer! **2** O men, how long shall my honor be turned into shame? How long will you love vain words and seek after lies? Selah **3** But know that the LORD has set apart the godly for himself; the LORD hears when I call to him. **4** Be angry, and do not sin; ponder in your own hearts on your beds, and be silent. Selah **5** Offer right sacrifices, and put your trust in the LORD. **6** There are many who say, "Who will show us some good? Lift up the light of your face upon us, O LORD!" **7** You have put more joy in my heart than they have when their grain and wine abound. **8** In peace I will both lie down and sleep; for you alone, O LORD, make me dwell in safety. (ESV)

Are there nights when you lay in bed, tossing and turning, troubled by the trials of the day or contemplating the challenges of tomorrow? God understands for He made us and knows us. And yet, we are told in verse 4 while we may tremble in fear or anger, we are not to sin in the process. How is that possible? The rest of that verse says to meditate within your heart and to be still. Our human response might be, "Sure, easier said than done" but it is the Lord who puts true joy in our hearts. In the stillness of your heart think back to the day's events and ask God to forgive you for those things where you missed the mark. Thank Him for His love and grace. Remember that He has provided the pathway for our righteousness through the sacrifice of Jesus. In the contentment of such knowledge, you can safely lie down and sleep in His peace.

O God, help me not to waste my time focusing on falsehoods or worshiping what is worthless; otherwise, I am just fooling myself. Help me remain a godly man and in so doing, You will set me apart and hear me when I call. As I lay on my bed, I will speak to You from my heart in meditation, yet I will also stay still and linger, listening to what You have for me to hear. Let my daily sacrifice be obedience in righteousness and to trust in You. The light of Your presence lifts me up and gives me a happy heart; my satisfied soul is like the festive farmer when he harvests his crops of plenty. When my faith is in You alone, I abide in Your peace and sleep secure in Your love. Amen

Psalm 5

To the Chief Musician. With flutes. A Psalm of David. **1** Give ear to my words, O Lord, Consider my meditation. **2** Give heed to the voice of my cry, My King and my God, For to You I will pray. **3** My voice You shall hear in the morning, O Lord; In the morning I will direct it to You, And I will look up. **4** For You are not a God who takes pleasure in wickedness, Nor shall evil dwell with You. **5** The boastful shall not stand in Your sight; You hate all workers of iniquity. **6** You shall destroy those who speak falsehood; The Lord abhors the bloodthirsty and deceitful man. **7** But as for me, I will come into Your house in the multitude of Your mercy; In fear of You I will worship toward Your holy temple. **8** Lead me, O Lord, in Your righteousness because of my enemies; Make Your way straight before my face. **9** For there is no faithfulness in their mouth; Their inward part is destruction; Their throat is an open tomb; They flatter with their tongue. **10** Pronounce them guilty, O God! Let them fall by their own counsels; Cast them out in the multitude of their transgressions, For they have rebelled against You. **11** But let all those rejoice who put their trust in You; Let them ever shout for joy, because You defend them; Let those also who love Your name Be joyful in You. **12** For You, O Lord, will bless the righteous; With favor You will surround him as with a shield. (NKJV)

While the previous Psalm was your bedtime prayer, this Psalm is your morning send off. Is there any better way to start your day than in a heartfelt conversation with the Lord, to tell Him your deepest desires? Don't be content with simply living in the present, satisfied with status quo. With resolution move forward. Ah, but don't blindly charge ahead and change for change's sake. You need to make sure you are heading in the right direction. Part of FBI SWAT training I received included land navigation exercises. We learned to read a map and "shoot an azimuth" with our compass to ensure we arrived at the desired designation. Even if you are just a couple feet off at the beginning of a trek, you might become lost, never finding your intended terminus. Like David, ask the Lord to lead you in His righteousness. Let God's Word be your compass and as He leads, pay close attention to your surroundings. Just like a walk in the woods, even though the end objective is desirable, sometimes, the greater goal is to simply enjoy each step, experiencing the beauty of God's handiwork and His presence as He leads you along the way.

O God, give ear to my prayer and consider my meditation, for You are my King and my God. May my mornings consistently commence with a sacrifice of prayer to You, and then, in eager expectancy, I will wait and watch for Your response. Lead me, O LORD, in Your righteousness and make the journey You have chosen for my life clearly set before me. And when I see it, with total trust in You, let me obediently follow it with a joyful and grateful heart. Amen

Psalm 6

For the choir director; with stringed instruments, upon an eight-string lyre. A Psalm of David. **1** O LORD, do not rebuke me in Your anger, Nor chasten me in Your wrath. **2** Be gracious to me, O LORD, for I am pining away; Heal me, O LORD, for my bones are dismayed. **3** And my soul is greatly dismayed; But You, O LORD -how long? **4** Return, O LORD, rescue my soul; Save me because of Your lovingkindness. **5** For there is no mention of You in death; In Sheol who will give You thanks? **6** I am weary with my sighing; Every night I make my bed swim, I dissolve my couch with my tears. **7** My eye has wasted away with grief; It has become old because of all my adversaries. **8** Depart from me, all you who do iniquity, For the LORD has heard the voice of my weeping. **9** The LORD has heard my supplication, The LORD receives my prayer. **10** All my enemies will be ashamed and greatly dismayed; They shall turn back, they will suddenly be ashamed. (NASB)

Let's face it – some days you just need someone to throw you a lifeline. Despite your best effort, you may find yourself aimlessly floating about, floundering in life's stormy sea. Sometimes it is the anchor of a particular sin that weighs us down. It might be the waves of fear we face that dwarf our faith. It could be the physical fatigue of frantically fighting against the currents of ongoing events. Whatever the cause of our dismay in the deluge, we have more than a lifesaver – we have a life Savior! We simply must acknowledge our weakness and cry out for help. It is only when a sinking swimmer who is about to drown recognizes his dilemma and ceases his futile fight against the waves, that the lifeguard is able to do his job and take them safely ashore. God proved His love for us in that while we were still pushing away His hand, He sent His Son to save us.

O God, forgive me for my sin, for You know how weak I am. Thank You for being gracious to me and healing me from the inside out. When my bones break or my shaken soul suffers, You are there to deliver me. When with weariness I groan and my eyes fill with tears, let me turn to You in thankfulness. For You hear me when I cry out to You in my prayers and supplication and You comfort me in my need. Amen

Psalm 7

A Shiggaion of David, which he sang to the LORD concerning the words of Cush, a Benjamite. 1 Lord my God, I seek refuge in you; save me from all my pursuers and rescue me 2 or they will tear me like a lion, ripping me apart with no one to rescue me. 3 Lord my God, if I have done this, if there is injustice on my hands, 4 if I have done harm to one at peace with me or have plundered my adversary without cause, 5 may an enemy pursue and overtake me; may he trample me to the ground and leave my honor in the dust. *Selah* 6 Rise up, Lord, in your anger; lift yourself up against the fury of my adversaries; awake for me; you have ordained a judgment. 7 Let the assembly of peoples gather around you; take your seat on high over it. 8 The Lord judges the peoples; vindicate me, Lord, according to my righteousness and my integrity. 9 Let the evil of the wicked come to an end, but establish the righteous. The one who examines the thoughts and emotions is a righteous God. 10 My shield is with God, who saves the upright in heart. 11 God is a righteous judge and a God who shows his wrath every day. 12 If anyone does not repent, he will sharpen his sword; he has strung his bow and made it ready. 13 He has prepared his deadly weapons; he tips his arrows with fire. 14 See, the wicked one is pregnant with evil, conceives trouble, and gives birth to deceit. 15 He dug a pit and hollowed it out but fell into the hole he had made. 16 His trouble comes back on his own head; his own violence comes down on top of his head. 17 I will thank the Lord for his righteousness; I will sing about the name of the Lord Most High. (CSB)

How many times have you been told, "Christians should not get angry" or "Don't you know anger is a sin?" Well, let's hold on a minute and remember a couple points: God is perfect and cannot sin and yet, this Psalm states that God is indignant or angry with the wicked every day. Why? Because He is a righteous judge! The Apostle Paul actually told us to be angry, but in our anger not to sin. How does that work? If we love justice as much as the Lord

26

does, there will be times when we not only can, but we should have a righteous anger. We need to be angry about the sin or the injustice. Our problem, however, comes when we let our own personal agendas and desires get in the way of what is truly just. We must remain focused on God's righteousness and let it be our standard and guidepost in life.

O God, I know there will be adversity and trials in my life but when I face them, let me longingly look to You as my refuge. Keep my hands pure and to act justly, to treat both my friends and foes with kindness. Someday, You will establish righteousness throughout the earth and the evil of the wicked will come to an end. But until that day, let me remember You are still in control and it is You who will judge – not me. Let me live with a heart of integrity and walk worthily of the righteous gift You have provided. Let me give thanks and sing Your praises forevermore. Amen

Psalm 8

For the choir director; on the Gittith. A Psalm of David. **1** O LORD, our Lord, How majestic is Your name in all the earth, Who have displayed Your splendor above the heavens! **2** From the mouth of infants and nursing babes You have established strength Because of Your adversaries, To make the enemy and the revengeful cease. **3** When I consider Your heavens, the work of Your fingers, The moon and the stars, which You have ordained; **4** What is man that You take thought of him, And the son of man that You care for him? **5** Yet You have made him a little lower than God, And You crown him with glory and majesty! **6** You make him to rule over the works of Your hands; You have put all things under his feet, **7** All sheep and oxen, And also the beasts of the field, **8** The birds of the heavens and the fish of the sea, Whatever passes through the paths of the seas. **9** O LORD, our Lord, How majestic is Your name in all the earth! (NASB)

Some of today's more commonly used sayings originated in the Bible. Here are just a few: Go the extra mile (Matthew). Saved by the skin of your teeth (Job). Eat, drink and be merry (Ecclesiastes). Nothing but skin and bones (Job). The writing is on the wall (Daniel). This Psalm also has such a saying: "Out of the mouth of babes…" In fact, even Jesus quoted this Psalm in Matthew 21:16. So what does it mean? I think Jesus sheds light where he prays in Matthew 11:25: "I thank You, Father, Lord of heaven and earth, that You have hidden these things from the wise and prudent and have revealed them to babes." God's power is so incredibly majestic, He can be glorified through the smallest and weakest instruments. We often focus too much on the messenger but in God's case, the true power lies in His message. Never think you are too insignificant to be God's ambassador.

O God, Your majesty permeates the earth and Your splendor penetrates the higher heavens above. The universe You created is too magnificent to comprehend and it reminds me how feebly fragile and insignificant I am in the scheme of things. And yet, You have given me a position in Your creation higher than I deserve, with the authority to rule in places over it. Give me grace and wisdom to properly interact with all earth's creatures, great and small. O LORD, my Lord, how majestic is Your name in all the earth! Amen

Psalm 9

To the Chief Musician. To the tune of 'Death of the Son.' A Psalm of David. **1** I will praise You, O Lord, with my whole heart; I will tell of all Your marvelous works. **2** I will be glad and rejoice in You; I will sing praise to Your name, O Most High. **3** When my enemies turn back, They shall fall and perish at Your presence. **4** For You have maintained my right and my cause; You sat on the throne judging in righteousness. **5** You have rebuked the nations, You have destroyed the wicked; You have blotted out their name forever and ever. **6** O enemy, destructions are finished forever! And you have destroyed cities; Even their memory has perished. **7** But the Lord shall endure forever; He has prepared His throne for judgment. **8** He shall judge the world in righteousness, And He shall administer judgment for the peoples in uprightness. **9** The Lord also will be a refuge for the oppressed, A refuge in times of trouble. **10** And those who know Your name will put their trust in You; For You, Lord, have not forsaken those who seek You. **11** Sing praises to the Lord, who dwells in Zion! Declare His deeds among the people. **12** When He avenges blood, He remembers them; He does not forget the cry of the humble. **13** Have mercy on me, O Lord! Consider my trouble from those who hate me, You who lift me up from the gates of death, **14** That I may tell of all Your praise In the gates of the daughter of Zion. I will rejoice in Your salvation. **15** The nations have sunk down in the pit which they made; In the net which they hid, their own foot is caught. **16** The Lord is known by the judgment He executes; The wicked is snared in the work of his own hands. Meditation. Selah **17** The wicked shall be turned into hell, And all the nations that forget God. **18** For the needy shall not always be forgotten; The expectation of the poor shall not perish forever. **19** Arise, O Lord, Do not let man prevail; Let the nations be judged in Your sight. **20** Put them in fear, O Lord, That the nations may know themselves to be but men. Selah (NKJV)

Who can you trust is today's world? In verse 10, David tells us those who know the Lord's name will put their trust in Him. So here is the next question: How can we know the Lord's name? Think back to Moses – even he asked what God's name was when first encountering Him. The answer: Yahweh. "I AM WHO I AM." We must truly believe that God exists and is preeminent in all things before we can trust in Him. As Proverbs 18:10 says, "The <u>name</u> of the Lord is a strong tower; the righteous man runs into it and is safe." But Yahweh isn't the God of only Moses, David and the nation of Israel. The rest of verse 10 provides a special promise of hope: God will not forsake those who seek Him. As God said through the prophet Jeremiah, "you will seek Me and find *Me,* when you search for Me with all your heart." Seek. Find. Trust.

O God, let me give thanks to You with my whole heart, not in half-hearted measures. Likewise, I want to love You with my whole heart. Let my joy be in You, O LORD, and help me to exhibit it inwardly and outwardly. I will put my trust in You, O LORD, for I know You will not forsake those who seek You. Whenever I become too big for my britches, let me remember, "You are God, I am not!" It is You who will judge and it is I who will be judged. My memory will falter and the memory of me will fade with time but You, O God, abide forever. Amen

Psalm 10

1 Why do You stand afar off, O LORD? Why do You hide Yourself in times of trouble? 2 In pride the wicked hotly pursue the afflicted; Let them be caught in the plots which they have devised. 3 For the wicked boasts of his heart's desire, And the greedy man curses and spurns the LORD. 4 The wicked, in the haughtiness of his countenance, does not seek Him. All his thoughts are, "There is no God." 5 His ways prosper at all times; Your judgments are on high, out of his sight; As for all his adversaries, he snorts at them. 6 He says to himself, "I will not be moved; Throughout all generations I will not be in adversity." 7 His mouth is full of curses and deceit and oppression; Under his tongue is mischief and wickedness. 8 He sits in the lurking places of the villages; In the hiding places he kills the innocent; His eyes stealthily watch for the unfortunate. 9 He lurks in a hiding place as a lion in his lair; He lurks to catch the afflicted; He catches the afflicted when he draws him into his net. 10 He crouches, he bows down, And the unfortunate fall by his mighty ones. 11 He says to himself, "God has forgotten; He has hidden His face; He will never see it." 12 Arise, O LORD; O God, lift up Your hand. Do not forget the afflicted. 13 Why has the wicked spurned God? He has said to himself, "You will not require it." 14 You have seen it, for You have beheld mischief and vexation to take it into Your hand. The unfortunate commits himself to You; You have been the helper of the orphan. 15 Break the arm of the wicked and the evildoer, Seek out his wickedness until You find none. 16 The LORD is King forever and ever; Nations have perished from His land. 17 O LORD, You have heard the desire of the humble; You will strengthen their heart, You will incline Your ear 18 To vindicate the orphan and the oppressed, So that man who is of the earth will no longer cause terror. (NASB)

Few Psalms provide a more poignant picture of the proud in pursuit of the poor or the arrogant ambushing the afflicted. We see the lion, laying low, lurking in his lair, positioned to pounce upon its prey; ready to spring suddenly, crouching with unconcealed claws to catch and crush its vulnerable victim. As a warning, we want to cry "watch-out!" The lion may be called the "king of beasts" but there is no royalty or regal bearing in this metaphor. For this heinous hunter is the wicked one with a haughty heart. In both verses 3 and 13, it says that in his pride he "spurns" God (scorns, reviles, disdains, shows utter contempt). There is no fear of the Lord in his heart. When it looks bleakest, the Psalmist reminds us that the Lord Jehovah is King and He will seek and destroy the wicked. God hears the desires of a humble heart and will strengthen it!

O God, remind me during those times when You seem far away from me that You are omnipresent – everywhere at all times. So, the truth is, it is I who has allowed my sin and pride to creep into the picture and put a wall between us. Forgive me and cause me to not be like those who have a haughty spirit refusing to seek You, who says, "there is no God." Instead, give me a humble heart so that the lines of communication are always clear. Amen

Psalm 11

For the choir director. A Psalm of David. **1** In the LORD I take refuge; How can you say to my soul, "Flee as a bird to your mountain; **2** For, behold, the wicked bend the bow, They make ready their arrow upon the string To shoot in darkness at the upright in heart. **3** If the foundations are destroyed, What can the righteous do?" **4** The LORD is in His holy temple; the LORD'S throne is in heaven; His eyes behold, His eyelids test the sons of men. **5** The LORD tests the righteous and the wicked, And the one who loves violence His soul hates. **6** Upon the wicked He will rain snares; Fire and brimstone and burning wind will be the portion of their cup. **7** For the LORD is righteous, He loves righteousness; The upright will behold His face. (NASB)

David gives us a Psalms making a bold statement, paints a picture of doom, asks a couple questions to get you thinking, then returns to his original premise. He begins by saying he trusts in the Lord, his refuge, and place of protection. But if that is the case, why would he need to flee like a bird elsewhere? The wicked are not just lying in wait to attack but the onslaught appears imminent – the bow is not only in hand but drawn back, arrow fitted and ready to fly! The only thing worse than facing such an enemy is to do so in the dark, unawares. When all seems lost, David turns the tables and reminds us: God is in His holy temple, enthroned in Heaven, scanning the earth looking deeply into the hearts of all. A talk of "fire and brimstone" may not be in vogue, but we clearly see what lies ahead for the wicked. There's no need to fear for our righteous God reigns!

O God, when everything around me is in free fall, devastation dominates, and I want to turn and hide, I will take refuge in You, O God, my Savior. You see all around You – the good and the bad, the righteous and the wicked. You love the righteous, O God, and it is only through Your gracious provision that the upright will be deemed worthy to one day see Your face. Amen

Psalm 12

To the Chief Musician. On an eight-stringed harp. A Psalm of David. **1** Help, Lord, for the godly man ceases! For the faithful disappear from among the sons of men. **2** They speak idly everyone with his neighbor; With flattering lips and a double heart they speak. **3** May the Lord cut off all flattering lips, And the tongue that speaks proud things, **4** Who have said, "With our tongue we will prevail; Our lips are our own; Who is lord over us?" **5** "For the oppression of the poor, for the sighing of the needy, Now I will arise," says the Lord; "I will set him in the safety for which he yearns." **6** The words of the Lord are pure words, Like silver tried in a furnace of earth, Purified seven times. **7** You shall keep them, O Lord, You shall preserve them from this generation forever. **8** The wicked prowl on every side, When vileness is exalted among the sons of men. (NKJV)

Have you felt abandoned in a wicked world, surrounded by evil at every turn? Recall Elijah, who singlehandedly took on all the prophets of Baal (of course, with a little help from God). But almost immediately, he was threatened and pursued by the king and queen and had to flee for his life. When God asked him what he was doing, he bemoaned the fact that he alone was left to be faithful to the Lord. God pointed out that He had reserved over 7,000 who remained loyal to Him. Our Psalmist David lived in Israel's "glory days" and yet, even then, he was surrounded by lying neighbors with flattering lips and boastful hearts. He saw his generation on the prowl, strutting about to exalt worthlessness. Sound familiar? And yet, we are never alone. If we will allow it, God's pure Word will saturate our soul and His Holy Spirit will remain with and in us!

O God, help me to see the upright path and walk it with a humble heart, no matter what those around me say or do. May I never become proud, possessing flattering lips or a double-heart nor see my success as my own doing and ability. Keep me from strutting about in self-exaltation. In the end, it is You, O God, who prevails with Your pure Word. Like silver refined in a fire, Your words will preserve me as I follow You, even in the midst of a crooked and depraved generation. Amen

Psalm 13

For the choir director. A psalm of David. **1** How long, Lord? Will you forget me forever? How long will you hide your face from me? **2** How long will I store up anxious concerns within me, agony in my mind every day? How long will my enemy dominate me? **3** Consider me and answer, Lord my God. Restore brightness to my eyes; otherwise, I will sleep in death. **4** My enemy will say, "I have triumphed over him," and my foes will rejoice because I am shaken. **5** But I have trusted in your faithful love; my heart will rejoice in your deliverance. **6** I will sing to the Lord because he has treated me generously. (CSB)

Do you have a problem with patience? For many in today's world, it is all about the present, the here-and-now, instant gratification. All must be done in accordance with our schedule and desire. As a sniper/observer for the FBI, there were times when I would deploy and watch and wait. Quietly laying in a prone position, sometimes hours on end, you had little or no control how long the situation might last. In this Psalm, David is struggling with God's timing, having the audacity to ask Him "how long?" David feels forgotten, separated and sorrowful. I like this Psalm because after he has "vented" it is as if he comes to his senses and boldly reminds himself, "But I will trust in the Lord…" For it is God who loves him and who has saved him and upon realizing this, his heart sings for joy. I wonder if this Psalm was in mind of the prophet Isaiah when he said, "the Lord waits to be gracious to you, and therefore He exalts Himself to show mercy to you. For the Lord is a God of justice; blessed are all those who wait for Him." Yes, let us learn to patiently wait for Him!

O God, there are days that seem bad, when I feel abandoned by everyone including You. But, may I never forget that You are always with me, surrounding me with Your lovingkindness. Let me always remember to remain joyful in Your salvation unto me. Give me the voice and place me in a positive posture to sing to You, O LORD, in appreciation for all You have done. Amen

Psalm 14

For the choir director. A Psalm of David. **1** The fool has said in his heart, "There is no God." They are corrupt, they have committed abominable deeds; There is no one who does good. **2** The LORD has looked down from heaven upon the sons of men To see if there are any who understand, Who seek after God. **3** They have all turned aside, together they have become corrupt; There is no one who does good, not even one. **4** Do all the workers of wickedness not know, Who eat up my people as they eat bread, And do not call upon the Lord? **5** There they are in great dread, For God is with the righteous generation. **6** You would put to shame the counsel of the afflicted, But the LORD is his refuge. **7** Oh, that the salvation of Israel would come out of Zion! When the LORD restores His captive people, Jacob will rejoice, Israel will be glad. (NASB)

It is a well-known fact that for the men and women who choose law enforcement as a career, they will likely see society at its worst. It has always been a difficult job, but as years go by, it seems to be ever more arduous and demanding. Each passing generation commits crimes more heinous than before. For those living in such a world, it can raise the question, "Where is God in the midst of all this pain and destruction?" Ironically, I think that question is really part of the answer. Our modern culture today has become too "progressive" to allow God to have His rightful place in our lives. Modern people see those who believe in God, and Christians in particular, as foolish. But this Psalm tells us the real fool is the one who deep-down denies God's very existence. Now, more than ever, it is time for all to earnestly seek after God.

O God, it is the fool who has said in his heart that You, O LORD, do not exist. They are the corrupt ones doing detestable deeds. Yes, no one can do good in and of themselves. When You look at this world which You have created, it is Your desire to find individuals who understand Your ways and seek after You. Instead, we have all turned away from You to do our own thing. Thank You for drawing me unto You, O God, for allowing me to call upon You to be my refuge and my salvation. By being saturated in Your Word, let me be a part of Your righteous generation. Through Your love, You have restored me and may I always rejoice in that! Amen

Psalm 15

A Psalm of David. **1** O LORD, who shall sojourn in your tent? Who shall dwell on your holy hill? **2** He who walks blamelessly and does what is right and speaks truth in his heart; **3** who does not slander with his tongue and does no evil to his neighbor, nor takes up a reproach against his friend; **4** in whose eyes a vile person is despised, but who honors those who fear the LORD; who swears to his own hurt and does not change; **5** who does not put out his money at interest and does not take a bribe against the innocent. He who does these things shall never be moved. (ESV)

I think of this Psalm as a message of consistent living. How so? The first verse asks two questions ("who shall sojourn?" and "who shall abide?") and then the rest of the Psalm provides the answers. I like the word "sojourn" as it connotes one traveling into a new place as a guest. Families of FBI Agents, and especially the military, are apt to move many times. Whether you are a constant mover or someone who tends to stay put, having never moved far from the place of your birth, the truth is, we are all travelers through this life. David isn't focusing on where you live or how often you move, but rather, what kind of person will you be on this journey called life? A person of integrity? Who acts rightly? Is truthful? Isn't swayed by the love of money? Here is the kicker question: Do life's challenges cause you to change how you live? No matter how often we move, let us never move from what God wants us to be and to do so with consistency!

O LORD, who could ever enjoy communion and fellowship with You? Only those whom You allow and draw near. May I walk each day with steps of integrity and my actions only bring glory to You. May the thoughts of my heart remain true and the words I speak about others be fair, honest and uprightly uttered with love. May I never compromise when I see the evil about me, but rather, honor You and those who obey You. May I remain faithful and consistent even when faced with difficult decisions. May I stand fast, unshaken in Your love. Amen

Psalm 16

A Michtam of David. 1 Preserve me, O God, for in You I put my trust. 2 O my soul, you have said to the Lord, "You are my Lord, My goodness is nothing apart from You." 3 As for the saints who are on the earth, "They are the excellent ones, in whom is all my delight." 4 Their sorrows shall be multiplied who hasten after another god; Their drink offerings of blood I will not offer, Nor take up their names on my lips. 5 O Lord, You are the portion of my inheritance and my cup; You maintain my lot. 6 The lines have fallen to me in pleasant places; Yes, I have a good inheritance. 7 I will bless the Lord who has given me counsel; My heart also instructs me in the night seasons. 8 I have set the Lord always before me; Because He is at my right hand I shall not be moved. 9 Therefore my heart is glad, and my glory rejoices; My flesh also will rest in hope. 10 For You will not leave my soul in Sheol, Nor will You allow Your Holy One to see corruption. 11 You will show me the path of life; In Your presence is fullness of joy; At Your right hand are pleasures forevermore. (NKJV)

Do you occasionally think you are just a little bit better than you really are? I call this my "proper perspective" Psalm. David reminds us that apart from God his goodness is nothing. It coincides to what Paul says in Romans 12:3 in that we are to use sound judgment to not think too highly of ourselves. Isaiah really hammers home this point when he says "all our righteous deeds are like filthy rags." OUCH! It remains so true for us today. Anything we do apart from God in our own power is weak and worthless. David's follow-up thought is interesting. He says his delight is in the saints on this earth – he calls them excellent, noble, majestic. As Christians, we too should delight in spending time with other believers. What a great way to keep the proper perspective when we see how God in His love has taken other broken vessels and made them whole.

O God, I pray that You will keep, protect and preserve me in Your perfect peace. In You I have everything and without You I am nothing. Thank You for surrounding me with those who love, seek and follow You – they are a joy to be around. As for those who have chosen not to follow You, I know they will not experience that same joy. May I be a light to them but never follow in their ways. Instead, I will continually keep my eyes upon You in the day and my thoughts upon You at night. By so doing, You will strengthen me as I joyfully follow the path that You have set before me. Amen

Psalm 17

A Prayer of David. **1** Hear a just cause, O LORD, give heed to my cry; Give ear to my prayer, which is not from deceitful lips. **2** Let my judgment come forth from Your presence; Let Your eyes look with equity. **3** You have tried my heart; You have visited me by night; You have tested me and You find nothing; I have purposed that my mouth will not transgress. **4** As for the deeds of men, by the word of Your lips I have kept from the paths of the violent. **5** My steps have held fast to Your paths. My feet have not slipped. **6** I have called upon You, for You will answer me, O God; Incline Your ear to me, hear my speech. **7** Wondrously show Your lovingkindness, O Savior of those who take refuge at Your right hand From those who rise up against them. **8** Keep me as the apple of the eye; Hide me in the shadow of Your wings **9** From the wicked who despoil me, My deadly enemies who surround me. **10** They have closed their unfeeling heart, With their mouth they speak proudly. **11** They have now surrounded us in our steps; They set their eyes to cast us down to the ground. **12** He is like a lion that is eager to tear, And as a young lion lurking in hiding places. **13** Arise, O LORD, confront him, bring him low; Deliver my soul from the wicked with Your sword, **14** From men with Your hand, O LORD, From men of the world, whose portion is in this life, And whose belly You fill with Your treasure; They are satisfied with children, And leave their abundance to their babes. **15** As for me, I shall behold Your face in righteousness; I will be satisfied with Your likeness when I awake. (NASB)

This is a Psalm of contrasts. Throughout it, David compares honesty and deceit in the context of hearts and lips. He points out that because God has tested (knows) his heart, He knows that his prayer is spoken in truth. What a great lesson for us today! We can't fool God, so the words that come forth from our lips in prayer must certainly be reflective of what resides in our heart. But David takes it to the next level in lesson two: He says, "I have purposed that my mouth will not transgress." This is not a simple statement of intent but a preemptive act of the will. In James 3 we are reminded of the challenges of controlling the tongue, especially where it says, "the tongue is a fire, a world of iniquity." David contrasts his desires with the wicked who with "fat" (unfeeling) hearts so arrogantly speak. God wants both our hearts and lips to be in tune with His. A physically fit heart is good; a spiritually fit heart is even better!

O God, may I remain in Your presence so my lips stay true and my judgment is pure. When You look into my heart may You find nothing offensive. I will make it my daily agenda to keep my mouth from transgressing. May each step I take remain firmly fastened to Your Word and ways. And when I feel like I'm slipping, I know You are there to hear and save me. When I awaken each morning, may You be my first and foremost thought. Amen

Psalm 18

For the choir director. Of the servant of the Lord, David, who spoke the words of this song to the Lord on the day the Lord rescued him from the grasp of all his enemies and from the power of Saul. He said: **1** I love you, Lord, my strength. **2** The Lord is my rock, my fortress, and my deliverer, my God, my rock where I seek refuge, my shield and the horn of my salvation, my stronghold. **3** I called to the Lord, who is worthy of praise, and I was saved from my enemies. **4** The ropes of death were wrapped around me; the torrents of destruction terrified me. **5** The ropes of Sheol entangled me; the snares of death confronted me. **6** I called to the Lord in my distress, and I cried to my God for help. From his temple he heard my voice, and my cry to him reached his ears. **7** Then the earth shook and quaked; the foundations of the mountains trembled; they shook because he burned with anger. **8** Smoke rose from his nostrils, and consuming fire came from his mouth; coals were set ablaze by it. **9** He bent the heavens and came down, total darkness beneath his feet. **10** He rode on a cherub and flew, soaring on the wings of the wind. **11** He made darkness his hiding place, dark storm clouds his canopy around him. **12** From the radiance of his presence, his clouds swept onward with hail and blazing coals. **13** The Lord thundered from heaven; the Most High made his voice heard. **14** He shot his arrows and scattered them; he hurled lightning bolts and routed them. **15** The depths of the sea became visible, the foundations of the world were exposed, at your rebuke, Lord, at the blast of the breath of your nostrils. **16** He reached down from on high and took hold of me; he pulled me out of deep water. **17** He rescued me from my powerful enemy and from those who hated me, for they were too strong for me. **18** They confronted me in the day of my calamity, but the Lord was my support. **19** He brought me out to a spacious place; he rescued me because he delighted in me. **20** The Lord rewarded me according to my righteousness; he repaid me according to the cleanness of my hands. **21** For I have kept the ways of the Lord and have not turned from my God to wickedness. **22** Indeed, I let all his ordinances guide me and have not disregarded his statutes. **23** I was blameless toward him and kept myself from my iniquity. **24** So the Lord repaid me according to my righteousness, according to the cleanness of my hands in his sight. **25** With the faithful you prove yourself faithful, with the blameless you prove yourself blameless, **26** with the pure you prove yourself pure; but with the crooked you prove yourself shrewd. **27** For you rescue an oppressed people, but you humble those with haughty eyes. **28** Lord, you light my lamp; my God illuminates my darkness. **29** With you I can attack a barricade, and with my God I can leap over a wall. **30** God—his way is perfect; the word of the Lord is pure. He is a shield to all who take refuge in him. **31** For who is God besides the Lord? And who is a rock? Only our God. **32** God—he clothes me with strength and makes my way perfect. **33** He makes my feet like the feet of a deer and sets me securely on the heights. **34** He trains my hands for war; my arms can bend a bow of bronze. **35** You have given me the shield of your salvation; your right hand upholds me, and your humility exalts me. **36** You make a spacious place beneath me for my steps, and my ankles do not give way. **37** I pursue my enemies and overtake them; I do not turn back until they are wiped out. **38** I crush them, and they cannot get up; they fall beneath my feet. **39** You have clothed me with strength for battle; you subdue my adversaries beneath me. **40** You have made my enemies retreat before me; I annihilate those who hate me. **41** They cry for help, but there is no one to save them—they cry to the Lord, but he does not answer them. **42** I pulverize them like dust before the wind; I trample them like mud in the streets. **43** You have freed me from the feuds among the people; you have appointed me the head of nations; a people I had not known serve me. **44** Foreigners submit to me cringing; as soon as they hear they obey me. **45** Foreigners lose heart and come trembling from their fortifications. **46** The Lord lives—blessed be my rock! The God of my salvation is exalted. **47** God—he grants me vengeance and subdues peoples under me. **48** He frees me from my enemies. You exalt me above my adversaries; you rescue me from violent men. **49** Therefore I will give thanks to you among the nations, Lord; I will sing praises about your name. **50** He gives great victories to his king; he shows loyalty to his anointed, to David and his descendants forever. (CSB)

In a single verse (vs. 2) David gives us many descriptive words to refer to God's protective nature: rock, fortress, deliverer, strength, shield, stronghold, and "horn of my salvation." Have you ever wondered what that last phrase means? All the other words are passive places of protection but the latter is an active defense. Animals use their horns to defend themselves, often quite aggressively. David's words were in the context of his enemies, yet our greatest enemy remains death due to sin. Notice twice (vv. 20, 24) David says the Lord rewarded him "in accordance with my righteousness." Most of us cringe to use such a lofty standard, but God took the offensive in saving us. As Zacharias prophesied in Luke 1:69, God has "raised up a horn of salvation for us in the house of His servant David." Our righteousness is now found in Jesus Christ.

O God, I love You LORD, for You are my Rock, my Fortress and my Deliverer, and worthy of all praise. Despite danger or desperation, I know when I call upon You, You hear me. When confronted by enemies You will rescue me, for You, O LORD, are my stay and sure support. Let my hands remain clean as I keep Your ways and walk the path of Your ordinances and statutes. Help me demonstrate Your mercy by being merciful. Keep my heart humble and my eyes focused on You. O God, it is only through You that I can find my way in the dark for You are my light. You gird me with strength; You steady my feet; You train me for battle, but it is Your salvation which shields me and hand that holds me up. I will sing Your praises as long as I have breath because You are Jehovah Keren Yish'i, the LORD and the Horn of My Salvation. Amen

Psalm 19

For the choir director. A Psalm of David. **1** The heavens are telling of the glory of God; And their expanse is declaring the work of His hands. **2** Day to day pours forth speech, And night to night reveals knowledge. **3** There is no speech, nor are there words; Their voice is not heard. **4** Their line has gone out through all the earth, And their utterances to the end of the world. In them He has placed a tent for the sun, **5** Which is as a bridegroom coming out of his chamber; It rejoices as a strong man to run his course. **6** Its rising is from one end of the heavens, And its circuit to the other end of them; And there is nothing hidden from its heat. **7** The law of the LORD is perfect, restoring the soul; The testimony of the LORD is sure, making wise the simple. **8** The precepts of the LORD are right, rejoicing the heart; The commandment of the LORD is pure, enlightening the eyes. **9** The fear of the LORD is clean, enduring forever; The judgments of the LORD are true; they are righteous altogether. **10** They are more desirable than gold, yes, than much fine gold; Sweeter also than honey and the drippings of the honeycomb. **11** Moreover, by them Your servant is warned; In keeping them there is great reward. **12** Who can discern his errors? Acquit me of hidden faults. **13** Also keep back Your servant from presumptuous sins; Let them not rule over me; Then I will be blameless, And I shall be acquitted of great transgression. **14** Let the words of my mouth and the meditation of my heart Be acceptable in Your sight, O LORD, my rock and my Redeemer. (NASB)

At first glance, this famous Psalm may appear a bit disconnected, shifting erratically from creation to God's Word. And yet, the message is seamless. God's heavens, highlighted in its vastness, speaks to us. The declaration is loud and clear, revealing God's majesty and glory. Technology has certainly enhanced man's ability to see into deep space but in reality, the naked eye and the Hubble telescope both fall short in seeing the full universe. God's created nature speaks to us of His infinite power, but He also uses His written Word to speak to us, declaring His truth and providing guidance. Most importantly, we see the influence and results in our lives if we pay attention: restoration, wisdom, joy, vision, endurance, and righteousness. O let us clearly listen to the Lord so that our words, thoughts, and actions are acceptable to Him!

O God, I praise and thank You for using Your creation to speak to me – it is Your unwritten Word. Heaven and earth resound with Your glory – give me the patience to quietly listen to it. Your written Word is just as powerful. It is perfect, true, sure and right – when I hear and obey it my soul is restored; my simple mind becomes wise; my heart becomes joyful; my eyes are enlightened. By hearing Your Word may I keep a heart submitted in worship and reverential awe of Your greatness and righteousness. May I desire Your Word above anything else – even above the purest gold. Each time I taste Your Word may I find it sweeter than before and want more. Your Word warns me of life's perilous pitfalls and rewards me when I obey it. It is my yardstick for life. It is only through Your power that I can overcome the sin of disobedience. It is only through Your grace that my faults are acquitted and my sins are forgiven. Let every word I speak and every thought deep within my heart become saturated in Your Word so that it may be acceptable to You, O LORD, my Rock and my Redeemer. Amen

Psalm 20

To the choirmaster. A Psalm of David. **1** May the LORD answer you in the day of trouble! May the name of the God of Jacob protect you! **2** May he send you help from the sanctuary and give you support from Zion! **3** May he remember all your offerings and regard with favor your burnt sacrifices! Selah **4** May he grant you your heart's desire and fulfill all your plans! **5** May we shout for joy over your salvation, and in the name of our God set up our banners! May the LORD fulfill all your petitions! **6** Now I know that the LORD saves his anointed; he will answer him from his holy heaven with the saving might of his right hand. **7** Some trust in chariots and some in horses, but we trust in the name of the LORD our God. **8** They collapse and fall, but we rise and stand upright. **9** O LORD, save the king! May he answer us when we call. (ESV)

Have you ever stopped to wonder, "Does God, the ruler of this entire vast universe want to pause and answer my prayer?" In this Psalm, David affirms no less than seven times, "May God" do something for us! What are those things? May He: (1) answer us in the day of trouble; (2) defend us; (3) send us help and strengthen us; (4) remember all our offerings; (5) grant us our heart's desires and fulfill our plans; (6) fulfill all our petitions; and (7) answer us when we call. Wow! Look at that entire list once again and ponder it. David reminds us that most people place their trust in the worldly power of man. At that time, horse and chariot were a symbol of ultimate power. Those who placed their trust in them were defeated, bowed down and fallen. But the ones who trust in the Lord rise up and stand firmly upright and are saved!

O God, I know You will answer me when I encounter everyday troubles. I look to You for my heart's desires and purpose in life. I will sing for joy of Your salvation. I know it's only You, O LORD, who sustains and saves me. While others trust in worldly weapons for their periodic power, I will remember my steadfast strength is in You and praise Your name all the days of my life. Amen

Psalm 21

To the Chief Musician. A Psalm of David. **1** The king shall have joy in Your strength, O Lord; And in Your salvation how greatly shall he rejoice! **2** You have given him his heart's desire, And have not withheld the request of his lips. Selah **3** For You meet him with the blessings of goodness; You set a crown of pure gold upon his head. **4** He asked life from You, and You gave it to him— Length of days forever and ever. **5** His glory is great in Your salvation; Honor and majesty You have placed upon him.**6** For You have made him most blessed forever; You have made him exceedingly glad with Your presence. **7** For the king trusts in the Lord, And through the mercy of the Most High he shall not be moved. **8** Your hand will find all Your enemies; Your right hand will find those who hate You. **9** You shall make them as a fiery oven in the time of Your anger; The Lord shall swallow them up in His wrath, And the fire shall devour them. **10** Their offspring You shall destroy from the earth, And their descendants from among the sons of men. **11** For they intended evil against You; They devised a plot which they are not able to perform. **12** Therefore You will make them turn their back; You will make ready Your arrows on Your string toward their faces. **13** Be exalted, O Lord, in Your own strength! We will sing and praise Your power. (NKJV)

For most of us, life under a monarchy is a thing of the past. Kings and queens still exist, yet their power is not what it once was. In David's time, he became a commanding king, for upon assuming the throne his military conquests established an extensive kingdom. From that perspective, David recognized it was not his own strength that brought true joy, but it came from the Lord's power and might. It was only by God he had been saved. He alluded to all the blessings he received from God to include the crown upon his head – not just one made of gold, but of very "fine" or "pure" gold – 14K simply wouldn't suffice! Because of God's great love for us, when we place our hope and trust in Him, He blesses us in ways far exceeding our expectations because that is His nature!

O God, it is only in Your strength that I can have genuine joy and in Your salvation, I will have happiness. Every blessing of life is a gift from You, O God. My greatest joy of all is to be in Your presence. You are my protection to keep me strong and unshaken. I will exalt You, O LORD, when I think of Your strength and praise You with song when I think of Your power. Amen

Psalm 22

For the choir director: according to "The Deer of the Dawn." A psalm of David.
1 My God, my God, why have you abandoned me? Why are you so far from my deliverance and from my words of groaning? **2** My God, I cry by day, but you do not answer, by night, yet I have no rest. **3** But you are holy, enthroned on the praises of Israel. **4** Our fathers trusted in you; they trusted, and you rescued them. **5** They cried to you and were set free; they trusted in you and were not disgraced. **6** But I am a worm and not a man, scorned by mankind and despised by people. **7** Everyone who sees me mocks me; they sneer and shake their heads: **8** "He relies on the Lord; let him save him; let the Lord rescue him, since he takes pleasure in him." **9** It was you who brought me out of the womb, making me secure at my mother's breast. **10** I was given over to you at birth; you have been my God from my mother's womb. **11** Don't be far from me, because distress is near and there's no one to help. **12** Many bulls surround me; strong ones of Bashan encircle me. **13** They open their mouths against me— lions, mauling and roaring. **14** I am poured out like water, and all my bones are disjointed; my heart is like wax, melting within me. **15** My strength is dried up like baked clay; my tongue sticks to the roof of my mouth. You put me into the dust of death. **16** For dogs have surrounded me; a gang of evildoers has closed in on me; they pierced my hands and my feet. **17** I can count all my bones; people look and stare at me. **18** They divided my garments among themselves, and they cast lots for my clothing. **19** But you, Lord, don't be far away. My strength, come quickly to help me. **20** Rescue my life from the sword, my only life from the power of these dogs. **21** Save me from the lion's mouth, from the horns of wild oxen. You answered me! **22** I will proclaim your name to my brothers and sisters; I will praise you in the assembly. **23** You who fear the Lord, praise him! All you descendants of Jacob, honor him! All you descendants of Israel, revere him! **24** For he has not despised or abhorred the torment of the oppressed. He did not hide his face from him but listened when he cried to him for help. **25** I will give praise in the great assembly because of you; I will fulfill my vows before those who fear you. **26** The humble

will eat and be satisfied; those who seek the Lord will praise him. May your hearts live forever! 27 All the ends of the earth will remember and turn to the Lord. All the families of the nations will bow down before you, 28 for kingship belongs to the Lord; he rules the nations. 29 All who prosper on earth will eat and bow down; all those who go down to the dust will kneel before him— even the one who cannot preserve his life. 30 Their descendants will serve him; the next generation will be told about the Lord. 31 They will come and declare his righteousness; to a people yet to be born they will declare what he has done. (CSB)

Have you ever felt sorry for yourself, thinking no one understands your dilemma? If so, this Psalm is a great reminder that no matter how bad things appear, there IS someone who truly understands. No other Psalm better captures Jesus' suffering - it is the most often quoted about His death in the New Testament. We tend to focus on Jesus' physical affliction, but as agonizing as it was, it pales compared to the emotional trauma He endured. Consider this: from eternity, Jesus was in perfect communion with His Father and just when He needs Him most, God turned away! Why? God's love for us allowed our sin to be placed upon Jesus causing a fathomless spiritual separation. Jesus died the death we deserved so that we can have a life that only He is justly due. When we see Jesus' love for us and obedience to the Father, how can we not do likewise?

O God, when I feel like You have forsaken me, when I feel You are far away, when I feel like You are not answering my cries for help – let me be still and think of who You are – You are holy! In ages past, Your people trusted in You and they were delivered. When I feel like an insignificant worm being belittled by those around me – remind me that before my birth, even in my mother's womb, You were my God. You are still my God! When my body begins to break down and my fortitude fails, stay near me to provide Your help. When all these things befall me, I will stand in awe of You and praise Your name. In the ages to come, Your name will be praised, from generation to generation. Amen

Psalm 23

A Psalm of David. 1 The Lord is my shepherd; I shall not want. 2 He makes me to lie down in green pastures; He leads me beside the still waters. 3 He restores my soul; He leads me in the paths of righteousness For His name's sake. 4 Yea, though I walk through the valley of the shadow of death, I will fear no evil; For You are with me; Your rod and Your staff, they comfort me 5 You prepare a table before me in the presence of my enemies; You anoint my head with oil; My cup runs over. 6 Surely goodness and mercy shall follow me All the days of my life; And I will dwell in the house of the Lord Forever. (NKJV)

Sometimes, passages of scripture have become so familiar that we no longer pause to ponder the point or meditate on the meaning. Surely, of all the Psalms this one is the best known. In fact, it may be one of the most famous chapters in the entire Bible. How sad when we let the majestic become mundane; exchange the extraordinary for the everyday; to pass up the preeminent to put up with the paltry. There is a reason this Psalm is so sublime – it is a rich story, a vivid vignette of our walk through life in the company of the Lord as our guide. You could write an entire book on this one chapter (and some have). As you read this Psalm, slow down and contemplate its content, meander through its meaning. It is in this context that I am drawn to the phrase, "You prepare a table before me in the presence of mine enemies." Why would God prepare a feast for us if we are surrounded by enemies? Might it be when we are with Him, we have nothing to fear and little else matters? It reminds me of the table that Jesus prepared for His disciples that actually had an enemy, a betrayer, present. He has made this table and then beckons us to join wherein we can have sweet communion with Him, to regularly recall what He did for us to atone for our sin and provide for our salvation. I wrote a poem to celebrate that table Christ has prepared for us:

O Let Us Now Come to His Table

O let us now come to His table, hearts joyful and so lifted up.
It is only in Christ we are able to receive the bread and the cup.
He displayed to His first disciples how to eat His memorial meal,
Heads bowed we pause now to ponder and before His altar we kneel.

O let us now come to His table, a banquet to be understood.
Not some custom attached to a fable, taste and see that the Lord is so good.
Jesus said 'twas His earnest desire to share His last supper on earth,
With those whom He loved and soon would provide a gift of infinite worth.

O let us now come to His table, beholding the bread and the wine,
Secured with an unbreaking cable to Christ the only true vine.
In remembrance of Him we the branches, gather now as His holy bride,
To receive the cup of salvation so that we in His love might abide.

O let us now come to His table and savor this morsel in time;
From angelic songs over stable until now with a Eucharist's chime.
Though tempted like us He was faultless, forsaking the enemy's lure,
Obedient heart, swaddled in love, to be slain for all of sin's cure.

O let us now come to His table, join those on that Passover night.
If asked, He is sure to enable our grasp of the depths of His plight.
Aware of His pending betrayal and the suffering soon to endure,
Jesus offered His blood and His body, a sacrifice perfect and pure.

O let us now come to His table, so we as one Body unite.
Christ's love we wear as a label, designed to be His salt and light.
Here in this moment we linger, to reflect on the victory won.
All praise to the Lamb who is worthy, our Savior and God's only Son.

O God, You are my Shepherd and You provide me everything I need. As I travel the path of life, keep my feet firmly planted in Your righteous ways so that my soul ever turns to You. Even when I find myself woefully walking near death's door, remind me I have nothing to fear because You are with me. You gently, yet firmly, use Your rod and staff to guide me, keeping me safe and secure. Even in the midst of my enemies You will provide what I need and do so more abundantly than I can imagine. Your love and mercy have been a companion for all my life and they will continue to remain with me, here on earth and forevermore. Amen

Psalm 24

A Psalm of David. **1** The earth is the LORD'S, and all it contains, The world, and those who dwell in it. **2** For He has founded it upon the seas And established it upon the rivers. **3** Who may ascend into the hill of the LORD? And who may stand in His holy place? **4** He who has clean hands and a pure heart, Who has not lifted up his soul to falsehood And has not sworn deceitfully. **5** He shall receive a blessing from the LORD And righteousness from the God of his salvation. **6** This is the generation of those who seek Him, Who seek Your face -even Jacob. Selah. **7** Lift up your heads, O gates, And be lifted up, O ancient doors, That the King of glory may come in! **8** Who is the King of glory? The LORD strong and mighty, The LORD mighty in battle. **9** Lift up your heads, O gates, And lift them up, O ancient doors, That the King of glory may come in! **10** Who is this King of glory? The LORD of hosts, He is the King of glory. Selah. (NASB)

The previous Psalm is the most famous, but can any of us quote even a snippet of the 24th Psalm? That is too bad for it is a glorious celebration song of the grand procession of our Great God entering Zion. An unusual set of phrases appear only here in the Old Testament: "Lift up your heads, O gates." They beckon the King to enter! We are also told who may join in this parade: the one who does not "lift up his soul" in vain. What I find intriguing is the only other place in the Bible we see a similar phrase is in Luke 21, where Jesus speaks of His return to earth. Jerusalem is encircled by enemy armies and about to be trampled. Our Lord says when these things begin to happen, straighten up and "lift up your heads" for your redemption is drawing near. Let us join the gates of old and lift up our heads that we may clearly see and focus on King Jesus our Redeemer!

O God, this is Your wonderful world. You have made it and everything in it. From the overwhelming oceans and rapid rivers to the majestic mountains and hallowed hills and all the people who live on it – they are all Yours! I ask for Your strength to keep my hands clean and my heart pure before You that I can come into Your presence. For You bless those who seek Your face. For You are Jehovah Gibbor Milchamah, the LORD Mighty in Battle, the King of Glory, the LORD of Hosts! Amen

Psalm 25

Of David. **1** To you, O LORD, I lift up my soul. **2** O my God, in you I trust; let me not be put to shame; let not my enemies exult over me. **3** Indeed, none who wait for you shall be put to shame; they shall be ashamed who are wantonly treacherous. **4** Make me to know your ways, O LORD; teach me your paths. **5** Lead me in your truth and teach me, for you are the God of my salvation; for you I wait all the day long. **6** Remember your mercy, O LORD, and your steadfast love, for they have been from of old. **7** Remember not the sins of my youth or my transgressions; according to your steadfast love remember me, for the sake of your goodness, O LORD! **8** Good and upright is the LORD; therefore he instructs sinners in the way. **9** He leads the humble in what is right, and teaches the humble his way. **10** All the paths of the LORD are steadfast love and faithfulness, for those who keep his covenant and his testimonies. **11** For your name's sake, O LORD, pardon my guilt, for it is great. **12** Who is the man who fears the LORD? Him will he instruct in the way that he should choose. **13** His soul shall abide in well-being, and his offspring shall inherit the land. **14** The friendship of the LORD is for those who fear him, and he makes known to them his covenant. **15** My eyes are ever toward the LORD, for he will pluck my feet out of the net. **16** Turn to me and be gracious to me, for I am lonely and afflicted. **17** The troubles of my heart are enlarged; bring me out of my distresses. **18** Consider my affliction and my trouble, and forgive all my sins. **19** Consider how many are my foes, and with what violent hatred they hate me. **20** Oh, guard my soul, and deliver me! Let me not be put to shame, for I take refuge in you. **21** May integrity and uprightness preserve me, for I wait for you. **22** Redeem Israel, O God, out of all his troubles. (ESV)

If you are like me, whenever you prepare a fancy dinner entrée you generally use a recipe from the Internet or a cookbook. If someone read this Psalm do you think they might be able to tell what's for dinner? In some ways, it appears to be David's recipe to ask the Lord to help get his life in order and keep it that way: One pound of protection from enemies; two ounces of knowledge to know the right path; a layer-cake of memory and forgetfulness – to remember His compassion and forget his youthful sins; a jar of justice to guide the humble of heart; a flask of fear of the Lord to remain close to Him; and a full measure of mercy to keep him from feeling lonely and afflicted. And after God has sprinkled us with integrity and uprightness we will be preserved in Him. All we have to do is wait upon the Lord to complete the good work He has begun in us and bring it to perfection!

O God, my soul is Yours. I entrust it to You because of who You are. There is no shame or fear for those who put their hope in You. Through Your relationship with me let me know Your ways and teach me Your paths so I may know Your truth. I praise You, O LORD, for being my salvation through Your love and compassion. Forgive me for my youthful sins and transgressions. Despite my nasty nature, You have instructed me in Your own way. Give me a humble heart to hear Your voice when You call to lead me in justice; a hearing heart to see Your hand when You point out Your path. When I am obedient I can see Your truth and lovingkindness even more clearly. When I become entangled in the snares and the stresses of life keep my eyes wholly focused on You, so I can walk evermore in a life of integrity and on Your straight path. Amen

Psalm 26

A Psalm of David. **1** Vindicate me, O LORD, for I have walked in my integrity, And I have trusted in the LORD without wavering. **2** Examine me, O LORD, and try me; Test my mind and my heart. **3** For Your lovingkindness is before my eyes, And I have walked in Your truth. **4** I do not sit with deceitful men, Nor will I go with pretenders. **5** I hate the assembly of evildoers, And I will not sit with the wicked. **6** I shall wash my hands in innocence, And I will go about Your altar, O LORD, **7** That I may proclaim with the voice of thanksgiving And declare all Your wonders. **8** O LORD, I love the habitation of Your house And the place where Your glory dwells. **9** Do not take my soul away along with sinners, Nor my life with men of bloodshed, **10** In whose hands is a wicked scheme, And whose right hand is full of bribes. **11** But as for me, I shall walk in my integrity; Redeem me, and be gracious to me. **12** My foot stands on a level place; In the congregations I shall bless the LORD. (NASB)

Within the FBI's seal are the words "Fidelity, Bravery, Integrity" and a saying regularly spoken within the FBI is "Don't embarrass the Bureau." They go hand in hand. Integrity is defined as having the quality of being honest and morally upright. It is walking in transparent truthfulness; it is consistently doing the right thing even when no one is watching. But someone is always watching. In this Psalm, David doesn't hesitate to ask God to look at him, and in fact, he pleads with God to examine, judge, test and try his mind and heart. In Hebrew, it actually says "my kidneys and my heart." Huh? The kidneys refer to our deepest, innermost being – the passionate side of us. The heart deals with our will and affections – our rational side. But think what those two organs do in our bodies. The kidneys act as a filter, removing impurities in our blood so the heart can pump the clean blood throughout the body. By being entirely transparent with God, the Holy Spirit can filter out those things in our life that shouldn't be there. Could that be what Jesus meant when He said, "Blessed are the pure in heart?"

O God, rule over me that I may always walk with integrity and trust in You with an unwavering heart. Examine me that I may daily demonstrate my love for You. Refine my mind and heart to keep it pure before You. Let me walk on Your path of truth with my eyes ever focused on Your lovingkindness. The world is full of deceitful, hypocritical and wicked people. May I never become comfortable amongst them or enjoy their company. Instead, may my hands remain clean, open to do Your work and pointing out Your ways to others. May my voice ever declare Your wondrous works with words of thankfulness. O LORD, I love to live in Your presence. Through Your love and mercy, You have redeemed me. Let me evermore walk with integrity and transparency before You and with each step bless Your Holy Name. Amen.

Psalm 27

Of David. **1** The LORD is my light and my salvation; whom shall I fear? The LORD is the stronghold of my life; of whom shall I be afraid? **2** When evildoers assail me to eat up my flesh, my adversaries and foes, it is they who stumble and fall. **3** Though an army encamp against me, my heart shall not fear; though war arise against me, yet I will be confident. **4** One thing have I asked of the LORD, that will I seek after: that I may dwell in the house of the LORD all the days of my life, to gaze upon the beauty of the LORD and to inquire in his temple. **5** For he will hide me in his shelter in the day of trouble; he will conceal me under the cover of his tent; he will lift me high upon a rock. **6** And now my head shall be lifted up above my enemies all around me, and I will offer in his tent sacrifices with shouts of joy; I will sing and make melody to the LORD. **7** Hear, O LORD, when I cry aloud; be gracious to me and answer me! **8** You have said, "Seek my face." My heart says to you, "Your face, LORD, do I seek." **9** Hide not your face from me. Turn not your servant away in anger, O you who have been my help. Cast me not off; forsake me not, O God of my salvation! **10** For my father and my mother have forsaken me, but the LORD will take me in. **11** Teach me your way, O LORD, and lead me on a level path because of my enemies. **12** Give me not up to the will of my adversaries; for false witnesses have risen against me, and they breathe out violence. **13** I believe that I shall look upon the goodness of the LORD in the land of the living! **14** Wait for the LORD; be strong, and let your heart take courage; wait for the LORD! (ESV)

Sometimes we read scripture and pass over it without much thought. Other times we find a verse so profound or difficult, that despite a great deal of thought we still wonder what it means. What is David's intent behind his confident declaration "The Lord is my light?" I think the best way to interpret scripture is through other scripture. Where else do we see the Lord described as light? The Apostle John spends a great deal of time in his gospel and his first letter doing just that. Jesus said He is the Light of the world and if we follow Him we will have the Light of Life. He also said if we believe in the Light we will become children of Light and not remain in darkness. David's deepest desire was sweet communion with God, to live in His presence, to seek His face. O that we too, may seek the Lord and let the Light of His face shine upon us each day!

O God, because You are my light, my salvation and the strength of my life, I have nothing to fear. When wicked enemies surrounded me, even though I'm severely outnumbered, my heart will remain calm and confident because You are greater than my enemies or my fears. Keep the desire of my life to always remain in Your peaceful presence and Your beauty behold. Despite my situation, may I daily offer sacrifices of joy and sing Your praises. May I always look to You first in the drama of life and obediently seek Your face, knowing that You are my salvation. Teach me Your ways, O LORD, so I can see the best path before me. And even when that path encounters adversities and adversaries, let my heart remain strong and courageous because I believed and waited upon You. Amen

Psalm 28

A Psalm of David. **1** To You, O LORD, I call; My rock, do not be deaf to me, For if You are silent to me, I will become like those who go down to the pit. **2** Hear the voice of my supplications when I cry to You for help, When I lift up my hands toward Your holy sanctuary. **3** Do not drag me away with the wicked And with those who work iniquity, Who speak peace with their neighbors, While evil is in their hearts. **4** Requite them according to their work and according to the evil of their practices; Requite them according to the deeds of their hands; Repay them their recompense. **5** Because they do not regard the works of the LORD Nor the deeds of His hands, He will tear them down and not build them up. **6** Blessed be the LORD, Because He has heard the voice of my supplication. **7** The LORD is my strength and my shield; My heart trusts in Him, and I am helped; Therefore my heart exults, And with my song I shall thank Him. **8** The LORD is their strength, And He is a saving defense to His anointed. **9** Save Your people and bless Your inheritance; Be their shepherd also, and carry them forever. (NASB)

To me, this is a Psalm all about hands – David sees the deeds of the wicked and asks God to repay them in accordance with the works of their hands. He predicts that God will destroy the wicked because they do not recognize or acknowledge the awesome deeds of God's hands. What does David do about this – does he fearfully wring his hands? No, he earnestly prays to God and as he does so, he stretches out his hands towards God's "holy sanctuary." The Hebrew word (debir) appears only in this Psalm besides Kings and Chronicles where it refers to the holy of holies – it is the innermost meeting place with the LORD. David's desire is to have his heart so close to God that his prayer is heard. We too can now enter into God's presence, not because of the work of our hands, but only because Jesus allowed His hands to be nailed to the cross.

O God, to You I call out for You are my Rock. I know You hear my cries for help - so let me longingly listen and patiently perceive Your response. The wicked have no such hope. May the thoughts of my heart, the words of my mouth and the action of my hands be consistent and in one accord, to demonstrate Your peace and love to all. May my eyes remain focused and alert to see Your mighty works and the deeds of Your hands. Because You hear my prayers I will bless You, O LORD. I will sing a thankful song from my heart to You, for You are Jehovah Magen, the LORD My Strength, my Shield, and my Shepherd! Amen

Psalm 29

A psalm of David. **1** Ascribe to the Lord, you heavenly beings, ascribe to the Lord glory and strength. **2** Ascribe to the Lord the glory due his name; worship the Lord in the splendor of his holiness. **3** The voice of the Lord is above the waters. The God of glory thunders— the Lord, above the vast water, **4** the voice of the Lord in power, the voice of the Lord in splendor. **5** The voice of the Lord breaks the cedars; the Lord shatters the cedars of Lebanon. **6** He makes Lebanon skip like a calf, and Sirion, like a young wild ox. **7** The voice of the Lord flashes flames of fire. **8** The voice of the Lord shakes the wilderness; the Lord shakes the wilderness of Kadesh. **9** The voice of the Lord makes the deer give birth and strips the woodlands bare. In his temple all cry, "Glory!" **10** The Lord sits enthroned over the flood; the Lord sits enthroned, King forever. **11** The Lord gives his people strength; the Lord blesses his people with peace. (CSB)

In J.R.R. Tolkien's famous book, The Hobbit, there is a passage where Bilbo and the dwarves get caught in the midst of a terrible storm. One dwarf cries out, "This is no thunderstorm. This is a thunder battle!" Two "storm giants" begin hurling large chunks of rocks, the size of small mountains at one another. Of all the creatures contained in "Middle Earth," few appear as indestructible and powerful. And yet, they are but fiction. Our Psalm depicts violent thunderstorms passing over the plains of Palestine and we are reminded that we serve an omnipotent God whose very voice rumbles majesty and power. Human voices can deliver either a calming or threatening message, but the voice itself is impotent. God speaks and the universe is created. Jesus speaks and the storms stop. Let us ascribe to the Lord the glory and majesty that His name deserves!

O God, I give You the glory You are due and worship You in Your majestic might and holiness. Your voice, O LORD, is powerful and full of majesty - it thunders over the waters and even its secret sigh shatters the mightiest of forests into splinters; it sends forth lightning and shakes the wilderness. In Your strength, O God, I find my strength to live each day. Blessed are You, O LORD my God, for You are King over all Your creation and all who occupy it will cry out, sooner or later, "Glory to You, now and forever." Amen

Psalm 30

A Psalm; a Song at the Dedication of the House. A Psalm of David. **1** I will extol You, O LORD, for You have lifted me up, And have not let my enemies rejoice over me. **2** O LORD my God, I cried to You for help, and You healed me. **3** O LORD, You have brought up my soul from Sheol; You have kept me alive, that I would not go down to the pit. **4** Sing praise to the LORD, you His godly ones, And give thanks to His holy name. **5** For His anger is but for a moment, His favor is for a lifetime; Weeping may last for the night, But a shout of joy comes in the morning. **6** Now as for me, I said in my prosperity, "I will never be moved." **7** O LORD, by Your favor You have made my mountain to stand strong; You hid Your face, I was dismayed. **8** To You, O LORD, I called, And to the Lord I made supplication: **9** "What profit is there in my blood, if I go down to the pit? Will the dust praise You? Will it declare Your faithfulness? **10** Hear, O LORD, and be gracious to me; O LORD, be my helper." **11** You have turned for me my mourning into dancing; You have loosed my sackcloth and girded me with gladness, **12** That my soul may sing praise to You and not be silent. O LORD my God, I will give thanks to You forever. (NASB)

Do you ever wish you were fluent in Hebrew and Greek when reading the Bible? I sure do. The slightest nuance can alter our entire perspective of the message delivered in God's Word. In the first verse of this Psalm, David says he will extol the Lord because he has been "lifted up" by God. The Hebrew word for "extol" (rum) means to exalt and be lifted high; the word for "lifted up" (dalah) literally means to dangle and draw up (like a bucket of water). How cool is that? David wants to lift the Lord on high because God has lifted him up from the depths below. You can almost picture David dangling in a bucket in his enemy's dangerous dungeon, but God raises and rescues him. What a great visual picture of salvation! Each day we should show our gratitude for His grace, praise for His providence, and devotion for His deliverance.

O God, I praise You for protecting me with Your all-powerful hand – Your hand which lifts me up and brings healing to me with Your slightest touch. I will sing praises unto You and give thanks to Your Holy Name. You restrain Your anger but delightfully demonstrate Your goodwill and love throughout all my days on earth. Each morning I look forward to the start of a new day. I will call upon You because You are gracious and my helper. You have removed the fetters from my ankles and make my feet frolic, dancing with joy. You have removed the cloak of despair and robed me in a coat of gladness. My soul cannot help but sing praises of thankfulness to You forever. Amen

Psalm 31

To the choirmaster. A Psalm of David. **1** In you, O LORD, do I take refuge; let me never be put to shame; in your righteousness deliver me! **2** Incline your ear to me; rescue me speedily! Be a rock of refuge for me, a strong fortress to save me! **3** For you are my rock and my fortress; and for your name's sake you lead me and guide me; **4** you take me out of the net they have hidden for me, for you are my refuge. **5** Into your hand I commit my spirit; you have redeemed me, O LORD, faithful God. **6** I hate those who pay regard to worthless idols, but I trust in the LORD. **7** I will rejoice and be glad in your steadfast love, because you have seen my affliction; you have known the distress of my soul, **8** and you have not delivered me into the hand of the enemy; you have set my feet in a broad place. **9** Be gracious to me, O LORD, for I am in distress; my eye is wasted from grief; my soul and my body also. **10** For my life is spent with sorrow, and my years with sighing; my strength fails because of my iniquity, and my bones waste away. **11** Because of all my adversaries I have become a reproach, especially to my neighbors, and an object of dread to my acquaintances; those who see me in the street flee from me. **12** I have been forgotten like one who is dead; I have become like a broken vessel. **13** For I hear the whispering of many— terror on every side!— as they scheme together against me, as they plot to take my life. **14** But I trust in you, O LORD; I say, "You are my God." **15** My times are in your hand; rescue me from the hand of my enemies and from my persecutors! **16** Make your face shine on your servant; save me in your steadfast love! **17** O LORD, let me not be put to shame, for I call upon you; let the wicked be put to shame; let them go silently to Sheol. **18** Let the lying lips be mute, which speak insolently against the righteous in pride and contempt. **19** Oh, how abundant is your goodness, which you have stored up for those who fear you and worked for those who take refuge in you, in the sight of the children of mankind! **20** In the cover of your presence you hide them from the plots of men; you store them in your shelter from the strife of tongues. **21** Blessed be the LORD, for he has wondrously shown his steadfast love to me when I was in a besieged city. **22** I had said in my alarm,

"I am cut off from your sight." But you heard the voice of my pleas for mercy when I cried to you for help. **23** Love the LORD, all you his saints! The LORD preserves the faithful but abundantly repays the one who acts in pride. **24** Be strong, and let your heart take courage, all you who wait for the LORD! (ESV)

Have you ever marveled at the knitted-nature of how the Bible is written? Words and phrases join books written many hundreds of years apart into a single cohesive story. We recall the children of Israel being saved by the outpouring of life-saving water from the Rock at Meribah. We well remember Jesus' parable about the need to build our house on the Rock and where Paul reminds the Corinthian church that they drank from the spiritual Rock and the Rock was Christ. In Matthew 16, Jesus uses two different Greek words to describe a rock when he speaks to Peter saying that his name is "Petros" (small rock or stone) and upon "this rock" (petra – solid mass of connected rock/cliff) He would build His church. Amazingly, in verses two and three of this Psalm, David uses two different Hebrew words for "rock." First, he uses a word meaning any size or shape rock, asking God to save him as his stronghold-rock, his fortress-house. He next uses a word meaning a lofty cliff and states emphatically that God is, in fact, his fortress. David's explanation points to God's plan of salvation and is captured in Jesus' last words on the cross from verse five of this Psalm, "into your hand I commit my spirit." God always provides a means of salvation for His people!

O God, in You I have taken refuge and placed my trust. How could I ever be ashamed of doing that? I can't! When I call out to You in desperation, You draw near, lowering Your ear to hear me. You have surrounded me with Your righteous hand to protect me – like a mighty fortress built upon the solid rock I am secure in Your keeping. Because You have ransomed and redeemed me at great cost, I graciously give my spirit into Your strong and loving hand. Let Your face shine upon me and save me from my enemies. Keep me in the secret place of Your presence where nothing can distract me or do me harm. Blessed are You, O LORD, for Your love preserves me as one of Your faithful. Because my hope is in You, I will praise Your name with a heart full of strength and courage. Amen

Psalm 32

A Psalm of David. A Maskil. **1** How blessed is he whose transgression is forgiven, Whose sin is covered! **2** How blessed is the man to whom the LORD does not impute iniquity, And in whose spirit there is no deceit! **3** When I kept silent about my sin, my body wasted away Through my groaning all day long. **4** For day and night Your hand was heavy upon me; My vitality was drained away as with the fever heat of summer. Selah. **5** I acknowledged my sin to You, And my iniquity I did not hide; I said, "I will confess my transgressions to the LORD"; And You forgave the guilt of my sin. Selah. **6** Therefore, let everyone who is godly pray to You in a time when You may be found; Surely in a flood of great waters they will not reach him. **7** You are my hiding place; You preserve me from trouble; You surround me with songs of deliverance. Selah. **8** I will instruct you and teach you in the way which you should go; I will counsel you with My eye upon you. **9** Do not be as the horse or as the mule which have no understanding, Whose trappings include bit and bridle to hold them in check, Otherwise they will not come near to you. **10** Many are the sorrows of the wicked, But he who trusts in the LORD, lovingkindness shall surround him. **11** Be glad in the LORD and rejoice, you righteous ones; And shout for joy, all you who are upright in heart. (NASB)

Sin. Today's "modern world" avoids talking about it; moreover, our western culture does not encourage us to admit we are sinners. This Psalm was one of Augustine's favorites and formed the basis for his statement, "the beginning of knowledge is to know yourself to be a sinner." Just like David, at one time or another, we have all felt the oppressive weight of sin upon us. He uses three different words to describe the cause of our fallen state: transgression (separation due to rebellion or turning away), sin (missing the mark), and iniquity (depravity or moral distortion). It almost seems to be a sequence in death's downward spiral. But like David, we can also experience the delight, the release, the freedom that forgiveness brings. It only happens when we confess our sin. God already knows it all so we can't hide it. He will remove its burden, cover it with Jesus' blood, and cancel its debt forever! What is your aim in life? Focus on the target and don't miss the mark!

O God, thank You for forgiving my sin and providing a covering over my transgression. May I always remain open and honest with You, for You know everything. When I ignore or fail to confess my sin, my spirit feels Your heavy hand and I groan throughout the day. But You remain ever faithful, O LORD. When I confess my sin, You forgive and cleanse me through and through. May I never try to hide my sin but instead, let me make You my hiding place. For You keep me from trouble and give me songs of deliverance. You instruct me to show me Your way. May I quickly follow, not dragging my feet like a bridled horse or stubborn mule, but as one who hears his Master's voice and obeys because I trust and love You. Yes, I will confess and follow – You will forgive and lead and my heart will rejoice in You, O LORD, my righteous Redeemer. Amen

Psalm 33

1 Shout for joy in the LORD, O you righteous! Praise befits the upright. 2 Give thanks to the LORD with the lyre; make melody to him with the harp of ten strings! 3 Sing to him a new song; play skillfully on the strings, with loud shouts. 4 For the word of the LORD is upright, and all his work is done in faithfulness. 5 He loves righteousness and justice; the earth is full of the steadfast love of the LORD. 6 By the word of the LORD the heavens were made, and by the breath of his mouth all their host. 7 He gathers the waters of the sea as a heap; he puts the deeps in storehouses. 8 Let all the earth fear the LORD; let all the inhabitants of the world stand in awe of him! 9 For he spoke, and it came to be; he commanded, and it stood firm. 10 The LORD brings the counsel of the nations to nothing; he frustrates the plans of the peoples. 11 The counsel of the LORD stands forever, the plans of his heart to all generations. 12 Blessed is the nation whose God is the LORD, the people whom he has chosen as his heritage! 13 The LORD looks down from heaven; he sees all the children of man; 14 from where he sits enthroned he looks out on all the inhabitants of the earth, 15 he who fashions the hearts of them all and observes all their deeds. 16 The king is not saved by his great army; a warrior is not delivered by his great strength. 17 The war horse is a false hope for salvation, and by its great might it cannot rescue. 18 Behold, the eye of the LORD is on those who fear him, on those who hope in his steadfast love, 19 that he may deliver their soul from death and keep them alive in famine. 20 Our soul waits for the LORD; he is our help and our shield. 21 For our heart is glad in him, because we trust in his holy name. 22 Let your steadfast love, O LORD, be upon us, even as we hope in you. (ESV)

What is hope? Some might call it "wishful thinking." Others might define it as having the desire for positive results of future plans. When I led the Critical Incident Response Group of the FBI, we were responsible for developing contingency plans for a multitude of crisis situations. One thing was certain, hope is never considered a plan! For Christians, hope goes far beyond that. It is inextricably tied to faith. It is not only the anticipation for an outcome but the assurance we have that God is in control and will work everything out according to His perfect plan, consistent with His love and mercy. The Hebrew word used for hope in verse 18 is yachal which can also mean "wait." Yes, with faith, we can wait patiently – we can hope in His steadfast love and mercy. Hope placed in anything other than the Lord – whether manmade works or military might – is a false hope. Our hope is not only in Him, but it is from Him. When we faithfully and patiently place our hopeful expectation in God alone, only then our souls find the solace we seek.

O God, because of who You are I will sing for joy and praise You with a thankful heart. When I consider Your Word and deeds and how they are true and faithful, how can I not help but to love You, for You are righteous and just? You spoke and the world was created and with Your breath all came to life. To think of it all makes me stand in awe of You. Nations around the globe chart their intended course but none know the outcome but You. Only those nations who put their trust in You are blessed, for You know each person's heart and their desires – for You made each one of us. Even the greatest nation on earth with all its worldly wealth and might is nothing in Your sight. For You see those who fear and put their hope in You. O LORD, may our nation seek You once again to be our shield and to put our trust in Your Holy Name. Amen

Psalm 34

A Psalm of David when he feigned madness before Abimelech, who drove him away and he departed. **1** I will bless the LORD at all times; His praise shall continually be in my mouth. **2** My soul will make its boast in the LORD; The humble will hear it and rejoice. **3** O magnify the LORD with me, And let us exalt His name together. **4** I sought the LORD, and He answered me, And delivered me from all my fears. **5** They looked to Him and were radiant, And their faces will never be ashamed. **6** This poor man cried, and the LORD heard him And saved him out of all his troubles. **7** The angel of the LORD encamps around those who fear Him, And rescues them. **8** O taste and see that the LORD is good; How blessed is the man who takes refuge in Him! **9** O fear the LORD, you His saints; For to those who fear Him there is no want. **10** The young lions do lack and suffer hunger; But they who seek the LORD shall not be in want of any good thing. **11** Come, you children, listen to me; I will teach you the fear of the LORD. **12** Who is the man who desires life And loves length of days that he may see good? **13** Keep your tongue from evil And your lips from speaking deceit. **14** Depart from evil and do good; Seek peace and pursue it. **15** The eyes of the LORD are toward the righteous And His ears are open to their cry. **16** The face of the LORD is against evildoers, To cut off the memory of them from the earth. **17** The righteous cry, and the LORD hears And delivers them out of all their troubles. **18** The LORD is near to the brokenhearted And saves those who are crushed in spirit. **19** Many are the afflictions of the righteous, But the LORD delivers him out of them all. **20** He keeps all his bones, Not one of them is broken. **21** Evil shall slay the wicked, And those who hate the righteous will be condemned. **22** The LORD redeems the soul of His servants, And none of those who take refuge in Him will be condemned. (NASB)

Have you noticed how hard mankind tries to replicate the original? Slogans confidently proclaim, "just like" or "better than" or "as good as." Whether it be jelly beans or air freshener, we try to make things that taste like or smell similar to the real deal. But for all our efforts, we always fall short of what God designed. It is a grand reminder of how great our God is and the praise He is due, at all times and in every place. As we encounter the daily grind of learning the lessons of life, instead of letting them crush our souls, let each event mold us into the image God desires. Let them scratch away the odor of our pride and release the full fragrance of Christ for all to inhale, not a phony forgery issued by man, but an authentic aroma of the One who humbled Himself unto death to set us free. Let us steadily savor the Savior so with palpable palates we can truly taste and see that the Lord is good!

O God, when I awaken in the morning may my first conscious conduct be to bless You. At the end of the day may my final fancy be to praise Your Holy Name. And in the moments in between, may my lips continuously exalt You, for You alone are worthy. May my greatest ambition and highest sense of accomplishment be that I have begun to understand who You are O LORD, and comprehend Your faithful love, justice, and righteousness. May my voice be one of many to proclaim Your greatness. Thank You, O LORD, for drawing me unto You, to seek You; for when I cried out to You, You heard me and relieved me of my fears. Let my face radiate with Your joy so when others see me, You alone are glorified. And when anyone asks me about my joy let me unashamedly tell them how I have tasted Your love and how good it is! May I teach my children and my children's children to fear You O LORD; to not speak harmful words or lie; to turn away from evil and do good; to not only seek peace but to passionately pursue it. May my heart ever remain humble and contrite before You, O LORD, my Redeemer. Amen

Psalm 35

A Psalm of David. **1** Plead my cause, O Lord, with those who strive with me; Fight against those who fight against me. **2** Take hold of shield and buckler, And stand up for my help. **3** Also draw out the spear, And stop those who pursue me. Say to my soul, "I am your salvation." **4** Let those be put to shame and brought to dishonor Who seek after my life; Let those be turned back and brought to confusion Who plot my hurt. **5** Let them be like chaff before the wind, And let the angel of the Lord chase them. **6** Let their way be dark and slippery, And let the angel of the Lord pursue them. **7** For without cause they have hidden their net for me in a pit, Which they have dug without cause for my life. **8** Let destruction come upon him unexpectedly, And let his net that he has hidden catch himself; Into that very destruction let him fall. **9** And my soul shall be joyful in the Lord; It shall rejoice in His salvation. **10** All my bones shall say, "Lord, who is like You, Delivering the poor from him who is too strong for him, Yes, the poor and the needy from him who plunders him?" **11** Fierce witnesses rise up; They ask me things that I do not know. **12** They reward me evil for good, To the sorrow of my soul. **13** But as for me, when they were sick, My clothing was sackcloth; I humbled myself with fasting; And my prayer would return to my own heart. **14** I paced about as though he were my friend or brother; I bowed down heavily, as one who mourns for his mother. **15** But in my adversity they rejoiced And gathered together; Attackers gathered against me, And I did not know it; They tore at me and did not cease; **16** With ungodly mockers at feasts They gnashed at me with their teeth. **17** Lord, how long will You look on? Rescue me from their destructions, My precious life from the lions. **18** I will give You thanks in the great assembly; I will praise You among many people. **19** Let them not rejoice over me who are wrongfully my enemies; Nor let them wink with the eye who hate me without a cause. **20** For they do not speak peace, But they devise deceitful matters Against the quiet ones in the land. **21** They also opened their mouth wide against me, And said, "Aha, aha! Our eyes have seen it." **22** This You have seen, O Lord; Do not keep silence. O Lord, do not be far from me. **23** Stir up Yourself, and awake to my vindication, To my cause, my God and my Lord. **24** Vindicate me, O Lord my God, according to Your righteousness; And let them not rejoice over me. **25** Let them not say in their hearts, "Ah, so we would have it!" Let them not say, "We have swallowed him up." **26** Let them be ashamed and brought to mutual confusion Who rejoice at my hurt; Let them be clothed with shame and dishonor Who exalt themselves against me. **27** Let them shout for joy and be glad, Who favor my righteous cause; And let them say continually, "Let the Lord be magnified, Who has pleasure in the prosperity of His servant." **28** And my tongue shall speak of Your righteousness And of Your praise all the day long. (NKJV)

This great Psalm is so demonstrative of God's love in action on our behalf. When we feel forsaken and secluded in the world, this Psalm places us in two venues where we need God's help. First, we find ourselves on trial in a courtroom; second, we are standing isolated on a battlefield. Both situations are wrought with peril and we need a helping hand. Initially, David asks God to plead his cause, to contend with the contentious, to litigate his case. In Him, we have a heavenly counselor. David then asks God to fight his battles here on earth with both defensive (shield) and offensive (spear) weapons. Imagine it, we have the Creator of the universe as both our legal and physical defender. Fast forward 1000 years and Jesus comes to earth to live the life we should each live but can never accomplish on our own and He died the unduly death we so deserve. In so doing, He fought the battle and forever conquered sin and death and is now our eternal advocate to intercede and plead our case. Does He plead for mercy on our behalf? No, He demands justice! Because Jesus has already paid the price in full for our transgression, justice can and will prevail!

O God, Mighty are You, LORD of Hosts, for You oppose those who are my enemy and use all the weapons of Your arsenal – You use Your shield to protect me and Your spear and battle-axe to pursue those against me. Even in the midst of the heated battle, let my heart hear Your voice say, "Be still, I am Your salvation." A simple puff from Your lips and my enemies fly like chaff in the wind. For no reason, my enemies lay a net to ensnare me or dig pits to try to trap me, yet in the end, they will be the ones caught and destroyed. And when they are on the receiving end of Your almighty hand, let me remain humble and in constant prayer to You. May my behavior always be worthy of the words uttered by those who rejoice in my vindication, but more importantly, may everything I say and do magnify Your Holy Name. May my voice proclaim Your righteousness, O LORD, and praise You all the day long. Amen

Psalm 36

For the choir director: A psalm of David, the servant of the Lord. **1** Sin whispers to the wicked, deep within their hearts. They have no fear of God at all. **2** In their blind conceit, they cannot see how wicked they really are. **3** Everything they say is crooked and deceitful. They refuse to act wisely or do good. **4** They lie awake at night, hatching sinful plots. Their actions are never good. They make no attempt to turn from evil. **5** Your unfailing love, O LORD, is as vast as the heavens; your faithfulness reaches beyond the clouds. **6** Your righteousness is like the mighty mountains, your justice like the ocean depths. You care for people and animals alike, O LORD. **7** How precious is your unfailing love, O God! All humanity finds shelter in the shadow of your wings. **8** You feed them from the abundance of your own house, letting them drink from your river of delights. **9** For you are the fountain of life, the light by which we see. **10** Pour out your unfailing love on those who love you; give justice to those with honest hearts. **11** Don't let the proud trample me or the wicked push me around. **12** Look! Those who do evil have fallen! They are thrown down, never to rise again. (NLT)

When your life's career has been working as an FBI Agent, it was always important to focus on the letter of the law, and yet, it was easy to feel you were in a battle of right versus wrong. This Psalm is a great contrast between evil and righteousness, darkness and light, death and life. Sin approaches as if personified, and calls out with a wily whisper to the wicked person's heart. It blinds him with words of flattery and disguised in arrogance, it obscures his ability to recognize iniquity and thereby despise it. It murmurs words of wickedness and deceit that leads to a path where goodness cannot be found. In time, his hardened heart is consumed with devising schemes of evil, ever justified in his own mind. The Psalmist then dissipates despair's dark dream and lifts us heavenward, high above the mountains, to witness the steadfast love and mercy of God. It is only with the realization of God's lovingkindness that we can be fully satisfied as we drink from the streams of His delights, for He is our true fountain of life. With an upright heart may we ever drink deeply!

O God, let my heart never become like the wicked who have no fear of You or Your holiness. Instead of confessing their sin, they allow their haughty hearts to flatter themselves. They speak malicious lies, have lost any sense of wisdom, and no longer try to do good. Even while lying in bed they think up wicked plans. O may I never lead such a life. Instead, O LORD, let me always ponder and proclaim how great You are – the universe itself cannot contain Your mercy, faithfulness, righteousness, and judgments. You, O God, are my perfect protector and provider. You are my fountain of life and it is only through the lens of Your light that I can see the true light. Do not let the foot of pride creep near me or into my heart, but let me remain humble and kneeling before You in praise and adoration all the days of my life. Amen

Psalm 37

A Psalm of David. **1** Do not fret because of evildoers, Be not envious toward wrongdoers. **2** For they will wither quickly like the grass And fade like the green herb. **3** Trust in the LORD and do good; Dwell in the land and cultivate faithfulness. **4** Delight yourself in the LORD; And He will give you the desires of your heart. **5** Commit your way to the LORD, Trust also in Him, and He will do it. **6** He will bring forth your righteousness as the light And your judgment as the noonday. **7** Rest in the LORD and wait patiently for Him; Do not fret because of him who prospers in his way, Because of the man who carries out wicked schemes. **8** Cease from anger and forsake wrath; Do not fret; it leads only to evildoing. **9** For evildoers will be cut off, But those who wait for the LORD, they will inherit the land. **10** Yet a little while and the wicked man will be no more; And you will look carefully for his place and he will not be there. **11** But the humble will inherit the land And will delight themselves in abundant prosperity. **12** The wicked plots against the righteous And gnashes at him with his teeth. **13** The Lord laughs at him, For He sees his day is coming. **14** The wicked have drawn the sword and bent their bow To cast down the afflicted and the needy, To slay those who are upright in conduct. **15** Their sword will enter their own heart, And their bows will be broken. **16** Better is the little of the righteous Than the abundance of many wicked. **17** For the arms of the wicked will be broken, But the LORD sustains the righteous. **18** The LORD knows the days of the blameless, And their inheritance will be forever. **19** They will not be ashamed in the time of evil, And in the days of famine they will have abundance. **20** But the wicked will perish; And the enemies of the LORD will be like the glory of the pastures, They vanish -like smoke they vanish away. **21** The wicked borrows and does not pay back, But the righteous is gracious and gives. **22** For those blessed by Him will inherit the land, But those cursed by Him will be cut off. **23** The steps of a man are established by the LORD, And He delights in his way. **24** When he falls, he will not be hurled headlong, Because the LORD is the One who holds his hand. **25** I have been young and now I am old, Yet I have not seen the righteous forsaken Or his descendants begging bread. **26** All day long he is gracious and lends, And his descendants are a blessing. **27** Depart from evil and do good, So you will abide forever. **28** For the LORD loves justice And does not forsake His godly ones; They are preserved forever, But the descendants of the wicked will be cut off. **29** The righteous will inherit the land And dwell in it forever. **30** The mouth of the righteous utters wisdom, And his tongue speaks justice. **31** The law of his God is in his heart; His steps do not slip. **32** The wicked spies upon the righteous And seeks to kill him. **33** The LORD will not leave him in his hand Or let him be condemned when he is judged. **34** Wait for the LORD and keep His way, And He will exalt you to inherit the land; When the wicked are cut off, you will see it. **35** I have seen a wicked, violent man Spreading himself like a luxuriant tree in its native soil. **36** Then he passed away, and lo, he was no more; I sought for him, but he could not be found. **37** Mark the blameless man, and behold the upright; For the man of peace will have a posterity. **38** But transgressors will be altogether destroyed; The posterity of the wicked will be cut off. **39** But the salvation of the righteous is from the LORD; He is their strength in time of trouble. **40** The LORD helps them and delivers them; He delivers them from the wicked and saves them, Because they take refuge in Him. (NASB)

At some point growing up you probably said, "that's not fair" only to hear your parents or teachers say to you, "Don't worry about them, just focus on yourself." In many ways, David is using this Psalm, almost like a chapter from Proverbs, to tell us exactly the same thing. Three times he says, "Don't fret" about the wicked or evildoers. The Hebrew word used for fret goes way beyond just worrying, but actually means "to burn with anger." We must not get so upset about what others are doing that it negatively impacts our own behavior. The thing is, our view of life can be so inaccurate – our perspective is short-sighted and so subjective. God is limited by neither so our focus needs to remain entirely on Him. Our salvation is in Him and with Him, justice is certain!

O God, keep me calm this day and especially when I'm around those who do evil. Let me never envy their possessions. Remind me that they and their belongings will wither away like the grass. Instead, let me daily trust in You, O God, and to do good. As I contemplate Your faithfulness and grow content in You, my heart's desires will be fulfilled. Let my trust grow in Your truth and my faith increase in Your faithfulness. Help me to not worry or be angry but instead to quietly be patient in Your presence. While the world around me strives to gain riches, remind me that it is the humble of heart whom You bless and prosper. It is better to be righteous in Your eyes with few possessions than to have all the wealth of the wicked. Let me not forget that they and their wealth will vanish. Guide my steps dear LORD so I walk a path pleasing to You. When I stumble, I know Your hand is holding mine to protect and sustain me. Because I know You love justice let me speak it. Because I know You love righteousness let me walk it. But in all I say or do, I know my salvation is from You, O LORD, my Helper, Deliverer, and the One in whom I take my refuge. Amen

Psalm 38

A Psalm of David, for a memorial. **1** O LORD, rebuke me not in Your wrath, And chasten me not in Your burning anger. **2** For Your arrows have sunk deep into me, And Your hand has pressed down on me. **3** There is no soundness in my flesh because of Your indignation; There is no health in my bones because of my sin. **4** For my iniquities are gone over my head; As a heavy burden they weigh too much for me. **5** My wounds grow foul and fester Because of my folly. **6** I am bent over and greatly bowed down; I go mourning all day long. **7** For my loins are filled with burning, And there is no soundness in my flesh. **8** I am benumbed and badly crushed; I groan because of the agitation of my heart. **9** Lord, all my desire is before You; And my sighing is not hidden from You. **10** My heart throbs, my strength fails me; And the light of my eyes, even that has gone from me. **11** My loved ones and my friends stand aloof from my plague; And my kinsmen stand afar off. **12** Those who seek my life lay snares for me; And those who seek to injure me have threatened destruction, And they devise treachery all day long. **13** But I, like a deaf man, do not hear; And I am like a mute man who does not open his mouth. **14** Yes, I am like a man who does not hear, And in whose mouth are no arguments. **15** For I hope in You, O LORD; You will answer, O Lord my God. **16** For I said, "May they not rejoice over me, Who, when my foot slips, would magnify themselves against me." **17** For I am ready to fall, And my sorrow is continually before me. **18** For I confess my iniquity; I am full of anxiety because of my sin. **19** But my enemies are vigorous and strong, And many are those who hate me wrongfully. **20** And those who repay evil for good, They oppose me, because I follow what is good. **21** Do not forsake me, O LORD; O my God, do not be far from me! **22** Make haste to help me, O LORD, my salvation! (NASB)

Have you ever felt so weighed down by sin that you didn't want to take another step or even seek relief? No Psalm better captures the depravity of human nature or the oppressiveness of unforgiven sin. After his introductory plea for mercy, David provides some rather vivid word-pictures to describe the effects of sin, resulting in a soul that is: inflicted by deeply penetrated arrows; pressed down by God's heavy hand; so sick it has led to a broken body; unable to breathe because the waves of sin are drowning him; unable to carry the unbearable burden alone; full of groans because his heart is in turmoil; forsaken by family, friends and foes alike. So, what does David do? He not only confesses his sin but he is genuinely sorry (in anguish and full of anxiety over it). Like David, if we confess our sin, God is faithful and just to forgive us and wash our soul anew!

O God, have mercy on me, a sinner. Let me always be responsive to Your Holy Spirit when Your hand of conviction weighs down on me, that I will quickly turn from my sin, confessing it to You and cry out for Your forgiveness. O may I never let sin, in my folly, fester within. For You, O LORD, know all my desires and nothing is hid from Your sight. May my heart beat in Your strength and my eyes stay focused on You. For even if my friends and family forsake me, my faith will remain in You. Even if I am speechless and cannot hear, You, O God, will hear and answer. For when I confess my sin, my anxiety and despair depart and I can draw close to You, O LORD, my salvation. Amen

Psalm 39

To the Chief Musician. To Jeduthun. A Psalm of David. **1** I said, "I will guard my ways, Lest I sin with my tongue; I will restrain my mouth with a muzzle, While the wicked are before me." **2** I was mute with silence, I held my peace even from good; And my sorrow was stirred up. **3** My heart was hot within me; While I was musing, the fire burned. Then I spoke with my tongue: **4** "Lord, make me to know my end, And what is the measure of my days, That I may know how frail I am. **5** Indeed, You have made my days as handbreadths, And my age is as nothing before You; Certainly every man at his best state is but vapor. Selah **6** Surely every man walks about like a shadow; Surely they busy themselves in vain; He heaps up riches, And does not know who will gather them. **7** And now, Lord, what do I wait for? My hope is in You. **8** Deliver me from all my transgressions; Do not make me the reproach of the foolish. **9** I was mute, I did not open my mouth, Because it was You who did it. **10** Remove Your plague from me; I am consumed by the blow of Your hand. **11** When with rebukes You correct man for iniquity, You make his beauty melt away like a moth; Surely every man is vapor. Selah **12** Hear my prayer, O Lord, And give ear to my cry; Do not be silent at my tears; For I am a stranger with You, A sojourner, as all my fathers were. **13** Remove Your gaze from me, that I may regain strength, Before I go away and am no more." (NKJV)

Everyone has likely seen the image of the three wise sitting monkeys covering their eyes, ears or mouth conferring the wisdom to "see no evil, hear no evil, speak no evil." David uses this Psalm to show a more enlightened perspective. He says he will "guard" his ways – the Hebrew word used (shamar) means to carefully, diligently keep watch – there is no eye covering here! He watches to keep from sinning with his tongue. Yet, he goes one step further because he DOES cover his mouth. The Hebrew word used here (machsom) appears only here in the entire Bible and it means to muzzle. With his eyes wide open and mouth closed shut he feels the pressure building up inside until he cries out to God, pleading to know the "measure of his days." He is not asking to know the length of his life, but to fully realize just how short it is. As such, he places his hope in the Lord. May we do the same and make the most of each day we live!

O God, keep me mindful this day of all I say and do. Help guard my tongue and muzzle my mouth that I may not sin against You or speak ill of others. Remind me daily, O LORD, that my days are numbered and compared to You, my life is just a puff of air and then gone. I walk as a mere shadow in Your light – And yet, it is all I have so let me make the most of it! Let me never become trapped in the ways of the world, trying to pile up possessions and round up riches that in the end, I will leave behind to others, including some I don't even know. Instead, I will wait upon You, O LORD, in whom I put my trust. Deliver me from all my transgressions for I am speechless in the presence of Your glory. My sin separates me from You and Your Holy Hand presses down on me for I am but a vapor. Hear my prayer, O LORD, as I cry out to You. Help me to realize that this world is not my home; it is just my temporary residence as I pass through this life. And as I travel through it, I will seek only after You, my Hope in whom I trust. Amen

Psalm 40

To the choirmaster. A Psalm of David. **1** I waited patiently for the LORD; he inclined to me and heard my cry. **2** He drew me up from the pit of destruction, out of the miry bog, and set my feet upon a rock, making my steps secure. **3** He put a new song in my mouth, a song of praise to our God. Many will see and fear, and put their trust in the LORD. **4** Blessed is the man who makes the LORD his trust, who does not turn to the proud, to those who go astray after a lie! **5** You have multiplied, O LORD my God, your wondrous deeds and your thoughts toward us; none can compare with you! I will proclaim and tell of them, yet they are more than can be told. **6** In sacrifice and offering you have not delighted, but you have given me an open ear. Burnt offering and sin offering you have not required. **7** Then I said, "Behold, I have come; in the scroll of the book it is written of me: **8** I delight to do your will, O my God; your law is within my heart." **9** I have told the glad news of deliverance in the great congregation; behold, I have not restrained my lips, as you know, O LORD. **10** I have not hidden your deliverance within my heart; I have spoken of your faithfulness and your salvation; I have not concealed your steadfast love and your faithfulness from the great congregation. **11** As for you, O LORD, you will not restrain your mercy from me; your steadfast love and your faithfulness will ever preserve me! **12** For evils have encompassed me beyond number; my iniquities have overtaken me, and I cannot see; they are more than the hairs of my head; my heart fails me. **13** Be pleased, O LORD, to deliver me! O LORD, make haste to help me! **14** Let those be put to shame and disappointed altogether who seek to snatch away my life; let those be turned back and brought to dishonor who delight in my hurt! **15** Let those be appalled because of their shame who say to me, "Aha, Aha!" **16** But may all who seek you rejoice and be glad in you; may those who love your salvation say continually, "Great is the LORD!" **17** As for me, I am poor and needy, but the Lord takes thought for me. You are my help and my deliverer; do not delay, O my God! (ESV)

How often have you felt "down in the dumps" or as David puts it in this Psalm, stuck in "the miry bog?" Most of us don't live near a bog but we can easily picture one in our mind – the slime, smell, decay, dead plant material. Is there a better picture of death and destruction? But that isn't the only focus here. It is also the lack of footing we will experience while we are standing in a bog and how it is only the Lord who can provide the stability and security we need to remain upright and get out. Note how we cannot remedy the situation alone. By ourselves, we will simply squirm without resolution. Our only hope is to look to the Lord and practice patience in allowing Him to work His way in us and in His perfect timing. The sequence for escape is clear: we call, He comes; we reach, He rescues; He saves, we sing His praises.

O LORD, help me wait patiently for You, knowing You hear me and will respond in accordance with Your perfect timing. This world is beset with perilous pits and slippery slopes but You have placed me on Your solid Rock where I am safe and secure. May I sing anew each day a song of praise unto You, O God, which leads many to put their trust in You. For I know that I am blessed when I put my trust in You instead of the worldly know-it-alls who base their lives on lies. Your wondrous blessings are incomparable and too numerous to count. You care less about sacrifices of routine procedures and more about a personal relationship - with ears that listen and a heart that is drenched in Your Word. Lead me daily to proclaim Your good news instead of keeping it to myself; to tell all about Your compassion and lovingkindness that preserves me and how You delivered me from my sin. For I have tasted of Your salvation and will continually proclaim Your greatness, O God, my Help and Deliverer. Amen

Psalm 41

To the Chief Musician. A Psalm of David. **1** Blessed is he who considers the poor; The Lord will deliver him in time of trouble. **2** The Lord will preserve him and keep him alive, And he will be blessed on the earth; You will not deliver him to the will of his enemies. **3** The Lord will strengthen him on his bed of illness; You will sustain him on his sickbed. **4** I said, "Lord, be merciful to me; Heal my soul, for I have sinned against You." **5** My enemies speak evil of me: "When will he die, and his name perish?" **6** And if he comes to see me, he speaks lies; His heart gathers iniquity to itself; When he goes out, he tells it. **7** All who hate me whisper together against me; Against me they devise my hurt. **8** "An evil disease," they say, "clings to him. And now that he lies down, he will rise up no more." **9** Even my own familiar friend in whom I trusted, Who ate my bread, Has lifted up his heel against me. **10** But You, O Lord, be merciful to me, and raise me up, That I may repay them. **11** By this I know that You are well pleased with me, Because my enemy does not triumph over me. **12** As for me, You uphold me in my integrity, And set me before Your face forever. **13** Blessed be the Lord God of Israel From everlasting to everlasting! Amen and Amen. (NKJV)

Who are the poor and needy? When you see a shabby-looking person standing at an intersection holding a scribbled sign, "Homeless, please help" what do you do? I must confess, I regularly fall short of a proper response. Far too often I speculate on how the person came to their plight. Worse yet, my cynical side may even doubt their apparent status, wondering if it is a charade to "make a buck." In the last verse of the preceding Psalm, David states, "But as for me, I am poor and needy." It is hard to picture a king in such dire straits but there are three primary Hebrew words used for poor. Financial poverty is the foremost use, but other times it means being afflicted due to personal trauma. In that sense, like David, we are ALL needy. Despite our own condition, God wants us to care for the poor. He blesses those who are His instruments to bless those in need.

O LORD, remind me that I'm blessed when I care about the poor and helpless. For You have promised to deliver the poor in their time of trouble, to protect and bless them. As for me, O LORD, I pray for Your mercy and healing hand as I confess my sin before You. I know that enemies may speak evil of me and wish for my demise, and there may be times when even trusted friends abandon me. May I always remember that You above all know what that is like, for You had to endure it. But You, O God, are gracious and raise me up in the midst of those who oppose me. Let me always walk with integrity and draw me into Your presence forevermore. Blessed are You, O LORD, from everlasting to everlasting. Amen

Psalm 42

To the Chief Musician. A Contemplation of the sons of Korah. **1** As the deer pants for the water brooks, So pants my soul for You, O God. **2** My soul thirsts for God, for the living God. When shall I come and appear before God? **3** My tears have been my food day and night, While they continually say to me, "Where is your God?" **4** When I remember these things, I pour out my soul within me. For I used to go with the multitude; I went with them to the house of God, With the voice of joy and praise, With a multitude that kept a pilgrim feast. **5** Why are you cast down, O my soul? And why are you disquieted within me? Hope in God, for I shall yet praise Him For the help of His countenance. **6** O my God, my soul is cast down within me; Therefore I will remember You from the land of the Jordan, And from the heights of Hermon, From the Hill Mizar. **7** Deep calls unto deep at the noise of Your waterfalls; All Your waves and billows have gone over me. **8** The Lord will command His lovingkindness in the daytime, And in the night His song shall be with me— A prayer to the God of my life. **9** I will say to God my Rock, "Why have You forgotten me? Why do I go mourning because of the oppression of the enemy?" **10** As with a breaking of my bones, My enemies reproach me, While they say to me all day long, "Where is your God?" **11** Why are you cast down, O my soul? And why are you disquieted within me? Hope in God; For I shall yet praise Him, The help of my countenance and my God. (NKJV)

Have you ever been so thirsty that all you can think about is getting a drink of cool water? I have never seen a deer pant but my Doberman Pinscher is another story. She loves to run and will chase a frisbee or ball for hours if you let her. But at some point, her thirst overrides her desire to "play catch." She will stop and stand in front of her water bowl, heavily panting and staring at me, begging me with her eyes to provide her some water. The Hebrew word for pant (arag) appears only three times in the Bible (twice in this Psalm and once in Joel 1). In all three uses, it emphasizes a sustained languishing and overwhelming cry of desire to quench a thirst. The Psalmist is saying his soul has such an unquenchable thirst or longing for God. When we feel spiritually parched and cast down, we must drink deeply from God's Word and let it saturate our soul. I wrote this poem to capture my thoughts on this Psalm:

A Peace That is Deeper Still

O soul of mine, be not cast down,
Packing burdens and overly marched.
A life dried up, fading to brown,
With a heart that is desperately parched.

A fountain is flowing, ready to pour,
Ever calling you deep unto deep.
Like waves ever crashing on to the shore,
To mingle with tears as you weep.

Pour out your soul, sing out your praise,
Place your hope in God's lasting love.
His peace will shine forth in glorious rays,
Then calmly descend like a dove.

O God, my soul thirsts for You. When I can't come into Your presence I become dry and parched, even while my eyes are wet with ever-flowing tears. It is then that I must stop, pour out my heart to You and ask myself, "Why am I so down in the dumps?" For You are my hope and I will praise You. No matter how deep my depression, Your faithful love is deeper still, roaring like a waterfall and washing over me like billowing waves. I am comforted by Your love and mercy in the daytime and Your song by night – a prayer to You, the God of my life! And when those downtrodden urges return, I will praise You, O God, for You are Jehovah Sel'i, the LORD My Rock, my Hope, and my Savior. Amen

Psalm 43

1 Vindicate me, O God, and plead my case against an ungodly nation; O deliver me from the deceitful and unjust man! 2 For You are the God of my strength; why have You rejected me? Why do I go mourning because of the oppression of the enemy? 3 O send out Your light and Your truth, let them lead me; Let them bring me to Your holy hill And to Your dwelling places. 4 Then I will go to the altar of God, To God my exceeding joy; And upon the lyre I shall praise You, O God, my God. 5 Why are you in despair, O my soul? And why are you disturbed within me? Hope in God, for I shall again praise Him, The help of my countenance and my God. (NASB)

Think back to how we traveled before the invention of GPS devices when a good map was key to getting to our destination. As a brand-new FBI Agent arriving in the booming Dallas Metroplex in 1985, one of the most important items we were issued was a map book called a "Mapsco." With well-defined grids and a detailed index, even the most obscure street was possible to locate. In today's world, we simply punch in an address and sojourn our merry way to a robotic voice of "turn left" or an occasional "recalculating" followed by "make a U-turn." Our Psalmist seeks the proper guidance to be led, finding that direction from the Lord. He has a bold confidence knowing that God is in complete control, able to overcome any obstacles or "traffic jams." Sometimes the signal of God's intersection is red to stop, green to go, and yellow for caution, but it is always a light of truth! For our destination isn't a local business or friend's house but the Lord's very presence. It is the place where we joyfully commune with God to present our offering of praise and thanksgiving for the great redemption He has provided. There is no need to doubt or worry when we let God be our guide!

O God, You are my advocate to plead my case and deliver me from an ungodly and hostile world. Because You are the God of my strength I have no fear of rejection or oppression from others. Send out Your light and truth to lead me and let me remain ever vigilant and obedient to follow; to come into Your holy presence with a heart full of joy. I have no need to worry or despair for my hope is in You. I will continually praise Your Holy Name for You are my salvation. Amen.

Psalm 44

For the choir director. A Maskil of the sons of Korah. **1** God, we have heard with our ears— our ancestors have told us— the work you accomplished in their days, in days long ago: **2** In order to plant them, you displaced the nations by your hand; in order to settle them, you brought disaster on the peoples. **3** For they did not take the land by their sword— their arm did not bring them victory— but by your right hand, your arm, and the light of your face, because you were favorable toward them. **4** You are my King, my God, who ordains victories for Jacob. **5** Through you we drive back our foes; through your name we trample our enemies. **6** For I do not trust in my bow, and my sword does not bring me victory. **7** But you give us victory over our foes and let those who hate us be disgraced. **8** We boast in God all day long; we will praise your name forever. *Selah* **9** But you have rejected and humiliated us; you do not march out with our armies. **10** You make us retreat from the foe, and those who hate us have taken plunder for themselves. **11** You hand us over to be eaten like sheep and scatter us among the nations. **12** You sell your people for nothing; you make no profit from selling them. **13** You make us an object of reproach to our neighbors, a source of mockery and ridicule to those around us. **14** You make us a joke among the nations, a laughingstock among the peoples. **15** My disgrace is before me all day long, and shame has covered my face, **16** because of the taunts of the scorner and reviler, because of the enemy and avenger. **17** All this has happened to us, but we have not forgotten you or betrayed your covenant. **18** Our hearts have not turned back; our steps have not strayed from your path. **19** But you have crushed us in a haunt of jackals and have covered us with deepest darkness. **20** If we had forgotten the name of our God and spread out our hands to a foreign god, **21** wouldn't God have found this out, since he knows the secrets of the heart? **22** Because of you we are being put to death all day long; we are counted as sheep to be slaughtered. **23** Wake up, Lord! Why are you sleeping? Get up! Don't reject us forever! **24** Why do you hide and forget our affliction and oppression? **25** For we have sunk down to the dust; our bodies cling to the ground. **26** Rise up! Help us! Redeem us because of your faithful love. (CSB)

Why is it we all love a good story? Whether an action-packed movie, a dramatic documentary or page-turning book, we are drawn to a well-told plot or message. For many, our love affair for lore began as children with "Once upon a time…" bedtime stories. This Psalm begins with the power of the epic tale to remind the reader of what God has done for His people "in days long ago." The Psalmist then looks at his present problems and proclaims that with God's power they will prevail by declaring it is "through you" that he will succeed. When things look grim for us, we are asked the key question in verse 21: Since God knows the secrets of the heart, do you really think the root cause of our problem is hidden from Him? Although we each desire a "happily ever after" ending in our life's tale, our real desire should be to hear: "Well done, good and faithful servant."

O God, through the annals of time we have heard and been reminded of Your great deeds. The accomplishments of man are only done by Your grace and through Your power. You, O God, are my King. I kneel in Your presence – command me to do Your bidding and I will obey. Even when my situation appears overwhelming, keep my heart faithful unto You and to You alone. Keep me humble and focused on Your love even when things appear dismal as if You have abandoned me. Yet, I know You remain true and have redeemed me for Your mercies' sake. Amen

Psalm 45

For the choir director; according to the Shoshannim. A Maskil of the sons of Korah. A Song of Love. **1** My heart overflows with a good theme; I address my verses to the King; My tongue is the pen of a ready writer. **2** You are fairer than the sons of men; Grace is poured upon Your lips; Therefore God has blessed You forever. **3** Gird Your sword on Your thigh, O Mighty One, In Your splendor and Your majesty! **4** And in Your majesty ride on victoriously, For the cause of truth and meekness and righteousness; Let Your right hand teach You awesome things. **5** Your arrows are sharp; The peoples fall under You; Your arrows are in the heart of the King's enemies. **6** Your throne, O God, is forever and ever; A scepter of uprightness is the scepter of Your kingdom. **7** You have loved righteousness and hated wickedness; Therefore God, Your God, has anointed You With the oil of joy above Your fellows. **8** All Your garments are fragrant with myrrh and aloes and cassia; Out of ivory palaces stringed instruments have made You glad. **9** Kings' daughters are among Your noble ladies; At Your right hand stands the queen in gold from Ophir. **10** Listen, O daughter, give attention and incline your ear: Forget your people and your father's house; **11** Then the King will desire your beauty. Because He is your LORD, bow down to Him. **12** The daughter of Tyre will come with a gift; The rich among the people will seek your favor. **13** The King's daughter is all glorious within; Her clothing is interwoven with gold. **14** She will be led to the King in embroidered work; The virgins, her companions who follow her, Will be brought to You. **15** They will be led forth with gladness and rejoicing; They will enter into the King's palace. **16** In place of your fathers will be your sons; You shall make them princes in all the earth. **17** I will cause Your name to be remembered in all generations; Therefore the peoples will give You thanks forever and ever. (NASB)

Many Psalms are prophetic in nature, allusions to the promised Messiah. Most Bible scholars consider this Psalm to be a picture of Christ in relationship to His kingdom and His bride, the Church. From the start, the Psalmist can barely contain himself in expressing the good theme or wonderful word about which he is writing. The Hebrew word used here for "overflows" (rachash) appears only here in the entire Bible and it means to be constantly astir. The inexpressible joy bubbles up from the author's heart and out through his lips to perfectly pronounce his King's beauty, grace, splendor, glory, truth, humility, and righteousness. May we also be of like-mind with hearts astir in love and worship, eager engines that allow our tongues to be obedient tools to proclaim Christ as King and Lord of all.

O LORD, You have made my heart overflow with a theme of goodness as I compose my prayer to You. Let my tongue be a skillful pen ready to write the words of praise from my heart. O LORD, as God's mighty and Anointed One, You await in majesty ready to ride victoriously in Your truth, humility, and righteousness to claim Your Bride. With a sword on Your thigh and a scepter of justice in hand, come soon to take Your Bride home. Let Your people listen intently for Your arrival, focusing only on You. May our beauty be in our obedience before You. I long for that day when You lead us in gladness and rejoicing into Your Palace on high. And finally, Your name will be remembered by all people, to be praised in thankfulness forevermore. Amen

Psalm 46

For the choir director. *A Psalm* of the sons of Korah, set to Alamoth. A Song. **1** God is our refuge and strength, A very present help in trouble. **2** Therefore we will not fear, though the earth should change And though the mountains slip into the heart of the sea; **3** Though its waters roar and foam, Though the mountains quake at its swelling pride. Selah. **4** There is a river whose streams make glad the city of God, The holy dwelling places of the Most High. **5** God is in the midst of her, she will not be moved; God will help her when morning dawns. **6** The nations made an uproar, the kingdoms tottered; He raised His voice, the earth melted. **7** The LORD of hosts is with us; The God of Jacob is our stronghold. Selah. **8** Come, behold the works of the LORD, Who has wrought desolations in the earth. **9** He makes wars to cease to the end of the earth; He breaks the bow and cuts the spear in two; He burns the chariots with fire. **10** "Cease striving and know that I am God; I will be exalted among the nations, I will be exalted in the earth." **11** The LORD of hosts is with us; The God of Jacob is our stronghold. Selah. (NASB)

Nearly 500 years ago, Martin Luther used this Psalm as the basis for his famous hymn, "A Mighty Fortress is Our God." The Psalm's first verse says God is not only our refuge and shelter but our very present help in trouble. The words, "very present" can be interpreted a couple ways: it might mean nearby, readily accessible and available. But the Hebrew word (matsa) means "proven" through experience. For emphasis, God has been "exceedingly" proven. No matter the situation, He is there to help. The thought of this made me pen this short poem:

Run to the Refuge

When life's winds wail and tempest's roar
and all seems in dire straits,
Run to the Lord, our Refuge and God,
and into His mighty gates.
The earth may quake and tremble,
as fear grows into deep distress,
Yet God remains true, solid and firm,
we are safe in His mighty fortress.

When we fear the Lord, we have nothing else to fear.

O God, You are my refuge and strength, always there to help me in the midst of troubles. No matter how crazy things get in this world, I will not fear. Earthquakes, floods, wars – You, O LORD, are in control. With a word, You created this world and all in it and with a word, You could melt it away. The greatest nations in all their might are nothing in Your presence. Put my heart at peace. Keep me from striving and let me always remember that You are God Almighty, to be exalted above all the earth. For You are always with me as my Mighty Fortress. Amen.

Psalm 47

To the choirmaster. A Psalm of the Sons of Korah. **1** Clap your hands, all peoples! Shout to God with loud songs of joy! **2** For the LORD, the Most High, is to be feared, a great king over all the earth. **3** He subdued peoples under us, and nations under our feet. **4** He chose our heritage for us, the pride of Jacob whom he loves. Selah **5** God has gone up with a shout, the LORD with the sound of a trumpet. **6** Sing praises to God, sing praises! Sing praises to our King, sing praises! **7** For God is the King of all the earth; sing praises with a psalm! **8** God reigns over the nations; God sits on his holy throne. **9** The princes of the peoples gather as the people of the God of Abraham. For the shields of the earth belong to God; he is highly exalted! (ESV)

Many Psalms tell us to "zamar" (the Hebrew verb to make music/sing in praise of God) but this one is unique as it tells us HOW to do it. The acronym "P-R-A-I-S-E" reminds us to praise God:

Physically (v.1 "clap your hands") bring applause to recognize God's greatness.

Reciprocally (v. 1 "all you people") do so collectively, together in one accord.

Audibly (v. 2 "shout with loud songs") there is no need to be shy about this.

Inspirationally (v. 2 "a voice of joy") to recognize our victory through Him.

Singing (v. 7 "sing praises") where we find the word zamar.

Expertly (v.7 "with understanding" or "with Psalms") in Hebrew it is "maskil" which you might recognize from many introductions. A maskil is a song/psalm done with a purpose, with understanding and consideration, to make you wise. Let us expertly sing praises to our Lord!

O God, I join with all people to clap my hands, singing and shouting for joy unto You. For You, O LORD, are supreme over all the earth and worthy of all praise. You set the course of nations and decide what will be the legacy and inheritance of all! For as You, O God, are high and lifted up, I lift up my voice in praise to You. Let all peoples and all nations know it is You who sits on Your holy throne and reigns. You protect those on earth whom You will with Your shield of love. My voice alone is not enough to exalt You. The voice of all the nations does not suffice Your glory, and so, it is only through Your own doing and majesty that You are highly exalted. Let me never stop praising Your Holy Name. Amen.

Psalm 48

A song. A psalm of the descendants of Korah. **1** How great is the LORD, how deserving of praise, in the city of our God, which sits on his holy mountain! **2** It is high and magnificent; the whole earth rejoices to see it! Mount Zion, the holy mountain, is the city of the great King! **3** God himself is in Jerusalem's towers, revealing himself as its defender. **4** The kings of the earth joined forces and advanced against the city. **5** But when they saw it, they were stunned; they were terrified and ran away. **6** They were gripped with terror and writhed in pain like a woman in labor. **7** You destroyed them like the mighty ships of Tarshish shattered by a powerful east wind. **8** We had heard of the city's glory, but now we have seen it ourselves— the city of the LORD of Heaven's Armies. It is the city of our God; he will make it safe forever. Interlude **9** O God, we meditate on your unfailing love as we worship in your Temple. **10** As your name deserves, O God, you will be praised to the ends of the earth. Your strong right hand is filled with victory. **11** Let the people on Mount Zion rejoice. Let all the towns of Judah be glad because of your justice. **12** Go, inspect the city of Jerusalem. Walk around and count the many towers. **13** Take note of the fortified walls, and tour all the citadels, that you may describe them to future generations. **14** For that is what God is like. He is our God forever and ever, and he will guide us until we die. (NLT)

Have you come upon some magnificent building and marveled at its beauty and architectural design? When my wife and I traveled to Italy we visited the Milan Cathedral. Walking on its roof among the 135 spires you feel as if you are in another world. When Mark Twain visited it, he wrote: "What a wonder it is! So grand, so solemn, so vast! And yet so delicate, so airy, so graceful! A very world of solid weight, and yet it seems …a delusion of frostwork that might vanish with a breath!" Sometimes, it is easy to focus too much on the building and not enough on the builder. At first glance, this Psalm's emphasis seems to be on the great city of Jerusalem. But closer inspection shows it is

God who is great and He who has imparted His beauty and greatness upon Mount Zion. His righteousness and steadfast love make the city and its inhabitants sing for joy. His power and majesty make enemies tremble in fear. Whether walking in a great city, grand cathedral or a quiet woodland path, let our focus and worship remain on the Maker of all things, without becoming distracted by the things that are made.

O LORD, how great You are and worthy of all praise. You chose Israel to be Your people and make Jerusalem Your Holy city to be a light and bring joy to the whole earth. No temple, palace or city, despite its splendor, can contain You and yet, just the mere presence of Your glory is enough to make all who pass by tremble with amazement and fear – And in Your presence, it is easy to meditate, to contemplate Your faithful love for me. Your name and the praise You are entitled reaches to the ends of the earth for You are just and righteous. Manmade temples and cathedrals built in Your honor can be impressive and remind us of Your majesty, and yet, they pale in comparison to Your glory. May such structures only remind me to worship You; to remember to tell my children and my children's children of who You are O God. For You are my God forever and ever and will remain my guide in life, through death and beyond. Amen.

Psalm 49

1 To the Chief Musician. A Psalm of the sons of Korah. Hear this, all peoples; Give ear, all inhabitants of the world, 2 Both low and high, Rich and poor together. 3 My mouth shall speak wisdom, And the meditation of my heart shall give understanding. 4 I will incline my ear to a proverb; I will disclose my dark saying on the harp. 5 Why should I fear in the days of evil, When the iniquity at my heels surrounds me? 6 Those who trust in their wealth And boast in the multitude of their riches, 7 None of them can by any means redeem his brother, Nor give to God a ransom for him— 8 For the redemption of their souls is costly, And it shall cease forever— 9 That he should continue to live eternally, And not see the Pit. 10 For he sees wise men die; Likewise the fool and the senseless person perish, And leave their wealth to others. 11 Their inner thought is that their houses will last forever, Their dwelling places to all generations; They call their lands after their own names. 12 Nevertheless man, though in honor, does not remain; He is like the beasts that perish. 13 This is the way of those who are foolish, And of their posterity who approve their sayings. Selah 14 Like sheep they are laid in the grave; Death shall feed on them; The upright shall have dominion over them in the morning; And their beauty shall be consumed in the grave, far from their dwelling. 15 But God will redeem my soul from the power of the grave, For He shall receive me. Selah 16 Do not be afraid when one becomes rich, When the glory of his house is increased; 17 For when he dies he shall carry nothing away; His glory shall not descend after him. 18 Though while he lives he blesses himself (For men will praise you when you do well for yourself), 19 He shall go to the generation of his fathers; They shall never see light. 20 A man who is in honor, yet does not understand, Is like the beasts that perish. (NKJV)

This Psalm is full of "rich" wisdom that applies to everyone no matter what their financial status. It provides relativity to the rich and perspective for the poor. Anyone trying to save their own soul or that of a friend or relative will find they are sitting alone in an empty bank vault, checkbook in hand with "insufficient funds." Surely, Jesus had this Psalm in mind when He said, "For what profit is it to a man if he gains the whole world, and loses his own soul?" It is also the basis for the oft-quoted saying of martyred missionary Jim Elliot, "He is no fool who gives what he cannot keep, to gain that which he cannot lose." He knew that though he might give his life for the cause of Christ, his death wouldn't save him. Rather, it was Jesus' death and faith in Him that allows sin to be "paid in full." Only checks written on Jesus' account will never bounce!

O God, may all people hear, and the entire earth, whether rich or poor, remember that You only can redeem a man's soul. Because of this, I have nothing to fear. No matter how rich a person becomes or how important someone thinks they are on the world's stage, they cannot save themselves or the ones they love. The price to redeem one's soul is so great a cost that only You can provide. The folly of man is to think they can, of their own accord, live forever. Whether wise or simple, we all return to the dust by which You formed us. And upon our return, all the wealth we have gathered we leave behind. Even if we lived in grand mansions or became so great that lands or countries are named after us, in the end, we die just like the beasts of the earth. It is not worldly riches that matter but the spiritual richness of Your redemption that determines our success. In the end, all will come to realize, a lifetime of wealth, glory, pomp, praise and self-congratulation will fade and disappear. Only our humble praise offered to You our Redeemer will echo through the halls of eternity. Amen

Psalm 50

A Psalm of Asaph. **1** Hear this, all peoples; Give ear, all inhabitants of the world, **2** Both low and high, Rich and poor together. **3** My mouth will speak wisdom, And the meditation of my heart will be understanding. **4** I will incline my ear to a proverb; I will express my riddle on the harp. **5** Why should I fear in days of adversity, When the iniquity of my foes surrounds me, **6** Even those who trust in their wealth And boast in the abundance of their riches? **7** No man can by any means redeem his brother Or give to God a ransom for him- **8** For the redemption of his soul is costly, And he should cease trying forever - **9** That he should live on eternally, That he should not undergo decay. **10** For he sees that even wise men die; The stupid and the senseless alike perish And leave their wealth to others. **11** Their inner thought is that their houses are forever And their dwelling places to all generations; They have called their lands after their own names. **12** But man in his pomp will not endure; He is like the beasts that perish. **13** This is the way of those who are foolish, And of those after them who approve their words. Selah. **14** As sheep they are appointed for Sheol; Death shall be their shepherd; And the upright shall rule over them in the morning, And their form shall be for Sheol to consume So that they have no habitation. **15** But God will redeem my soul from the power of Sheol, For He will receive me. Selah. **16** Do not be afraid when a man becomes rich, When the glory of his house is increased; **17** For when he dies he will carry nothing away; His glory will not descend after him. **18** Though while he lives he congratulates himself - And though men praise you when you do well for yourself- **19** He shall go to the generation of his fathers; They will never see the light. **20** Man in his pomp, yet without understanding, Is like the beasts that perish. (NASB)

When the prophet Samuel was trying to discern who should replace Saul as king, he was reminded that while man looks at outward appearances God always looks at the heart. To the Lord, it has always been a heart-thing. A

113

common theme throughout scripture is the need for a sacrifice to atone for sin. God set forth the very process. But there are numerous times where God says how tired He is of everyone's burnt offerings and sacrifices – what He really wants are obedient hearts in love with Him. The Psalmist takes note of the shortcomings of all the offerings and sacrifices that are continually before God. He doesn't need all the cattle of this world placed on an altar because He already owns them. What God truly desires is your heart. He wants us to place our thankful and obedient hearts on the altar before Him as our daily sacrifice of praise.

O God, You are the LORD Almighty and You have spoken. After creating this universe, You have maintained it in perfect harmony and all can see You in the beauty of Your creation. When You come forth in Your glory, who can stand? Before You, a devouring fire and around You rages a swirling storm. And then You call out for all heaven and earth to hear, "Gather my saints unto me!" You know each and every sacrifice placed before You but is that what You really want? You certainly don't need them, for the earth and all it contains is Yours – every beast in the forest and meadow, every bird in the air or the cattle on a thousand hills – all is Yours! You, O God, do not hunger for food or drink, but hunger after righteousness. What You really desire are hearts full of thanksgiving that honor You. The wicked will continue in their ways but those who call out to You will be rescued. O God, help me to conduct my life aright in a way that honors You in all I say and do. Amen

Psalm 51

To the choirmaster. A Psalm of David, when Nathan the prophet went to him, after he had gone in to Bathsheba. **1** Have mercy on me, O God, according to your steadfast love; according to your abundant mercy blot out my transgressions. **2** Wash me thoroughly from my iniquity, and cleanse me from my sin! **3** For I know my transgressions, and my sin is ever before me. **4** Against you, you only, have I sinned and done what is evil in your sight, so that you may be justified in your words and blameless in your judgment. **5** Behold, I was brought forth in iniquity, and in sin did my mother conceive me. **6** Behold, you delight in truth in the inward being, and you teach me wisdom in the secret heart. **7** Purge me with hyssop, and I shall be clean; wash me, and I shall be whiter than snow. **8** Let me hear joy and gladness; let the bones that you have broken rejoice. **9** Hide your face from my sins, and blot out all my iniquities. **10** Create in me a clean heart, O God, and renew a right spirit within me. **11** Cast me not away from your presence, and take not your Holy Spirit from me. **12** Restore to me the joy of your salvation, and uphold me with a willing spirit. **13** Then I will teach transgressors your ways, and sinners will return to you. **14** Deliver me from bloodguiltiness, O God, O God of my salvation, and my tongue will sing aloud of your righteousness. **15** O Lord, open my lips, and my mouth will declare your praise. **16** For you will not delight in sacrifice, or I would give it; you will not be pleased with a burnt offering. **17** The sacrifices of God are a broken spirit; a broken and contrite heart, O God, you will not despise. **18** Do good to Zion in your good pleasure; build up the walls of Jerusalem; **19** then will you delight in right sacrifices, in burnt offerings and whole burnt offerings; then bulls will be offered on your altar. (ESV)

No Psalm better portrays the perfect process to deal with sin. David knows the heights of joy to be in fellowship with God, as well as despair's depths when sin separates us from Him. David doesn't run from his sin attempting to hide or minimize it, rather, with open honesty, he acknowledges and confesses it. He asks God to "blot out" (utterly obliterate) his transgressions and iniquities – to be wholly washed and cleansed of the stain. With past sin now forgiven, David moves forward looking to the future. He pleads with the Creator of all, to create a clean heart within him; to rightly renew his spirit to allow him into God's presence and bring back that bond of fellowship he once enjoyed. He is then able to become an evangelist of God's saving message. This Psalm is not only a record of redemption but a lesson of liberation; a sermon of salvation!

O God, because of Your great love have mercy on me, a sinner. Erase my rebellious attitude and thoroughly wash away my guilt and cleanse me of my sin. O yes, my sin – I am well aware of it for it is right in front of my face and only You can clean it from my heart. No matter what my sin, ultimately it is against You – the perfect and Holy God who is just and righteous in Your judgment. From my birth, the stain of Adam's sin has been upon me – only You can remove it. You don't want me to make excuses or play games about it but to be honest with a heart of integrity so You can teach me Your wisdom. Only You can clean me through and through and wash me whiter than the freshly fallen snow. Open my ears to hear Your joy and heal my broken bones so I can dance in Your gladness. O God, replace my sinful heart with a clean and pure one, and with it a spirit of obedience. Do not send me from Your presence or take Your Holy Spirit from me. Restore to me the joy of Your salvation and sustain me with a spirit of willingness so I can teach others of Your great love. Let me be a light in a dark world to help lead others to You. Only You, O God, can rescue me from my own guilt. Protect me from the violence of others. Remind me of these things so my heart remains thankful and my mouth sings Your praises. Don't let me think a simple sacrifice of my own will appease You – that is not what You want! Help me to give what You really desire – a humble spirit and repentant heart for these You will always accept. That is the true act of worship which You want and are worthy to receive. Amen

Psalm 52

For the choir director. A Maskil of David, when Doeg the Edomite came and told Saul and said to him, "David has come to the house of Ahimelech." 1 Why do you boast in evil, O mighty man? The lovingkindness of God endures all day long. 2 Your tongue devises destruction, Like a sharp razor, O worker of deceit. 3 You love evil more than good, Falsehood more than speaking what is right. Selah. 4 You love all words that devour, O deceitful tongue. 5 But God will break you down forever; He will snatch you up and tear you away from your tent, And uproot you from the land of the living. Selah. 6 The righteous will see and fear, And will laugh at him, saying, 7 "Behold, the man who would not make God his refuge, But trusted in the abundance of his riches And was strong in his evil desire." 8 But as for me, I am like a green olive tree in the house of God; I trust in the lovingkindness of God forever and ever. 9 I will give You thanks forever, because You have done it, And I will wait on Your name, for it is good, in the presence of Your godly ones. (NASB)

If you are like me, you might overlook the introductory titles written for three-quarters of the Psalms and miss their insights. You may ask, "Who is Doeg the Edomite and what did he do?" David's disdain for this man is clearly manifest and no wonder. He was King Saul's chief of servants who not only revealed David's hiding place but killed 85 unarmed priests along with their families and livestock. You can almost hear the sarcasm dripping from David's pen when he writes, "O mighty man" as he provides a clear contrast between a wicked man living only for himself in the present versus a righteous God who lives forever; a stark distinction between slanderous deceit and truthfulness seeking justice. The detailed description of Doeg's destruction is decisive: he is broken down, snatched up, torn away and uprooted. It is a candid reminder of our daily choices in life, between good and evil. Let us be as David and trust in the Lord and be like a green olive tree growing in the house of God!

O LORD, counter any boastful evil thoughts I might have and replace them with the recognition of Your enduring lovingkindness. Keep my tongue from deceit and devising destruction and help me love good instead of evil, truth instead of lies. I know my tongue tends towards deceit – break that desire, O God. Help me to always see You as my refuge and not put my faith in my own strength or efforts. Rather, keep my eyes clearly focused on Your mercy and lovingkindness, O God, so I may be like a flourishing tree with roots delving deeply into Your Word. Keep my heart forever thankful to see all You have done and let me wait patiently in Your presence forevermore. Amen

Psalm 53

For the choir director: A meditation; a psalm of David. **1** Only fools say in their hearts, "There is no God." They are corrupt, and their actions are evil; not one of them does good! **2** God looks down from heaven on the entire human race; he looks to see if anyone is truly wise, if anyone seeks God. **3** But no, all have turned away; all have become corrupt. No one does good, not a single one! **4** Will those who do evil never learn? They eat up my people like bread and wouldn't think of praying to God. **5** Terror will grip them, terror like they have never known before. God will scatter the bones of your enemies. You will put them to shame, for God has rejected them. **6** Who will come from Mount Zion to rescue Israel? When God restores his people, Jacob will shout with joy, and Israel will rejoice. (NLT)

What a contrast – the person who was described as a man after God's own heart is writing about the fool who in his heart says there is no God. In truth, that is the real definition of foolishness. We are not talking about a lack of mental capacity or intellect, but someone who makes a willful choice to disregard God's existence and His ways. Here is David's point: this choice is key to the development of a wicked heart. It is a process of decay leading to utter ruin. In his letter to the Romans, the Apostle Paul states that since the beginning of time (creation) everyone has known deep down that God exists. The fool chooses not to glorify or thank Him, resulting in a mind full of futile thoughts and a darkened heart. But God provided us the bridge from our foolishness to His righteousness in Christ Jesus – all we need to do is walk across it in faith.

O God, may I never become like the fools of this world who deny Your very existence. Deep down, they must know You are there and yet, they choose a path of corruption and injustice instead of following You. You look upon all mankind to see if anyone seeks after You and acts wisely. But alas, everyone has chosen the path they think suits them best. No one on their own accord does good, not even one. Keep me from being like those who live in constant dread, timid and terrified of faceless fears. But thanks be to You, O God, who has supplied salvation to set our captive hearts free. You crush the workers of wickedness but give life to those who follow You. Amen

Psalm 54

To the Chief Musician. With stringed instruments. A Contemplation of David when the Ziphites went and said to Saul, 'Is David not hiding with us?' **1** Save me, O God, by Your name, And vindicate me by Your strength. **2** Hear my prayer, O God; Give ear to the words of my mouth. **3** For strangers have risen up against me, And oppressors have sought after my life; They have not set God before them. Selah **4** Behold, God is my helper; The Lord is with those who uphold my life. **5** He will repay my enemies for their evil. Cut them off in Your truth. **6** I will freely sacrifice to You; I will praise Your name, O Lord, for it is good. **7** For He has delivered me out of all trouble; And my eye has seen its desire upon my enemies. (NKJV)

This short Psalm offers a clear contrast in where we should put our trust, namely God or man. The Psalm's introduction mentions the "Ziphites" which begs the question, who were they? They were Judeans who lived in the Desert of Ziph and despite being kindred, David calls them strangers. David, experiencing his own wilderness wandering trying to escape capture from Saul, is betrayed twice by the Ziphites who tell Saul where he was hiding. While the Ziphites saw David as a "sacrifice" to gain favor with Saul, David shows the proper response and cries out to God and freely offers his sacrifice to Him. Let's face it, we all have Ziphites in our lives – those who we should be able to trust but instead, at best let us down or worse, downright stab us in the back. That is when we must be like David and place our trust wholly and only in the LORD.

O God, Your name speaks to power and justice and through it, You have saved me. Hear my prayer O LORD and listen to the words I speak. When those who have no regard for You or Your ways oppose me, You will help me. For You, O LORD, are the one who sustains my soul and will deal justly with my foes. O LORD, everything I have is Yours and I freely give it back to You with a thankful and happy heart. Blessed be Your name, O God, for You are my deliverer from the troubles and enemies in this life. Amen

Psalm 55

To the choirmaster: with stringed instruments. A Maskil of David. **1** God, listen to my prayer and do not hide from my plea for help. **2** Pay attention to me and answer me. I am restless and in turmoil with my complaint, **3** because of the enemy's words, because of the pressure of the wicked. For they bring down disaster on me and harass me in anger. **4** My heart shudders within me; terrors of death sweep over me. **5** Fear and trembling grip me; horror has overwhelmed me. **6** I said, "If only I had wings like a dove! I would fly away and find rest. **7** How far away I would flee; I would stay in the wilderness. *Selah* **8** I would hurry to my shelter from the raging wind and the storm." **9** Lord, confuse and confound their speech, for I see violence and strife in the city; **10** day and night they make the rounds on its walls. Crime and trouble are within it; **11** destruction is inside it; oppression and deceit never leave its marketplace. **12** Now it is not an enemy who insults me— otherwise I could bear it; it is not a foe who rises up against me— otherwise I could hide from him. **13** But it is you, a man who is my peer, my companion and good friend! **14** We used to have close fellowship; we walked with the crowd into the house of God. **15** Let death take them by surprise; let them go down to Sheol alive, because evil is in their homes and within them. **16** But I call to God, and the Lord will save me. **17** I complain and groan morning, noon, and night, and he hears my voice. **18** Though many are against me, he will redeem me from my battle unharmed. **19** God, the one enthroned from long ago, will hear and will humiliate them *Selah* because they do not change and do not fear God. **20** My friend acts violently against those at peace with him; he violates his covenant. **21** His buttery words are smooth, but war is in his heart. His words are softer than oil, but they are drawn swords. **22** Cast your burden on the Lord, and he will sustain you; he will never allow the righteous to be shaken. **23** God, you will bring them down to the Pit of destruction; men of bloodshed and treachery will not live out half their days. But I will trust in you. (CSB)

Have you ever been betrayed by a close companion, someone in whom you had placed your utmost confidence? David contrasts the taunting of an enemy with the double-dealing duplicity of a friend. He can handle the former, but the latter causes him to become so unsettled that he feels like a restless wandering nomad, unable to focus on anything else. In response, morning, noon and night he cries out to God for help, knowing He will not only hear him but will bring peace to his soul. Can we have the same assurance as David? Yes, and more. Jesus was forsaken by a friend; left by a loved one. We immediately think of Judas' betrayal, but that pales in comparison to the moment the word "godforsaken" became the defining point of history. Because Jesus was abandoned on the cross we can now rest assured He will never leave us alone.

Hear my prayer, O LORD, and in Your gracious mercy pay heed to and answer my supplication before You. When I meditate on You and Your Word, I so often become restless and distracted by the things of this world. The pressure of the wicked and my enemies bring anguish to my heart. At times it can become overwhelming. The storms of life can become so great that it makes me want to fly away, to find peace and quiet in a place of restful refuge. And yet, no matter where my enemies are, from within or without, my only true peace is in You O LORD. I will call upon You day and night and You will save me. I will meditate on You and listen to Your voice. Upon hearing it, I will know it is You who has redeemed my soul and given me peace from the battles I face. I will cast all my burdens on You, O LORD, for I know You will sustain me. I will ever trust You for Your mighty hand will hold me fast and secure all the days of my life. Amen

Psalm 56

To the choirmaster: according to The Dove on Far-off Terebinths. A Miktam of David, when the Philistines seized him in Gath. **1** Be gracious to me, O God, for man tramples on me; all day long an attacker oppresses me; **2** my enemies trample on me all day long, for many attack me proudly. **3** When I am afraid, I put my trust in you. **4** In God, whose word I praise, in God I trust; I shall not be afraid. What can flesh do to me? **5** All day long they injure my cause; all their thoughts are against me for evil. **6** They stir up strife, they lurk; they watch my steps, as they have waited for my life. **7** For their crime will they escape? In wrath cast down the peoples, O God! **8** You have kept count of my tossings; put my tears in your bottle. Are they not in your book? **9** Then my enemies will turn back in the day when I call. This I know, that God is for me. **10** In God, whose word I praise, in the LORD, whose word I praise, **11** in God I trust; I shall not be afraid. What can man do to me? **12** I must perform my vows to you, O God; I will render thank offerings to you. **13** For you have delivered my soul from death, yes, my feet from falling, that I may walk before God in the light of life. (ESV)

Does it seem like some days, despite your best effort, everyone wants to walk all over you? Or, no matter who you talk to everyone wants to argue or ridicule you? The constant contempt and relentless hounding can be so disheartening. But in those times, it is important to remember that God understands how we feel. He perceives the pain behind each of our teardrops and He keeps tabs on the hurts within each of our heartbeats. To those who would ask, "How does God know how I feel" they only need to look at what Jesus had to endure. The mocking and disdain by His enemies and the failures and abandonment by those who loved Him would be enough to cause most to just give up. Yet He took that burden for us all the way to the cross. If He was willing to die for us He certainly will be with us in our daily lives.

O God, I pray for Your gracious hand of protection this day as I face the foes of this life that seek to oppress me and trample down the joy You provide. When those fears creep in, remind me to steadily place my trust in You. Your Word remains my steadfast foundation and standing firmly upon it my footing is secure. Despite the efforts of man to wish me harm, I will not fear. What can mortal flesh do to me in Your presence, O God? Even if my enemies are lurking nearby, watching my steps to plot my demise, it is You, O God, who has set my path before me. You know where I have been and where I am going. You know my thoughts and have bottled up the tears from the cry of my heart. No matter what I face, this I know: If You are for me, what shall I fear? The promises of Your Word bind my heart to Yours, O God. Your Word is not a fetter to my feet but wings of deliverance. It lights my path to keep me from stumbling so I may always walk upright in Your presence, in this life and forever more. Amen

Psalm 57

For the choir director; *set to* Al-tashheth. A Mikhtam of David, when he fled from Saul in the cave. **1** Be gracious to me, O God, be gracious to me, For my soul takes refuge in You; And in the shadow of Your wings I will take refuge Until destruction passes by. **2** I will cry to God Most High, To God who accomplishes all things for me. **3** He will send from heaven and save me; He reproaches him who tramples upon me. Selah. God will send forth His lovingkindness and His truth. **4** My soul is among lions; I must lie among those who breathe forth fire, Even the sons of men, whose teeth are spears and arrows And their tongue a sharp sword. **5** Be exalted above the heavens, O God; Let Your glory be above all the earth. **6** They have prepared a net for my steps; My soul is bowed down; They dug a pit before me; They themselves have fallen into the midst of it. Selah. **7** My heart is steadfast, O God, my heart is steadfast; I will sing, yes, I will sing praises! **8** Awake, my glory! Awake, harp and lyre! I will awaken the dawn. **9** I will give thanks to You, O LORD, among the peoples; I will sing praises to You among the nations. **10** For Your lovingkindness is great to the heavens And Your truth to the clouds. **11** Be exalted above the heavens, O God; Let Your glory be above all the earth. (NASB)

Since retiring from the FBI, I have witnessed an increased attack on my fellow brothers and sisters in law enforcement. It grieves me to see so many servants for good being wrongly mischaracterized far too often. Are they perfect? Of course not, but only those who have walked in their shoes can truly appreciate the challenges they face. We should daily remember them all in our prayers – for discernment in their duty and safety in their service. This Psalm, as well as Isaiah 54:14, make for a good prayer: "No weapon formed against you shall prosper, And every tongue *which* rises against you in judgment You shall condemn." In the midst of dangers faced in this life, we can always find sanctuary in His presence. God's grace is not a random act nor His mercy a thoughtless deed. He knows us, loves us and will care for us in our daily life.

O God, be gracious to me as my soul takes refuge in You. Even the shadow of Your presence provides protection. I will cry out to You, LORD God Most High, who is able to accomplish all things. From Heaven on high, You send forth Your truth and lovingkindness to set right the attacks of this world – from those who prowl like lions whose words scorch like fire with tongues as sharp as swords. But You O God, are exalted above the heavens and the earth. You protect me from the traps of those who wish me harm. My heart will remain thankful and steadfast, secure in Your great love and mercy and I will praise Your Holy Name above all the earth. Amen

Psalm 58

For the choir director: A psalm of David, to be sung to the tune "Do Not Destroy!" **1** Justice—do you rulers know the meaning of the word? Do you judge the people fairly? **2** No! You plot injustice in your hearts. You spread violence throughout the land. **3** These wicked people are born sinners; even from birth they have lied and gone their own way. **4** They spit venom like deadly snakes; they are like cobras that refuse to listen, **5** ignoring the tunes of the snake charmers, no matter how skillfully they play. **6** Break off their fangs, O God! Smash the jaws of these lions, O LORD! **7** May they disappear like water into thirsty ground. Make their weapons useless in their hands. **8** May they be like snails that dissolve into slime, like a stillborn child who will never see the sun. **9** God will sweep them away, both young and old, faster than a pot heats over burning thorns. **10** The godly will rejoice when they see injustice avenged. They will wash their feet in the blood of the wicked. **11** Then at last everyone will say, "There truly is a reward for those who live for God; surely there is a God who judges justly here on earth." (NLT)

If you are like millions of others, you probably saw "The Two Towers," a movie based on Tolkien's trilogy, "The Lord of the Rings." If so, you might recall the alarming scene wherein the wicked wizard Saruman has transformed the caverns of Isengard into a factory of destruction, decimating forests to feed the fires to forge weapons of war. It is there he also breads a new race of evil orcs, stronger than men and able to endure great pain in battle. It is the epitome of evil. In this Psalm, David captures the deep-seated sin in the heart of malevolent men – a heart not only a heinous home of depravity but an underground workshop, crafting wares of wickedness. He paints a picture of corruption and just about the time we say, "no more" he reminds us of the outcome: the righteous rejoice when they see their sovereign God judge. We must never be dismayed for our God reigns!

O God, there are so many self-righteous people in this world – they say one thing and do another. Help me to never act in such a way. From the time of their birth, the wicked seek to do violence, imparting their venomous lies. O God, I look to You to break off their fangs, to break the shafts of their arrows, to make them become like slimy snails, melting away on a hot summer day. Blow Your righteous breath and sweep them away and reward those who seek Your face and follow Your ways. Amen

Psalm 59

To the choirmaster: according to Do Not Destroy. A Miktam of David, when Saul sent men to watch his house in order to kill him. **1** Deliver me from my enemies, O my God; protect me from those who rise up against me; **2** deliver me from those who work evil, and save me from bloodthirsty men. **3** For behold, they lie in wait for my life; fierce men stir up strife against me. For no transgression or sin of mine, O LORD, **4** for no fault of mine, they run and make ready. Awake, come to meet me, and see! **5** You, LORD God of hosts, are God of Israel. Rouse yourself to punish all the nations; spare none of those who treacherously plot evil. Selah **6** Each evening they come back, howling like dogs and prowling about the city. **7** There they are, bellowing with their mouths with swords in their lips— for "Who," they think, "will hear us?" **8** But you, O LORD, laugh at them; you hold all the nations in derision. **9** O my Strength, I will watch for you, for you, O God, are my fortress. **10** My God in his steadfast love will meet me; God will let me look in triumph on my enemies. **11** Kill them not, lest my people forget; make them totter by your power and bring them down, O Lord, our shield! **12** For the sin of their mouths, the words of their lips, let them be trapped in their pride. For the cursing and lies that they utter, **13** consume them in wrath; consume them till they are no more, that they may know that God rules over Jacob to the ends of the earth. Selah **14** Each evening they come back, howling like dogs and prowling about the city. **15** They wander about for food and growl if they do not get their fill. **16** But I will sing of your strength; I will sing aloud of your steadfast love in the morning. For you have been to me a fortress and a refuge in the day of my distress. **17** O my Strength, I will sing praises to you, for you, O God, are my fortress, the God who shows me steadfast love. (ESV)

How do you feel about facing the new day when you first wake up? The Psalmist says he will joyfully sing each morning about God's strength and mercy in how He protects him. I wrote this poem/prayer to start the day anew:

Morning Prayer

Before I rise, O Lord, this day,
Upon my bed I now delay,
With humble heart to You I pray,
Mold me into Your hands like clay.
Please keep the enemy at bay,
So I will not become his prey,
Remove my sin with its decay,
And in Your peace my fears allay.
All wrong desires help me slay,
And each decision let me weigh,
For whether I'm at work or play,
I know my deeds are on display.
My yearning heart wants to obey,
To stay the course and not astray,
Let everything I do and say,
Be in accordance with Your way. Amen

O God, deliver me from those who wish me harm and lift me up, secure and accessible to only You and Your will. Even when I do good and my heart is right with You, there will be those who will stir up strife in my life. They are like howling dogs encircling the city, looking for their prey. Despite their evil intentions and their perceived power, You scoff at them. Despite their strength, it is You, Jehovah Maginnenu, the LORD Our Defense, who remains my stronghold and my shield. As their pride becomes their downfall let my heart ever remain humble before You. Let my heart sing for joy of Your strength and lovingkindness, each morning, throughout the day, and forevermore. Amen

Psalm 60

For the choir director; according to Shushan Eduth. A Mikhtam of David, to teach; when he struggled with Aram-naharaim and with Aram-zobah, and Joab returned, and smote twelve thousand of Edom in the Valley of Salt. **1** O God, You have rejected us. You have broken us; You have been angry; O, restore us. **2** You have made the land quake, You have split it open; Heal its breaches, for it totters. **3** You have made Your people experience hardship; You have given us wine to drink that makes us stagger. **4** You have given a banner to those who fear You, That it may be displayed because of the truth. Selah. **5** That Your beloved may be delivered, Save with Your right hand, and answer us! **6** God has spoken in His holiness: "I will exult, I will portion out Shechem and measure out the valley of Succoth. **7** Gilead is Mine, and Manasseh is Mine; Ephraim also is the helmet of My head; Judah is My scepter. **8** Moab is My washbowl; Over Edom I shall throw My shoe; Shout loud, O Philistia, because of Me!" **9** Who will bring me into the besieged city? Who will lead me to Edom? **10** Have not You Yourself, O God, rejected us? And will You not go forth with our armies, O God? **11** O give us help against the adversary, For deliverance by man is in vain. **12** Through God we shall do valiantly, And it is He who will tread down our adversaries. (NASB)

In this Psalm, we see a kingdom on the brink of falling, a king tottering on his throne. It may be that David is living in a time in which he has to contend with the ruinous results of Saul's sinful disobedience. His people have endured great difficulties and David is seeking total restoration from the LORD. He sees that God has provided a banner for those who will fear Him and upon displaying it, beckons all to come. There are two Hebrew words for "banner" – one is "degel" and refers to a standard that is distinct or unique to identify a particular group or tribe; the other is "nes" which is used here, and is a standard lifted high to draw everyone together, as a rallying point to unify a people. It is so reassuring that we serve a glorious

God who can take diverse people from all nations and unite us under a single banner of His great love!

O God, any rejection I feel from You is because I have said and done things that reject You and Your ways. In Your righteous anger, I pray that You will restore me. When the world around me trembles and feels like it is on the brink of destruction, I pray You will heal it and heal me. In Your loving discipline, there are times I will experience hardship. When I am confused and stagger around like a dazed drunk clear my mind and my eyes to see Your truth as I seek You and Your deliverance. In Your holiness, You give and take as You deem best. Remind me daily that there is no deliverance from man but only from You. It is only in You, Jehovah Nissi, the LORD My Banner, to Whom I can rally and be victorious against life's adversaries. Amen

Psalm 61

To the Chief Musician. On a stringed instrument. A Psalm of David. **1** Hear my cry, O God; Attend to my prayer. **2** From the end of the earth I will cry to You, When my heart is overwhelmed; Lead me to the rock that is higher than I. **3** For You have been a shelter for me, A strong tower from the enemy. **4** I will abide in Your tabernacle forever; I will trust in the shelter of Your wings. Selah **5** For You, O God, have heard my vows; You have given me the heritage of those who fear Your name. **6** You will prolong the king's life, His years as many generations. **7** He shall abide before God forever. Oh, prepare mercy and truth, which may preserve him! **8** So I will sing praise to Your name forever, That I may daily perform my vows. (NKJV)

Did you ever make pretend tents when you were a child growing up? They might have been as skimpy as some old blanket or sheets draped over the backs of chairs but for some reason, as simple and flimsy as they might have been, they still seemed to provide a sanctuary of shelter once you climbed under and were inside. Talk about a false sense of security! Now imagine being within the tent of the King of the Universe – the finest fabrics woven into a tapestry strong enough to weather any storm, withstand any wind and comfort in any inclement condition. And yet, it isn't the tent that protects you but the presence of Him within the tent that brings you peace and safety. In this Psalm, you can hear the yearning of David's heart, pleading that he be allowed to dwell in the Lord's tent forever. O that we may also share that same desire!

O God, hear my cry unto You and listen to my prayer. Whether close at home or abroad in far off lands, keep me close to You. From my first breath to the final beating of my heart, lead me to You, my firm foundation and the Rock of my salvation. In You and on Your promises I find my refuge and protection against my enemies. I am but a sojourner on earth in life's journey - let me forever find my peace dwelling in Your tent and not in man-made abodes. Let me find my shelter from Your wings. You know the promises of my heart unto You, O LORD. You have blessed me by calling me to be a member of Your everlasting family who fears Your name and recognizes You as the LORD God Almighty. You have prolonged that blessing from parents to children to my children's children. Your lovingkindness and truth are the linchpins connecting and preserving the generations. Keep my heart close to Yours, O God, that I may daily remain true to You and sing Your praises, now and forevermore. Amen

Psalm 62

1 For God alone my soul waits in silence; from him comes my salvation. 2 He only is my rock and my salvation, my fortress; I shall not be greatly shaken. 3 How long will all of you attack a man to batter him, like a leaning wall, a tottering fence? 4 They only plan to thrust him down from his high position. They take pleasure in falsehood. They bless with their mouths, but inwardly they curse. Selah 5 For God alone, O my soul, wait in silence, for my hope is from him. 6 He only is my rock and my salvation, my fortress; I shall not be shaken. 7 On God rests my salvation and my glory; my mighty rock, my refuge is God. 8 Trust in him at all times, O people; pour out your heart before him; God is a refuge for us. Selah 9 Those of low estate are but a breath; those of high estate are a delusion; in the balances they go up; they are together lighter than a breath. 10 Put no trust in extortion; set no vain hopes on robbery; if riches increase, set not your heart on them. 11 Once God has spoken; twice have I heard this: that power belongs to God, 12 and that to you, O Lord, belongs steadfast love. For you will render to a man according to his work. (ESV)

When planning a tactical operation in the FBI, you had to always develop alternative plans for various contingencies. In our daily life, we have a tendency to "hedge our bets" by looking for multiple options to ensure we will always be on the winning side. Isn't that the way we all are? Usually, we don't like to put all our eggs in a single basket. But David in this Psalm leaves no doubt where and in Whom he places his trust and confidence. He makes it clear that when you wait upon the Lord and place your hope solely in Him, there is no need to look for other options or a backup plan. But notice, David takes it one step further - not only are you wait solely on the Lord, but you are to do so patiently. You should wait in silence. Why? To hear what He has to say. To not let other things distract you when you see God in action and watch in amazement how He will come to your rescue.

O God, in You alone does my soul find its peace and quiet for You alone are my steadfast Rock and salvation. Unlike those who are assailed by men and have not Your protection – they are like a flimsy fence or weakened wall ready to come crashing down. They love living the lie, saying nice things to my face but cursing me in their heart. Despite this, my soul is at rest in You, O God, my Rock, and salvation. In all times and circumstances, I will put my trust in You. Whether someone is lowly and poor or high and mighty, in the end, without You all are but a vapor, a delusional puff of air. There are no rewards for evildoing so keep my heart unattached to the false and fleeting riches of this world. Let Your spoken and written Word echo in my heart and mind that all power and steadfast love belong to You O LORD, so that all I say and do are pleasing in Your sight. Amen

Psalm 63

A Psalm of David, when he was in the wilderness of Judah. **1** O God, You are my God; I shall seek You earnestly; My soul thirsts for You, my flesh yearns for You, In a dry and weary land where there is no water. **2** Thus I have seen You in the sanctuary, To see Your power and Your glory. **3** Because Your lovingkindness is better than life, My lips will praise You. **4** So I will bless You as long as I live; I will lift up my hands in Your name. **5** My soul is satisfied as with marrow and fatness, And my mouth offers praises with joyful lips. **6** When I remember You on my bed, I meditate on You in the night watches, **7** For You have been my help, And in the shadow of Your wings I sing for joy. **8** My soul clings to You; Your right hand upholds me. **9** But those who seek my life to destroy it, Will go into the depths of the earth. **10** They will be delivered over to the power of the sword; They will be a prey for foxes. **11** But the king will rejoice in God; Everyone who swears by Him will glory, For the mouths of those who speak lies will be stopped. (NASB)

As human beings, we have many needs – physical, emotional and spiritual. The latter two types can sometimes be difficult to fully express or accurately characterize, but we are completely aware of our physical cravings and demands. In this Psalm, David provides us physical feelings which we can all relate to that help describe his spiritual yearnings. He "yearns" for God (Hebrew word kamah) which is only used here in the Bible and it means to faint, long or turn pale. We have all been hot and thirsty, longing for a cool drink of water, only to be without any. The Hebrew word David uses for thirst (tsame) is the same one Sampson used when he told God he would die of thirst after killing the 1,000 Philistines. Let us pray we become so in tune with our spiritual needs that our physical desires pale in comparison!

O God, You are my God. Let my first waking thought in the morning be to earnestly seek You. May I yearn for You like the parched land awaits the rain. My longing heart has sought You out to behold Your power and glory. I will speak Your praises because Your merciful love is better than life itself. My hands are lifted high in prayer before You. Only You can satisfy the longing in my inner being so that it wells up within me and causes my lips to joyfully sing Your praises. When night falls and I lay my head on my pillow let me deeply meditate on You and how You have always been my help in times of need. Your wings of protection cover me and Your own right hand supports me. Anyone who seeks to destroy me in opposition to You will quickly see their own demise and ruin. Keep me ever faithful and obedient to You, for in You alone is my hope and glory and victory. Amen

Psalm 64

To the Chief Musician. A Psalm of David. **1** Hear my voice, O God, in my meditation; Preserve my life from fear of the enemy. **2** Hide me from the secret plots of the wicked, From the rebellion of the workers of iniquity, **3** Who sharpen their tongue like a sword, And bend their bows to shoot their arrows—bitter words, **4** That they may shoot in secret at the blameless; Suddenly they shoot at him and do not fear. **5** They encourage themselves in an evil matter; They talk of laying snares secretly; They say, "Who will see them?" **6** They devise iniquities: "We have perfected a shrewd scheme." Both the inward thought and the heart of man are deep. **7** But God shall shoot at them with an arrow; Suddenly they shall be wounded. **8** So He will make them stumble over their own tongue; All who see them shall flee away. **9** All men shall fear, And shall declare the work of God; For they shall wisely consider His doing. **10** The righteous shall be glad in the Lord, and trust in Him. And all the upright in heart shall glory. (NKJV)

Let's face it, we've all been wounded by words, brandished as weapons in heartless hands. This Psalm is a preservation prayer for protection against such plots. David descriptively compares these verbal attacks: the tongue is a sharpened sword and bitter words are arrows shot from the bended bow. If you have ever shot an arrow you know the procedure – carefully attaching the arrow to string, purposefully pulling it back and tactfully taking aim. It is a very deliberate process similar to those who maliciously speak their well-planned words. And yet, God fights for us, not only shooting His arrow to wound the wicked but giving us another mighty weapon. Like a two-edged sword, the Holy Spirit uses God's Word to cut to the heart and judge every person's thoughts and intentions. Drill daily into the Word and you will wield a weapon against the wiles of the world.

O God, when I come to You in prayer and meditation please hear my voice. Keep me safe in the palm of Your hand, hidden from those who plot evil, who use their tongues like a sword, who shoot out their bitter words like arrows. The world is full of such people – those who attack the innocent from their haughty heights of arrogance, thinking their secret snares and well-planned plots are unstoppable. But in their cunningly conceived crimes, they forget one thing – You, O God, know all there is. Before they know what hits them Your mighty arrow of truth will strike deep into their heart and they will stumble. Their sharp words will cut their own throats. All who see this will stop, and in awe and wonder, declare Your great deeds and proclaim with bended knee You are the LORD God Almighty. Let me be that righteous man who takes joy in You and Your protection, that my heart remains humble and upright before You so I may forevermore praise Your name. Amen

Psalm 65

For the choir director. A Psalm of David. A Song. **1** There will be silence before You, and praise in Zion, O God, And to You the vow will be performed. **2** O You who hear prayer, To You all men come. **3** Iniquities prevail against me; As for our transgressions, You forgive them. **4** How blessed is the one whom You choose and bring near to You To dwell in Your courts. We will be satisfied with the goodness of Your house, Your holy temple. **5** By awesome deeds You answer us in righteousness, O God of our salvation, You who are the trust of all the ends of the earth and of the farthest sea; **6** Who establishes the mountains by His strength, Being girded with might; **7** Who stills the roaring of the seas, The roaring of their waves, And the tumult of the peoples. **8** They who dwell in the ends of the earth stand in awe of Your signs; You make the dawn and the sunset shout for joy. **9** You visit the earth and cause it to overflow; You greatly enrich it; The stream of God is full of water; You prepare their grain, for thus You prepare the earth. **10** You water its furrows abundantly, You settle its ridges, You soften it with showers, You bless its growth. **11** You have crowned the year with Your bounty, And Your paths drip with fatness. **12** The pastures of the wilderness drip, And the hills gird themselves with rejoicing. **13** The meadows are clothed with flocks And the valleys are covered with grain; They shout for joy, yes, they sing. (NASB)

Have you ever longingly waited for a special event? This Psalm of expectancy begins in an unusual manner – silent praise. Typically, our praise is clapping, singing, shouts of joy, but here, we see a quiet repose of worship. There is a faithful expectation that God will save us – almost a thankful response even before receiving His gift. In many ways, it is apropos that this Psalm continues with a tribute to God's creation and the richness of the fruited plain. If you have ever driven across America's heartland you have seen firsthand the mile upon mile of fertile farmland. Each year, thousands of farmers plant their crops and then patiently, yet expectantly, await the miracle of life to take place. We too must allow God to perform His miracle in us. Patiently, yet expectantly in faith, we wait upon the Lord as He changes us into the person He desires us to become.

O God, I come before You in silence to offer You my praise and lift up my thank offerings to You. You are the God who hears my prayer and sooner or later all mankind will know it and come before You. When my sin is overwhelming and seems too heavy to bear, only You can provide atonement and forgive me – and with Your forgiveness comes the blessing of being drawn into Your presence, to abide with You in Your holy temple. I remain in awe of Your acts of righteousness, O God of my salvation. I humbly hope in You as does all the ends of the earth. For by Your strength and mighty power You multiplied mountains, silenced seas, and calmed clamoring nations. From east to west all stand in awe of You and wonder at Your marvelous signs. From sunrise to sunset You give reason to shout for joy! With sun and rain, You provide all that is needed for the fertile fields to produce abundantly. The flock-filled pastures and plentiful plains of grain shout together for joy singing Your praises. Let my voice join in the chorus to praise Your Holy Name. Amen

Psalm 66

To the Chief Musician. A Song. A Psalm. **1** Make a joyful shout to God, all the earth! **2** Sing out the honor of His name; Make His praise glorious. **3** Say to God, "How awesome are Your works! Through the greatness of Your power Your enemies shall submit themselves to You. **4** All the earth shall worship You And sing praises to You; They shall sing praises to Your name." Selah **5** Come and see the works of God; He is awesome in His doing toward the sons of men. **6** He turned the sea into dry land; They went through the river on foot. There we will rejoice in Him. **7** He rules by His power forever; His eyes observe the nations; Do not let the rebellious exalt themselves. Selah **8** Oh, bless our God, you peoples! And make the voice of His praise to be heard, **9** Who keeps our soul among the living, And does not allow our feet to be moved. **10** For You, O God, have tested us; You have refined us as silver is refined. **11** You brought us into the net; You laid affliction on our backs. **12** You have caused men to ride over our heads; We went through fire and through water; But You brought us out to rich fulfillment. **13** I will go into Your house with burnt offerings; I will pay You my vows, **14** Which my lips have uttered And my mouth has spoken when I was in trouble. **15** I will offer You burnt sacrifices of fat animals, With the sweet aroma of rams; I will offer bulls with goats. Selah **16** Come and hear, all you who fear God, And I will declare what He has done for my soul. **17** I cried to Him with my mouth, And He was extolled with my tongue. **18** If I regard iniquity in my heart, The Lord will not hear. **19** But certainly God has heard me; He has attended to the voice of my prayer. **20** Blessed be God, Who has not turned away my prayer, Nor His mercy from me! (NKJV)

Many Psalms are full of life-lessons and this is such a one. The messages included here are: God is great, has done wondrous deeds and one day everyone will bow before Him; He keeps us alive (or as the Psalmist puts it – God keeps our soul among the living); occasionally, the Lord will bring us through trials to refine us into the people He wants us to be. But to me, the essential lesson is this: although what we say about God is very important, including how we declare His glory and what we tell others about Him, the most important thing is what lies within our heart (and what is not in it). If we "regard" sin in our heart (if we cherish it or look at it with favor or pleasure), then God will not hear us when we pray. Unconfessed sin is a barrier between us and the Lord. When we confess our sin, God not only cleanses us and forgives it, but He will then hear our prayers.

O God, I raise my voice to join the whole earth with a joyful shout unto You. May I sing in a manner worthy, to gloriously praise Your name. The works of Your hand are awesome to consider. Your power is so great that even those who do not love You must submit, cringingly cowering before You. In the end, all on earth will bow before You in worship and songs of praise. Your marvelous accomplishments before mankind are too great to comprehend. You keep me serenely secure during the floods of life. And yet, help me to remember that the trials of life are one of the ways You refine my heart, to remove the impurities that keep me from loving You fully and completely. Whether in distress or in quiet solitude, may I always come before You with a contrite and humble heart, for that is the greatest offering I can bring You. Keep my heart pure and may I quickly confess any secret sin that has crept in, that my prayer will come before You clear and unencumbered. I bless You for hearing me and for Your lovingkindness. Amen

Psalm 67

To the choirmaster: with stringed instruments. A Psalm. A Song. **1** May God be gracious to us and bless us and make his face to shine upon us, Selah **2** that your way may be known on earth, your saving power among all nations. **3** Let the peoples praise you, O God; let all the peoples praise you! **4** Let the nations be glad and sing for joy, for you judge the peoples with equity and guide the nations upon earth. Selah **5** Let the peoples praise you, O God; let all the peoples praise you! **6** The earth has yielded its increase; God, our God, shall bless us. **7** God shall bless us; let all the ends of the earth fear him! (ESV)

This is one of three Psalms which mentions God "shining His face" upon us. That phrase originates in Numbers 6 where God gave Moses the specific words of blessing to be used by Aaron and the line of priests to follow. It is easy to understand the words, "the Lord bless you" and "be gracious" and "give you peace" but what does a shining face mean? Moses deeply desired to see God's glory but we are told no man can see God's face and live. Even Moses' face shined after returning from his time on Mt. Sinai. Why? Because he was in the presence of God. When God's face shines upon us it is more than just being in His presence because God is omnipresent. It is demonstrative of being in the interpersonal presence of God – to be in a relationship with Him. The light of God's face brings His favor, His truth, His blessing. The Aaronic Blessing and this Psalm are both a request to the Lord and a promise from Him. Let us daily ask God to shine His face upon us so that we in turn, can reflect His light to others!

O God, I praise You for being gracious to me, for Your blessings and for causing Your face to shine upon me. Thank You for showing me Your ways and providing my salvation. I pray, O LORD, that the nations seek You and that the people on earth can sing for joy and be guided by Your Holy Hand, for You will judge mankind equitably. With a cornucopia of crops and plentiful produce, the earth has demonstrated Your bountiful blessings. For You, O God, are my God and I pray that all the ends of the earth fear and honor You to praise Your Holy Name. Amen

Psalm 68

For the choir director: A song. A psalm of David. **1** Rise up, O God, and scatter your enemies. Let those who hate God run for their lives. **2** Blow them away like smoke. Melt them like wax in a fire. Let the wicked perish in the presence of God. **3** But let the godly rejoice. Let them be glad in God's presence. Let them be filled with joy. **4** Sing praises to God and to his name! Sing loud praises to him who rides the clouds. His name is the LORD — rejoice in his presence! **5** Father to the fatherless, defender of widows— this is God, whose dwelling is holy. **6** God places the lonely in families; he sets the prisoners free and gives them joy. But he makes the rebellious live in a sun-scorched land. **7** O God, when you led your people out from Egypt, when you marched through the dry wasteland, Interlude **8** the earth trembled, and the heavens poured down rain before you, the God of Sinai, before God, the God of Israel. **9** You sent abundant rain, O God, to refresh the weary land. **10** There your people finally settled, and with a bountiful harvest, O God, you provided for your needy people. **11** The Lord gives the word, and a great army brings the good news. **12** Enemy kings and their armies flee, while the women of Israel divide the plunder. **13** Even those who lived among the sheepfolds found treasures— doves with wings of silver and feathers of gold. **14** The Almighty scattered the enemy kings like a blowing snowstorm on Mount Zalmon. **15** The mountains of Bashan are majestic, with many peaks stretching high into the sky. **16** Why do you look with envy, O rugged mountains, at Mount Zion, where God has chosen to live, where the LORD himself will live forever? **17** Surrounded by unnumbered thousands of chariots, the Lord came from Mount Sinai into his sanctuary. **18** When you ascended to the heights, you led a crowd of captives. You received gifts from the people, even from those who rebelled against you. Now the LORD God will live among us there. **19** Praise the Lord; praise God our savior! For each day he carries us in his arms. Interlude **20** Our God is a God who saves! The Sovereign LORD rescues us from death. **21** But God will smash the heads of his enemies, crushing the skulls of those who love their guilty ways. **22** The Lord says, "I will bring my enemies down from

Bashan; I will bring them up from the depths of the sea. **23** You, my people, will wash your feet in their blood, and even your dogs will get their share!" **24** Your procession has come into view, O God— the procession of my God and King as he goes into the sanctuary. **25** Singers are in front, musicians behind; between them are young women playing tambourines. **26** Praise God, all you people of Israel; praise the LORD, the source of Israel's life. **27** Look, the little tribe of Benjamin leads the way. Then comes a great throng of rulers from Judah and all the rulers of Zebulun and Naphtali. **28** Summon your might, O God. Display your power, O God, as you have in the past. **29** The kings of the earth are bringing tribute to your Temple in Jerusalem. **30** Rebuke these enemy nations— these wild animals lurking in the reeds, this herd of bulls among the weaker calves. Make them bring bars of silver in humble tribute. Scatter the nations that delight in war. **31** Let Egypt come with gifts of precious metals; let Ethiopia bring tribute to God. **32** Sing to God, you kingdoms of the earth. Sing praises to the Lord. Interlude **33** Sing to the one who rides across the ancient heavens, his mighty voice thundering from the sky. **34** Tell everyone about God's power. His majesty shines down on Israel; his strength is mighty in the heavens. **35** God is awesome in his sanctuary. The God of Israel gives power and strength to his people. Praise be to God! (NLT)

This Psalm begins with the same words that Moses would speak whenever the children of Israel would lift up the Ark of the Covenant to begin the next stage during their sojourn in the wilderness (see Numbers 10:35). This was more than just a ceremonial phrase but was a proclamation promise of the very presence of God Almighty in midst of their company. God's existence was manifest in the pillar of fire by night and a pillar of cloud by day. For forty years it was a visible statement of the Lord's love, guidance, and protection. An entire generation saw God telling them when and where to go. With the departure of the pillars upon entering the promised land, they became the basis of the testimony of God's provision and promise for all. It also reminds us today how awesome our God is, who provides us the strength and power we need each and every day!

O God, there are two kinds of people on this earth – Your enemies who hate You and the righteous who love and worship You. When You rise in Your majesty Your enemies scatter and flee as smoke driven by the whirling wind or the wax melting before the fire's flame. They will all disappear and perish before You. But, those who love You sing Your praises in joyful jubilance, O LORD. For You are a father to the fatherless and the widow's advocate and protector. Whether it is lodging for the lonely or prosperity for the prisoner, You see all and provide according to Your wisdom, love, and mercy. The earth quakes in Your presence. You provide plentiful rain in a parched and thirsty land. When I see my simple surroundings, remind me that in You I have rich rewards beyond worldly wealth. For You, O God, cause the great on earth to envy those whose treasure is in You. Blessed are You, Jehovah Yowm Amas, the LORD Who Bears My Burdens daily. You are my salvation and my God of deliverance. In the end, all will sing Your praises as they witness You leading the triumphal procession – from Your foes in fear to Your friends in delight – all will bow to worship. Blessed be You, O God, who gives me strength and power to live each day. Amen

Psalm 69

For the choir director: according to "The Lilies." Of David. **1** Save me, God, for the water has risen to my neck. **2** I have sunk in deep mud, and there is no footing; I have come into deep water, and a flood sweeps over me. **3** I am weary from my crying; my throat is parched. My eyes fail, looking for my God. **4** Those who hate me without cause are more numerous than the hairs of my head; my deceitful enemies, who would destroy me, are powerful. Though I did not steal, I must repay. **5** God, you know my foolishness, and my guilty acts are not hidden from you. **6** Do not let those who put their hope in you be disgraced because of me, Lord God of Armies; do not let those who seek you be humiliated because of me, God of Israel. **7** For I have endured insults because of you, and shame has covered my face. **8** I have become a stranger to my brothers and a foreigner to my mother's sons **9** because zeal for your house has consumed me, and the insults of those who insult you have fallen on me. **10** I mourned and fasted, but it brought me insults. **11** I wore sackcloth as my clothing, and I was a joke to them. **12** Those who sit at the city gate talk about me, and drunkards make up songs about me. **13** But as for me, Lord, my prayer to you is for a time of favor. In your abundant, faithful love, God, answer me with your sure salvation. **14** Rescue me from the miry mud; don't let me sink. Let me be rescued from those who hate me and from the deep water. **15** Don't let the floodwaters sweep over me or the deep swallow me up; don't let the Pit close its mouth over me. **16** Answer me, Lord, for your faithful love is good. In keeping with your abundant compassion, turn to me. **17** Don't hide your face from your servant, for I am in distress. Answer me quickly! **18** Come near to me and redeem me; ransom me because of my enemies. **19** You know the insults I endure— my shame and disgrace. You are aware of all my adversaries. **20** Insults have broken my heart, and I am in despair. I waited for sympathy, but there was none; for comforters, but found no one. **21** Instead, they gave me gall for my food, and for my thirst they gave me vinegar to drink. **22** Let their table set before them be a snare, and let it be a trap for their allies. **23** Let their eyes grow too dim to see, and let their hips continually quake. **24** Pour out your rage on them, and let your burning anger overtake them. **25** Make their fortification desolate; may no one live in their tents. **26** For they persecute the one you struck and talk about the pain of those you wounded. **27** Charge them with crime on top of crime; do not let them share in your righteousness. **28** Let them be erased from the book of life and not be recorded with the righteous. **29** But as for me—poor and in pain— let your salvation protect me, God. **30** I will praise God's name with song and exalt him with thanksgiving. **31** That will please the Lord more than an ox, more than a bull with horns and hooves. 32 The humble will see it and rejoice. You who seek God, take heart! **33** For the Lord listens to the needy and does not despise his own who are prisoners. **34** Let heaven and earth praise him, the seas and everything that moves in them, **35** for God will save Zion and build up the cities of Judah. They will live there and possess it. **36** The descendants of his servants will inherit it, and those who love his name will live in it. (CSB)

Many believe this Psalm, like the 22nd, is an example of a Messianic Psalm. While New Testament verses refer to this Psalm in the course of Jesus' earthly life (being hated without reason; being disregarded by His own brothers; clearing the temple of money lenders; etc.), when you get to verse 5 you might pause and say, hey wait, how can this apply to Jesus, He who was sinless? This is a good example of the importance of reading scripture in the context of other scripture - both the New Testament verses that refer to it as well as the great "suffering servant" chapter, Isaiah 53. Yes, Jesus did NOT sin Himself, but He was "wounded for our transgressions, He was bruised for our iniquities...and the Lord has laid on Him the iniquity of us all." Since Jesus bore the flood of our sins, we can stand firm, and approach the throne of grace with confidence!

O God, on those days when the waters are rising and I feel mired in a sinking swamp, save me! For You are the only firm foothold in this life. I will wait on You, O LORD, even though my eyes are wet with tears and my throat is dry from weeping wearily. Many and mighty are those who are against me for no good reason; who want repayment for things not taken. If anyone has the right to oppose me it would be You, O LORD, for You know all my wrongful deeds and foolish thoughts. You have warned me that because of my love for You, there will be taunting from this world. But amidst all this, I will pray unto You, O LORD, and in Your great love and mercy, You will rescue me with Your saving truth. No matter the depth of the abyss Your peace is deeper still. The floods of life can never rise above the heights of Your great love. For You have redeemed my soul and ransomed me from my sin. So even if this world slaps away my outstretched hand in my time of need, in my suffering sorrow I will look to You, O God for Your salvation securely sets me on high. I will praise Your name in song and glorify You with thanksgiving and a humble heart. Let heaven and earth praise Your name forevermore. Amen

Psalm 70

To the Chief Musician. *A Psalm* of David. To bring to remembrance. **1** Make haste, O God, to deliver me! Make haste to help me, O Lord! **2** Let them be ashamed and confounded Who seek my life; Let them be turned back and confused Who desire my hurt. **3** Let them be turned back because of their shame, Who say, "Aha, aha!" **4** Let all those who seek You rejoice and be glad in You; And let those who love Your salvation say continually, "Let God be magnified!" **5** But I am poor and needy; Make haste to me, O God! You are my help and my deliverer; O Lord, do not delay. (NKJV)

Let's be honest, at one time or another, we have each felt the desperate desire for deliverance. It may be a result of some serious situation into which we have fallen ranging from financial hardship to physical or emotional pain. It may be due to regrettable relationships that have developed where individuals go out of their way to taunt and mock us. It is in those times we tend to frantically cry out for help. As both a Sheriff's Deputy and an FBI Agent, there were codes used when communicating of the radio. One was "11-99" which was "Officer needs help." It was used in those situations when it appeared things were about to or had already gotten out of hand. In other words, "send back-up now!" Notice how David asks God to "make haste" and not delay in saving him. But it is in those circumstances of daily life we must take pause and acknowledge these three things: our need to seek God and rejoice in Him; to recognize God's greatness and that He only is able to save us; and to humbly remember our lowly state without Him. It is only then we can confidently cry out for help: "Lord save me!"

O God, in my time of need, come quickly to my rescue with Your healing hand. Let those who delight in my despair, who seek my soul, who mock my misfortune draw back in their own confusion and be brought to shame. But I will continually seek You for in You I find jubilant joy. In power, You extend Your helping hand unto me. I love Your great salvation. All glory be unto You, my great and wonderful God. Make haste to rescue me O LORD, my deliverer. Amen

Psalm 71

1 In You, O LORD, I have taken refuge; Let me never be ashamed. 2 In Your righteousness deliver me and rescue me; Incline Your ear to me and save me. 3 Be to me a rock of habitation to which I may continually come; You have given commandment to save me, For You are my rock and my fortress. 4 Rescue me, O my God, out of the hand of the wicked, Out of the grasp of the wrongdoer and ruthless man, 5 For You are my hope; O Lord GOD, You are my confidence from my youth. 6 By You I have been sustained from my birth; You are He who took me from my mother's womb; My praise is continually of You. 7 I have become a marvel to many, For You are my strong refuge. 8 My mouth is filled with Your praise And with Your glory all day long. 9 Do not cast me off in the time of old age; Do not forsake me when my strength fails. 10 For my enemies have spoken against me; And those who watch for my life have consulted together, 11 Saying, "God has forsaken him; Pursue and seize him, for there is no one to deliver." 12 O God, do not be far from me; O my God, hasten to my help! 13 Let those who are adversaries of my soul be ashamed and consumed; Let them be covered with reproach and dishonor, who seek to injure me. 14 But as for me, I will hope continually, And will praise You yet more and more. 15 My mouth shall tell of Your righteousness And of Your salvation all day long; For I do not know the sum of them. 16 I will come with the mighty deeds of the Lord GOD; I will make mention of Your righteousness, Yours alone. 17 O God, You have taught me from my youth, And I still declare Your wondrous deeds. 18 And even when I am old and gray, O God, do not forsake me, Until I declare Your strength to this generation, Your power to all who are to come. 19 For Your righteousness, O God, reaches to the heavens, You who have done great things; O God, who is like You? 20 You who have shown me many troubles and distresses Will revive me again, And will bring me up again from the depths of the earth. 21 May You increase my greatness And turn to comfort me. 22 I will also praise You with a harp, Even Your truth, O my God; To

You I will sing praises with the lyre, O Holy One of Israel. **23** My lips will shout for joy when I sing praises to You; And my soul, which You have redeemed. **24** My tongue also will utter Your righteousness all day long; For they are ashamed, for they are humiliated who seek my hurt. (NASB)

Despite our desperate desire for self-sustainment and independence, we are a very dependent race! Is there anything more helpless than a newborn baby? As we age, the sad reality for many of us is we will once again become heavily dependent on others. This Psalm is both a prayer for protection and a testimony of truth about God's guidance. C. H. Spurgeon says "this Psalm may be regarded as the utterance of struggling, but unstaggering, faith." The Psalmist recalls how he leaned on the Lord from his birth and was consistently sustained and supported by Him. His faith endured in his youth and now, with old age and failing strength, he cries out for God's help, recalling His past provisions and promises. The Apostle Paul said, "we are afflicted in every way, but not crushed; perplexed, but not despairing." Yes, trust in the Lord and let our souls sing unto Him!

In You, O God, I have found my place of preservation, a shelter without shame, a fortress without fear. In Your righteousness You have rescued me. You have become my home hewn of rock to which I continually come – an invincible bastion constant and secure. Within Your hand of protection I am safe from the hand of my enemies. From my childhood I have been drawn to You even as You drew me from my mother's womb. Your love and protection is a marvelous mystery for which I will continuously praise You. As my temples gray and the vanishing vigor of youth yields to old age, I will exchange my subsiding strength for Your everlasting omnipotence. When I become easy prey for my enemies I will pray unto You, my God in whom I hope. Your wondrous works of righteousness and salvation lift my voice in praise and lowers me to my knees in adoration. My soul, which You have redeemed, will forevermore give glory to Your Holy Name. Amen

Psalm 72

Of Solomon. **1** Give the king your justice, O God, and your righteousness to the royal son! **2** May he judge your people with righteousness, and your poor with justice! **3** Let the mountains bear prosperity for the people, and the hills, in righteousness! **4** May he defend the cause of the poor of the people, give deliverance to the children of the needy, and crush the oppressor! **5** May they fear you while the sun endures, and as long as the moon, throughout all generations! **6** May he be like rain that falls on the mown grass, like showers that water the earth! **7** In his days may the righteous flourish, and peace abound, till the moon be no more! **8** May he have dominion from sea to sea, and from the River to the ends of the earth! **9** May desert tribes bow down before him, and his enemies lick the dust! **10** May the kings of Tarshish and of the coastlands render him tribute; may the kings of Sheba and Seba bring gifts! **11** May all kings fall down before him, all nations serve him! **12** For he delivers the needy when he calls, the poor and him who has no helper. **13** He has pity on the weak and the needy, and saves the lives of the needy. **14** From oppression and violence he redeems their life, and precious is their blood in his sight. **15** Long may he live; may gold of Sheba be given to him! May prayer be made for him continually, and blessings invoked for him all the day! **16** May there be abundance of grain in the land; on the tops of the mountains may it wave; may its fruit be like Lebanon; and may people blossom in the cities like the grass of the field! **17** May his name endure forever, his fame continue as long as the sun! May people be blessed in him, all nations call him blessed! **18** Blessed be the LORD, the God of Israel, who alone does wondrous things. **19** Blessed be his glorious name forever; may the whole earth be filled with his glory! Amen and Amen! **20** The prayers of David, the son of Jesse, are ended. (ESV)

Have you ever stopped to ponder what it would be like to live in a nation where the political leadership truly led in accordance with God's guidance and used His Word as a policy plan? Those of us who live in America usually recognize how fortunate we are in comparison to so many other peoples and nations who live under the incessant threat of bondage, disease, and death. Even so, we still see political bickering and personal agendas set the course for how our nation is ruled. This Psalm gives us a glimpse into the life of a nation living under a godly ruler. And yet, the description here appears to go beyond the capabilities of a mere mortal. Someday, the world will all fall under the rule of the true Righteous Judge and Prince of Peace, but in the meantime, we need to continue to pray for our leaders.

O God, I pray for my nation's leaders. Give them hearts that seek Your ways to rule righteously and judge justly. May those in power bring honor and glory to Your name, not to themselves. May they use their positions as a time of trust prior to the coming of Your Messiah's arrival. You, O LORD, will rule in glory, becoming the needy child's champion and crushing those who oppress others. Your reign will be like the refreshing rain upon the nations and peace will flourish on the righteous. All kings and all nations will fall at Your feet to serve You. You are the friend of the forsaken and deliver the destitute, saving the souls of the needy. May Your name, O LORD, endure forever, so one day, mankind will bless Your glorious name and the entire earth will be filled with Your glory. Amen

Psalm 73

A psalm of Asaph. **1** Truly God is good to Israel, to those whose hearts are pure. **2** But as for me, I almost lost my footing. My feet were slipping, and I was almost gone. **3** For I envied the proud when I saw them prosper despite their wickedness. **4** They seem to live such painless lives; their bodies are so healthy and strong. **5** They don't have troubles like other people; they're not plagued with problems like everyone else. **6** They wear pride like a jeweled necklace and clothe themselves with cruelty. **7** These fat cats have everything their hearts could ever wish for! **8** They scoff and speak only evil; in their pride they seek to crush others. **9** They boast against the very heavens, and their words strut throughout the earth. **10** And so the people are dismayed and confused, drinking in all their words. **11** "What does God know?" they ask. "Does the Most High even know what's happening?" **12** Look at these wicked people— enjoying a life of ease while their riches multiply. **13** Did I keep my heart pure for nothing? Did I keep myself innocent for no reason? **14** I get nothing but trouble all day long; every morning brings me pain. **15** If I had really spoken this way to others, I would have been a traitor to your people. **16** So I tried to understand why the wicked prosper. But what a difficult task it is! **17** Then I went into your sanctuary, O God, and I finally understood the destiny of the wicked. **18** Truly, you put them on a slippery path and send them sliding over the cliff to destruction. **19** In an instant they are destroyed, completely swept away by terrors. **20** When you arise, O Lord, you will laugh at their silly ideas as a person laughs at dreams in the morning. **21** Then I realized that my heart was bitter, and I was all torn up inside. **22** I was so foolish and ignorant— I must have seemed like a senseless animal to you. **23** Yet I still belong to you; you hold my right hand. **24** You guide me with your counsel, leading me to a glorious destiny. **25** Whom have I in heaven but you? I desire you more than anything on earth. **26** My health may fail, and my spirit may grow weak, but God remains the strength of my heart; he is mine forever. **27** Those who desert him will perish, for you destroy those who abandon you. **28** But as for me, how good it is to be near God! I have made the Sovereign LORD my shelter, and I will tell everyone about the wonderful things you do. (NLT)

Have you been around someone so arrogant, so full of pompous pride that you just want to walk away? Our Psalmist points to pride as a key feature of the wicked but quickly cautions himself not to become like them, envious of what they possess whether it be power or prosperity. Pride is the seed that cultivates mouths of mirth into malice and transforms tongues of truth into treachery. He is quick to place into perspective the fleeting limit of life we all live. There is no reason for any of us to wear pride like a necklace around our neck, for all we have is given to us by the Lord. As we rise to begin each day, it is so important that we remember God's grace to us, to let humility envelop us like a cloak held close to the vest of our heart. It is not something to be worn on our sleeve for all to see for then it becomes a garment of pride.

O God, You are so good. Keep my heart pure before You. Don't let my footsteps falter or allow me to take stumbling strides. When I see the sinful succeed and the profane prosper, let me not become envious of their arrogance. They seem so self-assured, fearing neither death nor disease. In pride, their hearts are full of futile fancies and deceitful desires. They speak malice toward mankind and scoff at You. When I witness the wealth of the wicked and ponder their prosperity, I can become frustrated and troubled. And yet, it is only in Your presence, O God, that I perceive life with the proper perspective. Turning to You sheds my self-pity and reminds me, in the end, You will judge justly and in righteousness. With an open hand and humble heart, I reach toward You and You are there to counsel and guide me. There is no one else to look to in heaven but You and besides You, nothing to desire here on earth. In time, I will come before You with a broken body and failing heart – but as I draw near to You I will remember You are my strength, my rock, and my refuge. Amen

Psalm 74

A Maskil of Asaph. **1** O God, why have You rejected us forever? Why does Your anger smoke against the sheep of Your pasture? **2** Remember Your congregation, which You have purchased of old, Which You have redeemed to be the tribe of Your inheritance; And this Mount Zion, where You have dwelt. **3** Turn Your footsteps toward the perpetual ruins; The enemy has damaged everything within the sanctuary. **4** Your adversaries have roared in the midst of Your meeting place; They have set up their own standards for signs. **5** It seems as if one had lifted up His axe in a forest of trees. **6** And now all its carved work They smash with hatchet and hammers. **7** They have burned Your sanctuary to the ground; They have defiled the dwelling place of Your name. **8** They said in their heart, "Let us completely subdue them." They have burned all the meeting places of God in the land. **9** We do not see our signs; There is no longer any prophet, Nor is there any among us who knows how long. **10** How long, O God, will the adversary revile, And the enemy spurn Your name forever? **11** Why do You withdraw Your hand, even Your right hand? From within Your bosom, destroy them! **12** Yet God is my king from of old, Who works deeds of deliverance in the midst of the earth. **13** You divided the sea by Your strength; You broke the heads of the sea monsters in the waters. **14** You crushed the heads of Leviathan; You gave him as food for the creatures of the wilderness. **15** You broke open springs and torrents; You dried up ever-flowing streams. **16** Yours is the day, Yours also is the night; You have prepared the light and the sun. **17** You have established all the boundaries of the earth; You have made summer and winter. **18** Remember this, O LORD, that the enemy has reviled, And a foolish people has spurned Your name. **19** Do not deliver the soul of Your turtledove to the wild beast; Do not forget the life of Your afflicted forever. **20** Consider the covenant; For the dark places of the land are full of the habitations of violence. **21** Let not the oppressed return dishonored; Let the afflicted and needy praise Your name. **22** Arise, O God, and plead Your own cause; Remember how the foolish man reproaches You all day long. **23** Do not forget the voice of Your adversaries, The uproar of those who rise against You which ascends continually. (NASB)

We likely have all heard the saying, "where there is smoke, there is fire." Sound reasoning lies behind these words for the presence of smoke means something is burning or soon will be. Our Psalmist asks God, "Why does your anger smoke against the sheep of your pasture?" Notice God's anger is not a consuming fire here; it is smoking, smoldering, on the verge of combustion. It reminds me of the Fall when you would burn a pile of dried leaves and see the gray smoke sneak from the cracks of the heap, watching it wander and whiff upwards and then, in a split second, ignites. But God's anger doesn't burst into flame against His people. The truth is, we, the sheep of His pasture have been made spiritually fireproof – not of our own doing – but because Jesus freely became our sacrificial Lamb. Worthy is the Lamb who was slain to take away our sin!

O God, when I despair with feelings that You have rejected me as one of Your sheep, return me to the peaceful pasture of Your presence. For I know I have been purchased and it is You and no other who has redeemed me as Your own. When I see the world at war against Your ways, it is no wonder Your righteous anger rises. The enemy has sought to destroy all that represents Your congregation and replace Your symbols of truth with their own boastful banners. Their desire to defile Your dwelling place will be their undoing. For You, O God, are my King of old – the One who brings salvation by working deeds of deliverance for Your people. Yours is the day and night - nothing can stand in Your way. You hold the boundaries of time and space in the palm of Your hand. When those who are Your enemies spurn Your name and afflict Your people, remember us, O LORD. Protect us who praise You and vindicate Your Holy Name. Amen

Psalm 75

For the choir director: A psalm of Asaph. A song to be sung to the tune "Do Not Destroy!" **1** We thank you, O God! We give thanks because you are near. People everywhere tell of your wonderful deeds. **2** God says, "At the time I have planned, I will bring justice against the wicked. **3** When the earth quakes and its people live in turmoil, I am the one who keeps its foundations firm. Interlude **4** "I warned the proud, 'Stop your boasting!' I told the wicked, 'Don't raise your fists! **5** Don't raise your fists in defiance at the heavens or speak with such arrogance.'" **6** For no one on earth—from east or west, or even from the wilderness— should raise a defiant fist. **7** It is God alone who judges; he decides who will rise and who will fall. **8** For the LORD holds a cup in his hand that is full of foaming wine mixed with spices. He pours out the wine in judgment, and all the wicked must drink it, draining it to the dregs. **9** But as for me, I will always proclaim what God has done; I will sing praises to the God of Jacob. **10** For God says, "I will break the strength of the wicked, but I will increase the power of the godly." (NLT)

A common perception by many is to see the God of the Bible only as a wrathful ruler ready to render judgment. This Psalm certainly shows God as Judge but does so in the proper light. It opens with a double acclamation of thanks to God for all the incomparable things He has done (wonderful deeds). Then suddenly, God Himself speaks, clearly informing us about His judgment: it is He who will judge; it is He who determines the proper time for it to happen; His verdicts are fair; and the same power that enables Him to carry out judgment also allows Him to keep things from getting out of control. And who are the recipients of this wrath? The easy answer is "the wicked" but what makes them so bad? The Psalm is clear – it is their haughty arrogance; their insolent pride. Let us always remember our proper place and to live with a humble heart before God.

O God, I give thanks to You for Your wondrous deeds and forever remaining near me. I know it is You who decides when and how to judge the earth and it will be done fairly and at the proper time. You silence boastful lying lips and bow the stiff-necked proud. There is no power on earth but You, O LORD, for You judge all, making the haughty humbled and exalting those who seek Your face. Your cup of wrathful wine awaits the wicked who in the end must drain its dreadful dregs. Let me sing Your praises now and forevermore. Amen

Psalm 76

For the choir director; on stringed instruments. A Psalm of Asaph, a Song. **1** God is known in Judah; His name is great in Israel. **2** His tabernacle is in Salem; His dwelling place also is in Zion. **3** There He broke the flaming arrows, The shield and the sword and the weapons of war. Selah. **4** You are resplendent, More majestic than the mountains of prey. **5** The stouthearted were plundered, They sank into sleep; And none of the warriors could use his hands. **6** At Your rebuke, O God of Jacob, Both rider and horse were cast into a dead sleep. **7** You, even You, are to be feared; And who may stand in Your presence when once You are angry? **8** You caused judgment to be heard from heaven; The earth feared and was still **9** When God arose to judgment, To save all the humble of the earth. Selah. **10** For the wrath of man shall praise You; With a remnant of wrath You will gird Yourself. **11** Make vows to the LORD your God and fulfill them; Let all who are around Him bring gifts to Him who is to be feared. **12** He will cut off the spirit of princes; He is feared by the kings of the earth. (NASB)

This Psalm provides a glimpse of God's power and majesty over all the earth. The Lord's judgment is clearly on display and yet, those who benefit from His wrath are the humble of the earth. In fact, verse 9 states that the very purpose His judgment is established is to save the humble. This picture of power and judgment is juxtaposed in Philippians 2 where we see Christ, being in the very form of God, humbling Himself by coming to earth in the form of a man. In an act of utter and complete humility, He willingly gives up His life. With this act of ultimate obedience, He laid low the majesty rightfully His to save us. It is only then that Jesus is returned to His proper place in power. Jesus did all this, not to receive glory, but for what was set before Him – the joy of demonstrating His love to save us. In humility and love, let us also receive that great salvation.

O God, You are known throughout the whole earth. You shatter the warring weapons of this world. Mountains' majesty pale in Your presence. You wisp away the spoils from the bravest warrior who cannot lift a finger in response. Your rebuke renders riders useless and stalls the stallion in his tracks, for no one can stand in Your presence. In Your judgment, You save the humble and silence the vacant vows of the proud. Let me humbly receive your gift of salvation, and in return, may my gifts of obedience and praise always be acceptable to You, O LORD. Amen

Psalm 77

To the choirmaster: according to Jeduthun. A Psalm of Asaph. **1** I cry aloud to God, aloud to God, and he will hear me. **2** In the day of my trouble I seek the Lord; in the night my hand is stretched out without wearying; my soul refuses to be comforted. **3** When I remember God, I moan; when I meditate, my spirit faints. Selah **4** You hold my eyelids open; I am so troubled that I cannot speak. **5** I consider the days of old, the years long ago. **6** I said, "Let me remember my song in the night; let me meditate in my heart." Then my spirit made a diligent search: **7** "Will the Lord spurn forever, and never again be favorable? **8** Has his steadfast love forever ceased? Are his promises at an end for all time? **9** Has God forgotten to be gracious? Has he in anger shut up his compassion?" Selah **10** Then I said, "I will appeal to this, to the years of the right hand of the Most High." **11** I will remember the deeds of the LORD; yes, I will remember your wonders of old. **12** I will ponder all your work, and meditate on your mighty deeds. **13** Your way, O God, is holy. What god is great like our God? **14** You are the God who works wonders; you have made known your might among the peoples. **15** You with your arm redeemed your people, the children of Jacob and Joseph. Selah **16** When the waters saw you, O God, when the waters saw you, they were afraid; indeed, the deep trembled. **17** The clouds poured out water; the skies gave forth thunder; your arrows flashed on every side. **18** The crash of your thunder was in the whirlwind; your lightnings lighted up the world; the earth trembled and shook. **19** Your way was through the sea, your path through the great waters; yet your footprints were unseen. **20** You led your people like a flock by the hand of Moses and Aaron. (ESV)

How do you pray? Of course, there are many methods and the "proper" way is often determined by the situation. In this Psalm, we see a person who is at wit's end, despondent and in deep distress. What does he do? He prays. Not some inaudible mental prayer, but ardently passionate and heartfelt cries rising up to the Lord. And then, as if to emphasize it, he says it twice! Our Psalmist's pleadings turn to languishing laments of reflective memories, giving weight to his internal arguments. It is only then he begins to meditate on the greatness of God and all the marvelous deeds He has performed. The Lord is well-aware of the inner conflicts we struggle with so there is no need to mull them over with murmurings or whispered words. Cry out to the Lord and share with Him the deepest longings of your heart – He is always there to hear us.

O God, I cry out to You with a troubled voice and You hear me. When the travailing trials of life linger from day into night I will seek Your face for guidance. For unless You rescue me my soul will never know solace. When I think of You, O LORD, and how much I depend on Your grace it can overwhelm both soul and spirit. With sleepless eyes and a speechless voice, I realize my dire dilemma – I am lost without You! When the doubts of despair creep like creatures in the night, I will recall my song to You and my heart will meditate on Your goodness and thereby depose distrust – away with any questions about Your acceptance, lovingkindness, gracious compassion or promises. Yes, I will meditate on Your mighty deeds and wondrous works for You have redeemed Your people. Water, wind, earth, and fire reside in the palm of Your hand. Without delay, they rapidly respond to Your commands. And while no one can trace Your footsteps, You lead Your people in love, if we will only listen, obey and follow. Amen

Psalm 78

A Maskil of Asaph. **1** My people, hear my instruction; listen to the words from my mouth. **2** I will declare wise sayings; I will speak mysteries from the past— **3** things we have heard and known and that our fathers have passed down to us. **4** We will not hide them from their children, but will tell a future generation the praiseworthy acts of the Lord, his might, and the wondrous works he has performed. **5** He established a testimony in Jacob and set up a law in Israel, which he commanded our fathers to teach to their children **6** so that a future generation— children yet to be born—might know. They were to rise and tell their children **7** so that they might put their confidence in God and not forget God's works, but keep his commands. **8** Then they would not be like their fathers, a stubborn and rebellious generation, a generation whose heart was not loyal and whose spirit was not faithful to God. **9** The Ephraimite archers turned back on the day of battle. **10** They did not keep God's covenant and refused to live by his law. **11** They forgot what he had done, the wondrous works he had shown them. **12** He worked wonders in the sight of their fathers in the land of Egypt, the territory of Zoan. **13** He split the sea and brought them across; the water stood firm like a wall. **14** He led them with a cloud by day and with a fiery light throughout the night. **15** He split rocks in the wilderness and gave them drink as abundant as the depths. **16** He brought streams out of the stone and made water flow down like rivers. **17** But they continued to sin against him, rebelling in the desert against the Most High. **18** They deliberately tested God, demanding the food they craved. **19** They spoke against God, saying, "Is God able to provide food in the wilderness? **20** Look! He struck the rock and water gushed out; torrents overflowed. But can he also provide bread or furnish meat for his people?" **21** Therefore, the Lord heard and became furious; then fire broke out against Jacob, and anger flared up against Israel **22** because they did not believe God or rely on his salvation. **23** He gave a command to the clouds above and opened the doors of heaven. **24** He rained manna for them to eat; he gave them grain from heaven. **25** People ate the bread of angels. He sent them an abundant supply of food. **26** He made the east wind blow in the skies and drove the south wind by his might. **27** He rained meat on them like dust, and winged birds like the sand of the seas. **28** He made them fall in the camp, all around the tents. **29** The people ate and were completely satisfied, for he gave them what they craved. **30** Before they had turned from what they craved, while the food was still in their mouths, **31** God's anger flared up against them, and he killed some of their best men. He struck down Israel's fit young men. **32** Despite all this, they kept sinning and did not believe his wondrous works. **33** He made their days end in futility, their years in sudden disaster. **34** When he killed some of them, the rest began to seek him; they repented and searched for God. **35** They remembered that God was their rock, the Most High God, their Redeemer. **36** But they deceived him with their mouths, they lied to him with their tongues, **37** their hearts were insincere toward him, and they were unfaithful to his covenant. **38** Yet he was compassionate; he atoned for their iniquity and did not destroy them. He often turned his anger aside and did not unleash all his wrath. **39** He remembered that they were only flesh, a wind that passes and does not return. **40** How often they rebelled against him in the wilderness and grieved him in the desert. **41** They constantly tested God and provoked the Holy One of Israel. **42** They did not remember his power shown on the day he redeemed them from the foe, **43** when he performed his miraculous signs in Egypt and his wonders in the territory of Zoan. **44** He turned their rivers into blood, and they could not drink from their streams. **45** He sent among them swarms of flies, which fed on them, and frogs, which devastated them. **46** He gave their crops to the caterpillar and the fruit of their labor to the locust. **47** He killed their vines with hail and their sycamore fig trees with a flood. **48** He handed over their livestock to hail and their cattle to lightning bolts. **49** He sent his burning anger against them: fury, indignation, and calamity— a band of deadly messengers. **50** He cleared a path for his anger. He did not spare them from death but delivered their lives to the plague. **51** He struck all the firstborn in Egypt, the first progeny of the tents of Ham. **52** He led his people out like sheep and guided them like a flock in the wilderness. **53** He led them safely, and they were not afraid; but the sea covered their enemies. **54** He brought them to his holy territory, to the mountain his right hand acquired. **55** He drove out nations before them. He apportioned their inheritance by lot and settled the tribes of Israel in their tents. **56** But they rebelliously tested the Most High God, for they did not keep his decrees. **57** They treacherously turned away like their fathers; they became warped like a faulty bow. **58** They enraged him with their high places and provoked his jealousy with their carved images. **59** God heard and became furious; he completely rejected Israel. **60** He abandoned the tabernacle at Shiloh, the tent where he resided among mankind. **61** He gave up his strength to captivity and his splendor to the hand of a foe. **62** He surrendered his people to the sword because he was enraged with his heritage. **63** Fire consumed his chosen young men, and his young women had no wedding songs. **64** His priests fell by the sword, and the widows could not lament. **65** The Lord awoke as if from sleep, like a warrior from the effects of wine. **66** He beat back his foes; he gave them lasting disgrace. **67** He rejected the tent of Joseph and did not choose the tribe of Ephraim. **68** He chose instead the tribe of Judah, Mount Zion, which he loved. **69** He built his sanctuary like the heights, like the earth that he established forever. **70** He chose David his servant and took him from the sheep pens; **71** he brought him from tending ewes to be shepherd over his people Jacob— over Israel, his inheritance. **72** He shepherded them with a pure heart and guided them with his skillful hands. (CSB)

Do you have a favorite family story or legend of lore that although the ending is known, it is still told, over and over again? When I joined the FBI in 1985, there was still a large percentage of FBI employees who had worked under the infamous J. Edgar Hoover. Many a story was told of decisions and directives issued by Mr. Hoover, some who could tell the tale from firsthand knowledge; most however, just passed it down from those who came before them. Here, the Psalmist weaves us a tale of wonder, stitching the stubbornness of his people into God's fabric of faithfulness. God just freed His people from slavery and instead of relishing their freedom, they are missing the "free fish" they had in Egypt. With an audacious taunt of the heart, they demand the "food they craved." In His wisdom and to keep them from starving, the Lord rains down miraculous manna, a daily portion of heavenly food. With mouths still stuffed, they complain, "Meat! Give us meat" and my how God delivers – quail until it comes out their nostrils! This is not a mere historical account but a spiritual lesson of life. God knows best what we need. If we seek Him first, our hearts will be transformed and with that change, our heart's desires will align with His.

O God, help me to tilt my head towards You to listen only to You and Your Word. Whether You speak in parables or riddles, may I closely pay attention. You have spoken truths from generation to generation – let me be bold and wise to speak Your Word to my children and children's children – to tell of Your wondrous works. May I instill in them the desire to put their confidence in You and keep Your commandments. Help me to remind them of Your miraculous deeds of old – how You divided the sea to provide Your people safe passage on dry ground; in the desert wilderness, You split the rock to provide abundant waters like the ocean deep. You provided them the heavenly bread of angels to satisfy their hunger, and yet, with mouths still full they complained. Let me ever be grateful for Your provisions. May I continually seek You with all diligence and remember that You, O God, are my redeeming rock and firm foundation. Keep my feet planted in You and not wandering off the wayward path. For You are my Great Shepherd who guides me with a loving heart and skillful hands. Amen

Psalm 79

A Psalm of Asaph. **1** O God, the nations have come into Your inheritance; Your holy temple they have defiled; They have laid Jerusalem in heaps. **2** The dead bodies of Your servants They have given as food for the birds of the heavens, The flesh of Your saints to the beasts of the earth. **3** Their blood they have shed like water all around Jerusalem, And there was no one to bury them. **4** We have become a reproach to our neighbors, A scorn and derision to those who are around us. **5** How long, Lord? Will You be angry forever? Will Your jealousy burn like fire? **6** Pour out Your wrath on the nations that do not know You, And on the kingdoms that do not call on Your name. **7** For they have devoured Jacob, And laid waste his dwelling place. **8** Oh, do not remember former iniquities against us! Let Your tender mercies come speedily to meet us, For we have been brought very low. **9** Help us, O God of our salvation, For the glory of Your name; And deliver us, and provide atonement for our sins, For Your name's sake! **10** Why should the nations say, "Where is their God?" Let there be known among the nations in our sight The avenging of the blood of Your servants which has been shed. **11** Let the groaning of the prisoner come before You; According to the greatness of Your power Preserve those who are appointed to die; **12** And return to our neighbors sevenfold into their bosom Their reproach with which they have reproached You, O Lord. **13** So we, Your people and sheep of Your pasture, Will give You thanks forever; We will show forth Your praise to all generations. (NKJV)

Most everyone has heard and many have quoted the famous opening line of Charles Dickens' *Tale of Two Cities*: "It was the best of times, it was the worst of times..." In many ways, this Psalm is the tale of two conditions in which one might live: imprisonment or freedom; extermination or preservation; destruction or restoration; and ultimately death or life. The Psalmist bemoans his people's dire condition – an R-rated landscape strewn with bodies and blood, surrounded by many enemies, full of taunting and derision – to be certain, a very dismal picture indeed. But despite the despair, the story ends with the words of comfort that only God can provide. It is only the Lord who can help us, deliver us, and ultimately save us by atoning for our sins. It is no wonder we take solace that the Good Shepherd of His sheep gives us rest in God's pasture.

O God, the people of this world no longer reverently respect You or Your ways. They consider Your followers to be of little or no worth, only to be mocked and ridiculed. How long, O LORD, will this continue? Open their eyes to Your loving light that they may repent and turn to You. But if not, bring to bear, I pray, Your just wrath on those who no longer acknowledge You in their arrogant defiance. I recognize my wrongful ways and seek salvation which only You gracefully give in Your mercy to those who ask. I thank You for redeeming me from my sins. I know that in Your time You will restore those whom the world reproaches. In Your power preserve the sheep of Your pasture that we may give thanks and praise Your name forevermore. Amen

Psalm 80

For the choir director: A psalm of Asaph, to be sung to the tune "Lilies of the Covenant." **1** Please listen, O Shepherd of Israel, you who lead Joseph's descendants like a flock. O God, enthroned above the cherubim, display your radiant glory **2** to Ephraim, Benjamin, and Manasseh. Show us your mighty power. Come to rescue us! **3** Turn us again to yourself, O God. Make your face shine down upon us. Only then will we be saved. **4** O LORD God of Heaven's Armies, how long will you be angry with our prayers? **5** You have fed us with sorrow and made us drink tears by the bucketful. **6** You have made us the scorn of neighboring nations. Our enemies treat us as a joke. **7** Turn us again to yourself, O God of Heaven's Armies. Make your face shine down upon us. Only then will we be saved. **8** You brought us from Egypt like a grapevine; you drove away the pagan nations and transplanted us into your land. **9** You cleared the ground for us, and we took root and filled the land. **10** Our shade covered the mountains; our branches covered the mighty cedars. **11** We spread our branches west to the Mediterranean Sea; our shoots spread east to the Euphrates River. **12** But now, why have you broken down our walls so that all who pass by may steal our fruit? **13** The wild boar from the forest devours it, and the wild animals feed on it. **14** Come back, we beg you, O God of Heaven's Armies. Look down from heaven and see our plight. Take care of this grapevine **15** that you yourself have planted, this son you have raised for yourself. **16** For we are chopped up and burned by our enemies. May they perish at the sight of your frown. **17** Strengthen the man you love, the son of your choice. **18** Then we will never abandon you again. Revive us so we can call on your name once more. **19** Turn us again to yourself, O LORD God of Heaven's Armies. Make your face shine down upon us. Only then will we be saved. (NLT)

Nearly everyone, at one time or another, has heard the 1965 song made famous by The Byrds, "Turn, Turn, Turn" based on Ecclesiastes 3. It is a great song but the truth is, this Psalm of restoration could rightly have the same title. Three times, in verses 3, 7, and 19, the Psalmist uses the Hebrew word (shub) to plead for the Lord to "turn us again." Most translations use the word "restore" in those places, but literally, it means to turn us back. Sadly, too often we instead turn our backs on God. But fortunately, God can restore us to Him. There is a great verse in II Chronicles 7 where God tells His people if they will humble themselves and pray, seek His face and TURN (shub) from their wicked ways, He will hear their prayer, forgive their sins, and heal them. It is only through the Lord's power that we are turned back and restored to Him and saved!

O God, You have led Your People Israel as only the Good Shepherd can – lead me also I pray. You are always there and Your face is always ready to shine upon me but sometimes I am misdirected – turn me towards You that I may be restored and saved. For my prayers are useless and unheard unless I seek forgiveness from my sin and turn toward You. In times when my tears are both my bread and weeping water, You are still there. When I hear my neighbor's ridicule and my enemies' scornful laugh, You are still there. Gently turn me back to You O God of Hosts that Your face will shine on me and I will be saved. You planted Your people like a vine in the desert and its roots grew deep. But sin stifled that growth – in our repentance return to us. Make this vine an image of the True Vine that we may thrive and bear fruit for You. May I never turn back from You for it is only Your breath of life that beckons me back to call upon Your name. Turn me once again toward You, O LORD God of Hosts so Your face will shine upon me and I will be saved. Amen

Psalm 81

To the Chief Musician. On an instrument of Gath. A Psalm of Asaph. **1** Sing aloud to God our strength; Make a joyful shout to the God of Jacob. **2** Raise a song and strike the timbrel, The pleasant harp with the lute. **3** Blow the trumpet at the time of the New Moon, At the full moon, on our solemn feast day. **4** For this is a statute for Israel, A law of the God of Jacob. **5** This He established in Joseph as a testimony, When He went throughout the land of Egypt, Where I heard a language I did not understand. **6** "I removed his shoulder from the burden; His hands were freed from the baskets. **7** You called in trouble, and I delivered you; I answered you in the secret place of thunder; I tested you at the waters of Meribah. Selah **8** "Hear, O My people, and I will admonish you! O Israel, if you will listen to Me! **9** There shall be no foreign god among you; Nor shall you worship any foreign god. **10** I am the Lord your God, Who brought you out of the land of Egypt; Open your mouth wide, and I will fill it. **11** "But My people would not heed My voice, And Israel would have none of Me. **12** So I gave them over to their own stubborn heart, To walk in their own counsels. **13** "Oh, that My people would listen to Me, That Israel would walk in My ways! **14** I would soon subdue their enemies, And turn My hand against their adversaries. **15** The haters of the Lord would pretend submission to Him, But their fate would endure forever. **16** He would have fed them also with the finest of wheat; And with honey from the rock I would have satisfied you." (NKJV)

How often do you hear people complain about the ills of this world, asking how a loving and just God would ever allow such misery to exist? The truth is, God didn't create a bunch of reasonless robots but a rational race with a free will to make decisions on how we will live our lives. All He asks is that we "Love the Lord your God with all your hearts." That is just another way of saying to put "no other gods" before Him. And yet, far too often that is exactly what we do. As a result, He gives us over to our own counsel and the stubbornness of our hearts. As C.S. Lewis wrote in *The Great Divorce*, "There are only two kinds of people in the end: those who say to God, 'Thy will be done,' and those to whom God says, in the end, 'Thy will be done.'" He so desires to provide us with blessings overflowing if we will only follow Him and His Word in obedience. When God says, "open wide" He means more than our mouths. He wants us to open wide our hearts in obedience and great expectancy. Our expectations of God can never be too great!

O God, let me sing for joy unto You and with whatever instruments are available let them in prayerful praise play – tambourines, trumpets, lyres, and harps – let all glorify Your name. For You, O LORD, take away my burdens and rescue me when I call upon You. Never let the idols of this world worm their way into my heart so that it can remain wholly Yours. For You and only You are the LORD, my God. When my headstrong heart summons me to follow my own desires, let me hearken to Your voice alone O LORD, and to consistently walk in Your ways. Let me seek and receive the blessings You want to give, for You bring sweetness even in the hard things in life like honey from a rock. But You, O LORD, are my only Rock and Redeemer. Amen

Psalm 82

A Psalm of Asaph. **1** God takes His stand in His own congregation; He judges in the midst of the rulers. **2** How long will you judge unjustly And show partiality to the wicked? Selah. **3** Vindicate the weak and fatherless; Do justice to the afflicted and destitute. **4** Rescue the weak and needy; Deliver them out of the hand of the wicked. **5** They do not know nor do they understand; They walk about in darkness; All the foundations of the earth are shaken. **6** I said, "You are gods, And all of you are sons of the Most High. **7** Nevertheless you will die like men And fall like any one of the princes." **8** Arise, O God, judge the earth! For it is You who possesses all the nations. (NASB)

Stop and think about the grandest ballroom, most majestic statehouse or intensely imposing courtroom you have ever seen or entered. Did it make you feel rather small, insignificant, unimportant? We are far too quickly dazzled by the outward opulence of man-made architecture and so easily impressed when we stand in the pompous presence of earthly nobility. This Psalm is a great reminder that nothing we have ever seen (or will see) on earth compares to the breadth, beauty, and grandeur of Heaven's court. It isn't the place that is so overpowering, but the presence of the One who stands therein. All the proud palaces ever made and all the mighty magistrates and monarchs who ever occupied them will eventually turn to dust. Let us humbly behold and praise the Lord who possesses all nations and will one day justly judge all.

O God, You alone rule in power and majesty. When You assemble the mighty in Your divine court – whether they be judges or rulers, principalities or powers – All must stand silent in Your judgment. You, O LORD, judge the judges and rule the rulers. You condemn injustice but champion integrity seeking vindication for the orphaned and the weak and for the destitute deliverance. You remind those You have placed in authority that even though they reign on earth with godlike ambition and power, You alone are the LORD Most High who reigns. Even the most powerful who do not honor You and follow Your ways will fail and fall to their doom, death, and destruction. You O God, judge the entire earth, holding it in the palm of Your hand, sifting the thoughts and hearts of the nations. Amen

Psalm 83

A Song. A psalm of Asaph. **1** God, do not keep silent. Do not be deaf, God; do not be quiet. **2** See how your enemies make an uproar; those who hate you have acted arrogantly. **3** They devise clever schemes against your people; they conspire against your treasured ones. **4** They say, "Come, let us wipe them out as a nation so that Israel's name will no longer be remembered." **5** For they have conspired with one mind; they form an alliance against you— **6** the tents of Edom and the Ishmaelites, Moab and the Hagrites, **7** Gebal, Ammon, and Amalek, Philistia with the inhabitants of Tyre. **8** Even Assyria has joined them; they lend support to the sons of Lot. *Selah* **9** Deal with them as you did with Midian, as you did with Sisera and Jabin at the Kishon River. **10** They were destroyed at En-dor; they became manure for the ground. **11** Make their nobles like Oreb and Zeeb, and all their tribal leaders like Zebah and Zalmunna, **12** who said, "Let us seize God's pastures for ourselves." **13** Make them like tumbleweed, my God, like straw before the wind. **14** As fire burns a forest, as a flame blazes through mountains, **15** so pursue them with your tempest and terrify them with your storm. **16** Cover their faces with shame so that they will seek your name, Lord. **17** Let them be put to shame and terrified forever; let them perish in disgrace. **18** May they know that you alone— whose name is the Lord— are the Most High over the whole earth. (CSB)

Have you ever pondered why Israel has been the targeted enemy of others for so long? Not just during our lifetime, but for much of all recorded history. Despite this Psalm being written over 3,000 years ago, you could easily exchange the names of the hostile nations back then to some very well-known countries today. Both sets shout out the same familiar battle cry: "Come, and let us wipe them out as a nation, That the name of Israel is remembered no more." How could such a little country generate so much hatred? Might it have something to do with Israel being God's "chosen" people? This Psalm points out that the enemies are not just Israel's, but that they are actually haters of God. It is not only a plea for protection but a proclamation that one day, all will know that the Lord is the Most High over all the earth. May we now also proclaim it!

O God, I know You will stay silent and remain restrained for only as long as Your perfect plan requires. But in the meantime, the haughty haters of You and Your people conspire in crafty counsel to destroy Your chosen ones. I pray protection for Your people Israel from those nations that seek her destruction. Make those enemies, become like stubble and straw strewn before the storm and blown into Your fiery furnace. Whether they remorsefully repent and seek Your face or in disgraceful dismay simply perish, in the end, all will know that You alone, O LORD, are God Most High over all the earth. Amen

Psalm 84

To the choirmaster: according to The Gittith, A Psalm of the Sons of Korah. **1** How lovely is your dwelling place, O LORD of hosts! **2** My soul longs, yes, faints for the courts of the LORD; my heart and flesh sing for joy to the living God. **3** Even the sparrow finds a home, and the swallow a nest for herself, where she may lay her young, at your altars, O LORD of hosts, my King and my God. **4** Blessed are those who dwell in your house, ever singing your praise! Selah **5** Blessed are those whose strength is in you, in whose heart are the highways to Zion. **6** As they go through the Valley of Baca they make it a place of springs; the early rain also covers it with pools. **7** They go from strength to strength; each one appears before God in Zion. **8** O LORD God of hosts, hear my prayer; give ear, O God of Jacob! Selah **9** Behold our shield, O God; look on the face of your anointed! **10** For a day in your courts is better than a thousand elsewhere. I would rather be a doorkeeper in the house of my God than dwell in the tents of wickedness. **11** For the LORD God is a sun and shield; the LORD bestows favor and honor. No good thing does he withhold from those who walk uprightly. **12** O LORD of hosts, blessed is the one who trusts in you! (ESV)

In this Psalm, we see references to God's "dwelling place" and "courts" and His "house." No single place can house God nor can a man make such a place. And yet, God gave guidance how to build His tabernacle and later His temple. The purpose was not a place to "house" God, but a place for His people to be in His presence. The first and greatest commandment is: "You shall love the Lord your God with all your heart and with all your soul and with all your mind." This would indicate such an intense desire to love God that nothing is left in you. We see a similar yearning by the Psalmist to be in God's courts – his soul not only longs for it but he "faints" over it. The Hebrew word (kaletah) means to be completely finished, spent, at an end – to be exhausted from the longing. May each day begin with a craving to love God with every fiber of our being!

*O God, to be in Your presence is the place of perfect peace. My entire being –
heart, soul, body, and mind – yearns for You, O LORD, for it is only then that
my joy is complete. For You alone are my God and King and I am blessed to dwell
in Your house and praise You. There is great happiness when my strength is in
You and my heart's highway is set in Your ways. Even if I travel through the valley
of hard times, You transform my tears into flowing fountains of refreshment and
with each step, You renew my strength. O LORD God of Hosts, hear my prayer,
for You are my shield of protection. It is better to spend one day in Your courtyard
communing with You than a thousand days anywhere else. I would rather stand
in Your dwelling's door than accept the luxurious living this wicked world offers.
In You, O LORD, my life is enlightened and protected; in Your love, You provide
favor and honor to those who walk with integrity. O LORD, let me be that man
who always puts my trust in You. Amen*

Psalm 85

To the Chief Musician. A Psalm of the sons of Korah. **1** Lord, You have been favorable to Your land; You have brought back the captivity of Jacob. **2** You have forgiven the iniquity of Your people; You have covered all their sin. Selah **3** You have taken away all Your wrath; You have turned from the fierceness of Your anger. **4** Restore us, O God of our salvation, And cause Your anger toward us to cease. **5** Will You be angry with us forever? Will You prolong Your anger to all generations? **6** Will You not revive us again, That Your people may rejoice in You? **7** Show us Your mercy, Lord, And grant us Your salvation. **8** I will hear what God the Lord will speak, For He will speak peace To His people and to His saints; But let them not turn back to folly. **9** Surely His salvation is near to those who fear Him, That glory may dwell in our land. **10** Mercy and truth have met together; Righteousness and peace have kissed. **11** Truth shall spring out of the earth, And righteousness shall look down from heaven. **12** Yes, the Lord will give what is good; And our land will yield its increase. **13** Righteousness will go before Him, And shall make His footsteps our pathway. (NKJV)

We know our God is a God of action and this Psalm clearly displays it. In the first three verses, the Psalmist says it is God who has shown us His favor, has restored us, has forgiven us, has covered our sin, has turned from His wrath and turned away from His anger. If actions speak louder than words, then God's action surely demonstrates His great love for us. We need to hear God speak, see His works and take action ourselves. How often have you seen something that needs done, thought "I should do it" only to let the moment slip away? In the New Testament, James tells us how important it is that our faith should be demonstrated with action. We can't work our way to Heaven, but on our way to Heaven, our way should be sprinkled with works of God's love. I wrote a poem to capture this message:

The Pathway to Do

How far is the path from your ear to your mind;
Do the words somehow wander and ever so wind?
Do they enter one ear and then out the other;
Have you not heard the cry of your sister or brother?

How far is the path from your mind to your heart;
Is this where the will and the way choose to part?
Do you think far too deeply but never employ
The deeds that will bring your heart so much joy?

How far is the path from your heart to your hands,
Or are you now gripping life's daily demands?
Clenched tight on the stuff that this world wants to give;
Let go, and let God show you how we should live.

Closed ears and closed minds we block the right thought,
With hearts that are calloused and hands that are not.
Attuned to the Spirit, your mind becomes new,
With a heart that is willing and hands that will do.

Your faith may be strong and come from above,
But has little use if it doesn't show love.
Hear, understand, believe and obey;
This is our path to follow God's way.

How far was the path from Heaven's great throne,
To that old rugged cross where Christ died all alone?
The distance was great but far greater still,
Was the love in His heart there on Calvary's Hill.

O God, You have shown favor to Your land and brought fortune to Your people. You have pardoned my guilt and forgiven my sins. In Your great mercy, You turned from Your righteous anger and turned me away from my sin and toward You and my salvation. You, O LORD, have given me a life anew and for that, I rejoice. Each day I will listen longingly to hear what You have to say to me...I hear "Peace." Keep me from returning to the foolish habits of old but to instead worship You for the great salvation You have provided. You bring harmony to this world and in my life, where mercy and faithfulness unite and righteousness and peace lovingly embrace. To earth extends Your righteous heavenly hand and lifting my eyes upward to You I reach right back in loyal love. For You, O LORD, bestow blessings to those on Your peaceful path of righteousness. Help me to always walk step by step with You. Amen

Psalm 86

A Prayer of David. **1** Incline your ear, O LORD, and answer me, for I am poor and needy. **2** Preserve my life, for I am godly; save your servant, who trusts in you—you are my God. **3** Be gracious to me, O Lord, for to you do I cry all the day. **4** Gladden the soul of your servant, for to you, O Lord, do I lift up my soul. **5** For you, O Lord, are good and forgiving, abounding in steadfast love to all who call upon you. **6** Give ear, O LORD, to my prayer; listen to my plea for grace. **7** In the day of my trouble I call upon you, for you answer me. **8** There is none like you among the gods, O Lord, nor are there any works like yours. **9** All the nations you have made shall come and worship before you, O Lord, and shall glorify your name. **10** For you are great and do wondrous things; you alone are God. **11** Teach me your way, O LORD, that I may walk in your truth; unite my heart to fear your name. **12** I give thanks to you, O Lord my God, with my whole heart, and I will glorify your name forever. **13** For great is your steadfast love toward me; you have delivered my soul from the depths of Sheol. **14** O God, insolent men have risen up against me; a band of ruthless men seeks my life, and they do not set you before them. **15** But you, O Lord, are a God merciful and gracious, slow to anger and abounding in steadfast love and faithfulness. **16** Turn to me and be gracious to me; give your strength to your servant, and save the son of your maidservant. **17** Show me a sign of your favor, that those who hate me may see and be put to shame because you, LORD, have helped me and comforted me. (ESV)

This Psalm contains a phrase found seven other times in the Bible, namely, God is "slow to anger, abounding in love…" He is our great example for if anyone has the right to be angry, it is God. So, what does "slow to anger" mean? Several Proverbs tell us that those who are slow to anger are better than the mighty, they have great understanding, they quiet contention and calm disputes, and it is a direct result of discretion. In James' epistle, we get advice on just how we should go about the process: we are to be quick to listen (why we have two ears) and slow to speak (why we have only one mouth). Our anger, even when justified, must be measured and aligned with God's word. Following Jesus' lead on the cross should be our goal: instead of being angry and justifiably crushing those killing Him, he said: "Father forgive them." May we always do likewise!

O God, You know my stupefied state of need and as I cry out to You in distress - tilt Your head toward my heart to hear my prayer. For only in You is my soul secure and any godliness I possess is solely a gift of Your grace. In Your mercy, hear my daily devotion to seek You first and as I lift my soul to You, give me a happy heart in Your service. For You are full of goodness and mercy to those who call upon You with a humble heart – hear my prayerful pleadings. There is no God but You and nothing compares to Your wondrous works. I look forward to that day when every nation will bow and worship before You and glorify Your name. But in the meantime, teach me Your way that I may understand Your truth and walk in it. Purify my heart so it can focus fully and solely in reverence to You, to praise and glorify You forevermore. In Your great mercy, You have saved my soul from the deepest despair. When enemies turn on me, I will turn to You, seeking strength that only You can provide. The heart of the opposition will soften in shame and I will be comforted knowing You will be glorified above all. Amen

Psalm 87

A Psalm of the sons of Korah. A Song. **1** His foundation is in the holy mountains. **2** The Lord loves the gates of Zion More than all the dwellings of Jacob. **3** Glorious things are spoken of you, O city of God! Selah **4** "I will make mention of Rahab and Babylon to those who know Me; Behold, O Philistia and Tyre, with Ethiopia: 'This one was born there.'" **5** And of Zion it will be said, "This one and that one were born in her; And the Most High Himself shall establish her." **6** The Lord will record, When He registers the peoples: "This one was born there." Selah **7** Both the singers and the players on instruments say, "All my springs are in you." (NKJV)

Citizenship has its privileges! This short Psalm speaks of those blessed to be born in Jerusalem and their status compared to those from other nations. We know that Jerusalem is a glorious city, for it was chosen by God to play a critical role in the history of His people. But it also will play a vital part in the future of the world. Even today, we see mankind's three major religions vying for position and possession there. This Psalm can also be interpreted to mean "even those people from other nations will one day be able to claim their citizenship from Jerusalem." How so? The Lord looks on the hearts of each of us as individuals, irrespective of our place of birth. Our rebirth in Christ, however, gives us the right, the privilege to proclaim our new citizenship in God's eternal kingdom so that we too can join in the song, "Glorious things of thee are spoken, Zion, City of our God."

O God, You have established Your city on the holy mount, the city Jerusalem that You love so much. Glorious things have been spoken of it. There are great cities and places in this world that others will sometimes claim as their boastful birthplace, but O to be from Jerusalem, a citizen of the city You have established. It has a heroic history to be sure, but a glorious future lies ahead when it will be made anew and all will sing about its springs of life and joy. Amen

Psalm 88

A Song. A Psalm of the sons of Korah. For the choir director; according to Mahalath Leannoth. A Maskil of Heman the Ezrahite. **1** O LORD, the God of my salvation, I have cried out by day and in the night before You. **2** Let my prayer come before You; Incline Your ear to my cry! **3** For my soul has had enough troubles, And my life has drawn near to Sheol. **4** I am reckoned among those who go down to the pit; I have become like a man without strength, **5** Forsaken among the dead, Like the slain who lie in the grave, Whom You remember no more, And they are cut off from Your hand. **6** You have put me in the lowest pit, In dark places, in the depths. **7** Your wrath has rested upon me, And You have afflicted me with all Your waves. Selah. **8** You have removed my acquaintances far from me; You have made me an object of loathing to them; I am shut up and cannot go out. **9** My eye has wasted away because of affliction; I have called upon You every day, O LORD; I have spread out my hands to You. **10** Will You perform wonders for the dead? Will the departed spirits rise and praise You? Selah. **11** Will Your lovingkindness be declared in the grave, Your faithfulness in Abaddon? **12** Will Your wonders be made known in the darkness? And Your righteousness in the land of forgetfulness? **13** But I, O LORD, have cried out to You for help, And in the morning my prayer comes before You. **14** O LORD, why do You reject my soul? Why do You hide Your face from me? **15** I was afflicted and about to die from my youth on; I suffer Your terrors; I am overcome. **16** Your burning anger has passed over me; Your terrors have destroyed me. **17** They have surrounded me like water all day long; They have encompassed me altogether. **18** You have removed lover and friend far from me; My acquaintances are in darkness. (NASB)

In the seasons of our life, we will surely encounter sorrow and despair and of all the Psalms, this one is probably the darkest and most dismal. It is as if someone is standing on a precipice, looking over the edge into the depths of despondency and knowing he is about to take the plunge. But even amidst the gloom, the first verse shines out one beam of hope and a reminder of redemption – no matter how bleak things appear, it is God who provides salvation. This is not someone who has surrendered his faith and is wallowing in self-pity. No, he has taken the course we must all choose in troublesome times and call out to the Lord. His prayers are passionate and persistent – crying out constantly, day and night. But our cry isn't <u>about</u> our sorrows, rather, it is <u>to</u> the only one who can lift us up and deliver us – in fact, He has already done so. Thanks be to God!

O God, When my soul despairs and faces the troubles of this life I will cry out to You. For You are Jehovah Elohe Yeshuathi, the LORD God of My Salvation. Whether it be day or night, let my prayer come into Your presence so You will hear and answer. Like all mankind, each day I am one step closer to the edge of the grave. Even from my youth, the thought of death is present for it is the relentless reminder of our frail flesh and mortality. But amidst the waves of despair, I will cry out to You for even the darkness cannot hide Your wondrous works. Even when walking in the land of forgetfulness I will always remember Your righteousness. Amen

Psalm 89

A Maskil of Ethan the Ezrahite. **1** I will sing about the Lord's faithful love forever; I will proclaim your faithfulness to all generations with my mouth. **2** For I will declare, "Faithful love is built up forever; you establish your faithfulness in the heavens." **3** The Lord said, "I have made a covenant with my chosen one; I have sworn an oath to David my servant: **4** 'I will establish your offspring forever and build up your throne for all generations.'" *Selah* **5** Lord, the heavens praise your wonders— your faithfulness also— in the assembly of the holy ones. **6** For who in the skies can compare with the Lord? Who among the heavenly beings is like the Lord? **7** God is greatly feared in the council of the holy ones, more awe-inspiring than all who surround him. **8** Lord God of Armies, who is strong like you, Lord? Your faithfulness surrounds you. **9** You rule the raging sea; when its waves surge, you still them. **10** You crushed Rahab like one who is slain; you scattered your enemies with your powerful arm. **11** The heavens are yours; the earth also is yours. The world and everything in it— you founded them. **12** North and south—you created them. Tabor and Hermon shout for joy at your name. **13** You have a mighty arm; your hand is powerful; your right hand is lifted high. **14** Righteousness and justice are the foundation of your throne; faithful love and truth go before you. **15** Happy are the people who know the joyful shout; Lord, they walk in the light from your face. **16** They rejoice in your name all day long, and they are exalted by your righteousness. **17** For you are their magnificent strength; by your favor our horn is exalted. **18** Surely our shield belongs to the Lord, our king to the Holy One of Israel. **19** You once spoke in a vision to your faithful ones and said: "I have granted help to a warrior; I have exalted one chosen from the people. **20** I have found David my servant; I have anointed him with my sacred oil. **21** My hand will always be with him, and my arm will strengthen him. **22** The enemy will not oppress him; the wicked will not afflict him. **23** I will crush his foes before him and strike those who hate him. **24** My faithfulness and love will be with him, and through my name his horn will be exalted. **25** I will extend his power to the sea and his right hand to the rivers. **26** He will call to me, 'You are my Father, my God, the rock of my salvation.' **27** I will also make him my firstborn, greatest of the kings of the earth. **28** I will always preserve my faithful love for him, and my covenant with him will endure. **29** I will establish his line forever, his throne as long as heaven lasts. **30** If his sons abandon my instruction and do not live by my ordinances, **31** if they dishonor my statutes and do not keep my commands, **32** then I will call their rebellion to account with the rod, their iniquity with blows. **33** But I will not withdraw my faithful love from him or betray my faithfulness. **34** I will not violate my covenant or change what my lips have said. **35** Once and for all I have sworn an oath by my holiness; I will not lie to David. **36** His offspring will continue forever, his throne like the sun before me, **37** like the moon, established forever, a faithful witness in the sky." *Selah* **38** But you have spurned and rejected him; you have become enraged with your anointed. **39** You have repudiated the covenant with your servant; you have completely dishonored his crown. **40** You have broken down all his walls; you have reduced his fortified cities to ruins. **41** All who pass by plunder him; he has become an object of ridicule to his neighbors. **42** You have lifted high the right hand of his foes; you have made all his enemies rejoice. **43** You have also turned back his sharp sword and have not let him stand in battle. **44** You have made his splendor cease and have overturned his throne. **45** You have shortened the days of his youth; you have covered him with shame. *Selah* **46** How long, Lord? Will you hide forever? Will your anger keep burning like fire? **47** Remember how short my life is. Have you created everyone for nothing? **48** What courageous person can live and never see death? Who can save himself from the power of Sheol? *Selah* **49** Lord, where are the former acts of your faithful love that you swore to David in your faithfulness? **50** Remember, Lord, the ridicule against your servants— in my heart I carry abuse from all the peoples— **51** how your enemies have ridiculed, Lord, how they have ridiculed every step of your anointed. **52** Blessed be the Lord forever. Amen and amen. (CSB)

For this Psalmist, one of the best ways to convey a message was in song. It was foundational to the Jewish culture to verbally pass along a story to the next generation. Video has now become the favorite form of media, and yet, the written word remains the most enduring way to communicate. With e-books, e-mail and twitter, more written words are floating around the earth in a single day than what was once published in an entire century. How much thought do you put into what you write? As Charles Spurgeon once said, "We ought to have an eye to posterity in all that we write, for we are the schoolmasters of succeeding ages." Most of us will never become a famous author, but if we season our message with scripture, surely our words will linger long after the ink fades or voices falter. Like the grass, we too will wither, but the Word of our Lord lasts forever!

O God, I will sing of Your mercies forever and proclaim Your faithfulness from one generation to the next. For You have firmly formed Your lasting love and mercy without end and Your faithfulness to heaven's hallowed heights. To Your servant David, You swore a continuing covenant; a dynasty of lasting legacy. For generations since, people over all the earth have marveled at Your mercies. The angels You created are majestic, but even in heaven, they gather in awe and reverence to praise Your wonders and faithfulness. For there is none like You our great God, the LORD of Hosts. The oceans You created are mighty but even when they rage as a turbulent tempest You silence the white capped waves. Even the greatest of nations are crushed and crumbled into pieces under the awesome power of Your mighty arm. Heaven and earth are Yours and everything in them. Your throne is secure with Your righteousness and justice; mercy and truth usher me into Your presence. Hearing the joyful trumpet call I am blessed as I walk in the light of Your countenance. My daily delight is in Your name and in Your righteousness I rejoice. I can hold my head high, not because of anything I have done but only because of Your glorious strength. For You are my sword and shield, O LORD, my defender and protector. For You are my Father, my God and the Rock of my salvation. I know far too well that as a man my measured life will one day end and that no one but You can deliver me from the power of the grave. Blessed are You, O LORD forevermore. Amen

Psalm 90

A prayer of Moses, the man of God. **1** Lord, through all the generations you have been our home! **2** Before the mountains were born, before you gave birth to the earth and the world, from beginning to end, you are God. **3** You turn people back to dust, saying, "Return to dust, you mortals!" **4** For you, a thousand years are as a passing day, as brief as a few night hours. **5** You sweep people away like dreams that disappear. They are like grass that springs up in the morning. **6** In the morning it blooms and flourishes, but by evening it is dry and withered. **7** We wither beneath your anger; we are overwhelmed by your fury. **8** You spread out our sins before you— our secret sins—and you see them all. **9** We live our lives beneath your wrath, ending our years with a groan. **10** Seventy years are given to us! Some even live to eighty. But even the best years are filled with pain and trouble; soon they disappear, and we fly away. **11** Who can comprehend the power of your anger? Your wrath is as awesome as the fear you deserve. **12** Teach us to realize the brevity of life, so that we may grow in wisdom. **13** O LORD, come back to us! How long will you delay? Take pity on your servants! **14** Satisfy us each morning with your unfailing love, so we may sing for joy to the end of our lives. **15** Give us gladness in proportion to our former misery! Replace the evil years with good. **16** Let us, your servants, see you work again; let our children see your glory. **17** And may the Lord our God show us his approval and make our efforts successful. Yes, make our efforts successful! (NLT)

Of the 150 Psalms, this is the only one attributed to Moses. It was likely written near the end of his life after leading the children of Israel through the wilderness. For forty years, they walked....and walked. If they had obeyed, the trip would have been much shorter. Moses recognized how short and transitory our life is as humans and the need to make the most of it. So then, how should we walk? The Apostle Paul gave us clear instruction in the fifth and sixth chapters in his letter to the Ephesians. Based on that, I wrote a poem to capture how we should walk:

Walk in a Manner So Worthy

Walk in a manner so worthy
of the calling with which you were called,
Maintaining the Spirit of oneness
and the strength which He has installed.
Be gentle, humble and patient
so that all contention will cease.
Live tranquil your life with each other
and keep the bond of His peace.

Walk not anymore in your old ways,
with futility set in your minds,
Hold fast to what is important,
let go of the sin that so binds.
It darkens your deep understanding
and causes a hard-calloused heart,
To undo your life as intended
and keep you and God far apart.

Walk in Christ's love as He loved us
and gave up Himself as our price;
A sweet-smelling scent up to Heaven,
presented as our sacrifice.
Following God's perfect model
to live life as His holy saint,
And not the life of your old self
but one full of thankful restraint.

Walk in the light as God tells us.
Yes, walk in the light of the Lord!

Discern every act that will please Him
and result in a mind thus restored.
Fruitless dark deeds that once held you,
prior old habits from youth,
Exposed by the light of His glory,
transformed into goodness and truth.

Walk not in the ways of the foolish,
rather choose the path of the wise.
Keep watch for the things to delight Him,
fooled not by the enemy's guise.
Because of these days that are evil,
redeem your time for the best;
Keeping a heart that is thankful
and living a life God has blessed.

O God, from one generation to the next You have been our place of refuge and shelter. Even before You formed the earth and universe You eternally existed. Our time on earth is but a fleeting flash that fades but You are forever. A thousand years to You is but a passing dream from yesterday. We glide along the river of time thinking how important our lives are but in reality, we are like a blade of green grass, sprouting anew in the morning and mowed down in the evening. You divulge our deceitful disguises and lay bare our secret sins - nothing is hidden from You, O God. And when our life's drama draws to a close we simply sigh and pass on. Whether we last seventy or even eighty years, unless our life's work isn't done for You, it doesn't amount to much in the scheme of things. Before we know it, we are gone and drift away. With this in mind, teach me to make the most of every day; to start each morning with a heart given wholly to You with a desire to walk in Your wisdom. In Your mercy, have pity on me so that when the sun rises I am filled with Your love; a love that sustains me the rest of my life. Make each new day better than the past one. In doing Your work, may I have hands that are calloused but a heart that is not. Help me to clearly behold Your majesty so that Your beauty fills me. May it guide and strengthen me so that even in my very temporary and limited life the work of my hands will bring permanent glory to Your name. Amen

Psalm 91

1 He who dwells in the shelter of the Most High Will abide in the shadow of the Almighty. 2 I will say to the LORD, "My refuge and my fortress, My God, in whom I trust!" 3 For it is He who delivers you from the snare of the trapper And from the deadly pestilence. 4 He will cover you with His pinions, And under His wings you may seek refuge; His faithfulness is a shield and bulwark. 5 You will not be afraid of the terror by night, Or of the arrow that flies by day; 6 Of the pestilence that stalks in darkness, Or of the destruction that lays waste at noon. 7 A thousand may fall at your side And ten thousand at your right hand, But it shall not approach you. 8 You will only look on with your eyes And see the recompense of the wicked. 9 For you have made the LORD, my refuge, Even the Most High, your dwelling place. 10 No evil will befall you, Nor will any plague come near your tent. 11 For He will give His angels charge concerning you, To guard you in all your ways. 12 They will bear you up in their hands, That you do not strike your foot against a stone. 13 You will tread upon the lion and cobra, The young lion and the serpent you will trample down. 14 "Because he has loved Me, therefore I will deliver him; I will set him securely on high, because he has known My name. 15 He will call upon Me, and I will answer him; I will be with him in trouble; I will rescue him and honor him. 16 With a long life I will satisfy him And let him see My salvation." (NASB)

Often considered a Psalm of protection, the benefit of abiding in the secret place of God is extensive: refuge, fearlessness, safekeeping, deliverance, assurance, and security. But it is really about so much more! It is being in close communion with God. The imagery is as if we have entered into the Holy Place, giving us direct access to God and allowing us to worship "behind the veil." Amazingly, the foulest of all trappers, Satan, tried to snare Jesus using this very passage. But the verses directly following the ones quoted by the devil gives us a unique view of Jesus' relationship with His Father –

"Because He has set His love (wholly and completely) on Me…I will set Him securely on high!" The precipice of temptation didn't lose its luster or danger by the wings of angels, but due to Jesus taking refuge under His Father's wings. May we always desire the same!

O God, my God, You are the Almighty, Jehovah Elyown, the LORD Most High. I dwell under the shadow of Your secret shelter where nothing can touch me except by Your leave. I will ever trust You as my mighty fortress. It is You, O LORD, who delivers me from the treacherous traps and deadly diseases of this life. Your truth surrounds me like a shield of armor. I will not dread danger, whether it stalks me by night as a plague or commutes chaos in broad daylight. No matter what is happening around me, I am Yours as I gaze in awe while You repay evil its just reward. Because You are my secure shelter no evil will befall me without Your leave. You have ordered Your angels to protect me as they support me on life's path. Because I know You, love You, and call upon You, I am delivered from danger when You answer me. During my hardships, You are at my side bringing deliverance and honor. You, O LORD, make life worth living and in You I am satisfied for You have shown me the way of salvation. Amen

Psalm 92

A psalm. A song to be sung on the Sabbath Day. **1** It is good to give thanks to the LORD, to sing praises to the Most High. **2** It is good to proclaim your unfailing love in the morning, your faithfulness in the evening, **3** accompanied by a ten-stringed instrument, a harp, and the melody of a lyre. **4** You thrill me, LORD, with all you have done for me! I sing for joy because of what you have done. **5** O LORD, what great works you do! And how deep are your thoughts. **6** Only a simpleton would not know, and only a fool would not understand this: **7** Though the wicked sprout like weeds and evildoers flourish, they will be destroyed forever. **8** But you, O LORD, will be exalted forever. **9** Your enemies, LORD, will surely perish; all evildoers will be scattered. **10** But you have made me as strong as a wild ox. You have anointed me with the finest oil. **11** My eyes have seen the downfall of my enemies; my ears have heard the defeat of my wicked opponents. **12** But the godly will flourish like palm trees and grow strong like the cedars of Lebanon. **13** For they are transplanted to the LORD's own house. They flourish in the courts of our God. **14** Even in old age they will still produce fruit; they will remain vital and green. **15** They will declare, "The LORD is just! He is my rock! There is no evil in him!" (NLT)

Who doesn't love music? There are so many different kinds and choices, and while you may not like a specific style, there is certainly one type that suits your taste. Apparently, God loves music too! This Psalm is called a "song" for the Sabbath day and whether it is singing or playing instruments, whether it is harmony or melody, whether it is morning or nighttime, God wants to be praised in a musical manner. In the early 1970s, the brother/sister musical tandem "The Carpenters" recorded a popular song named "Sing." The lyrics of this simplistic jingle included this catchy line: "Sing, sing a song, make it simple to last your whole life long." God isn't so concerned with the quality of your singing voice, but He does care about the sincerity of your singing heart. Let us make our time here on earth a life-long song thanking our Lord who is worthy to be praised!

O God, what a joy it is to give thanks to You and to sing Your praises. Each morning I will proclaim Your lovingkindness and throughout the night whisper words recalling Your faithfulness. With whatever instrument I can play and with the voice You have given me, I will make a joyful song of Your great works. Your plans and purposes are too great for my comprehension. Give me the sense and understanding to grasp Your designs in life. Even though the wicked appear to flourish on earth, their destructive doom is sure; for You, O LORD, are the Most High forevermore. You give me strength and honor against my enemies each day anew. When I keep my eyes focused on You I grow straight and tall like the finest tree in the forest. Let me be like a healthy tree bearing fruit only for You for many years to come. For You, O God, are holy and just, my Rock in whom there is no unrighteousness. Amen

Psalm 93

1 The LORD reigns, He is clothed with majesty; The LORD has clothed and girded Himself with strength; Indeed, the world is firmly established, it will not be moved. **2** Your throne is established from of old; You are from everlasting. **3** The floods have lifted up, O LORD, The floods have lifted up their voice, The floods lift up their pounding waves. **4** More than the sounds of many waters, Than the mighty breakers of the sea, The LORD on high is mighty. **5** Your testimonies are fully confirmed; Holiness befits Your house, O LORD, forevermore. (NASB)

There is something enchanting about watching the waves on the seashore. Our face feels the fine spray of mist. Our eyes see the back-and-forth mesmerizing motion. Our ears hear the ebb-and-flow duel between roaring thunder and retreating whispers. Waves certainly can be described as a combination of strength and beauty. That strength is manifest in two ways: repetitious consistency over many millennia can transform a mighty mountain into a sandy seashore; or, in an instant, a single tsunami can level a city leaving death and destruction in its wake. But despite the power of those waves, it is our God who reigns supreme. Praise God, we have a Savior, Christ Jesus, who is the same yesterday, today and forever. His command transforms the mightiest waves into the calmest sea! He can do the same with the storms in our life if we let Him.

O God, You reign as King, surrounding Yourself in majestic might and perfect power. The world You have firmly fashioned is sustained by Your supreme sovereignty and Your throne eternally existing. Even the greatest thundering waves will wane and cease in silence before You. But You, O LORD, endure eternal in might. Your proclamations are unwavering and faithful and holiness is forever the hallmark of Your house. Amen

Psalm 94

1 O LORD, the God of vengeance, O God of vengeance, let your glorious justice shine forth! 2 Arise, O Judge of the earth. Give the proud what they deserve. 3 How long, O LORD? How long will the wicked be allowed to gloat? 4 How long will they speak with arrogance? How long will these evil people boast? 5 They crush your people, LORD, hurting those you claim as your own. 6 They kill widows and foreigners and murder orphans. 7 "The LORD isn't looking," they say, "and besides, the God of Israel doesn't care." 8 Think again, you fools! When will you finally catch on? 9 Is he deaf—the one who made your ears? Is he blind—the one who formed your eyes? 10 He punishes the nations—won't he also punish you? He knows everything— doesn't he also know what you are doing? 11 The LORD knows people's thoughts; he knows they are worthless! 12 Joyful are those you discipline, LORD, those you teach with your instructions. 13 You give them relief from troubled times until a pit is dug to capture the wicked. 14 The LORD will not reject his people; he will not abandon his special possession. 15 Judgment will again be founded on justice, and those with virtuous hearts will pursue it. 16 Who will protect me from the wicked? Who will stand up for me against evildoers? 17 Unless the LORD had helped me, I would soon have settled in the silence of the grave. 18 I cried out, "I am slipping!" but your unfailing love, O LORD, supported me. 19 When doubts filled my mind, your comfort gave me renewed hope and cheer. 20 Can unjust leaders claim that God is on their side— leaders whose decrees permit injustice? 21 They gang up against the righteous and condemn the innocent to death. 22 But the LORD is my fortress; my God is the mighty rock where I hide. 23 God will turn the sins of evil people back on them. He will destroy them for their sins. The LORD our God will destroy them. (NLT)

Let's face it – as a race, we humans are generally a rather impatient lot, often prone to great doubt. The most frequently asked question in the Psalms is,

"How long, O Lord?" and it isn't just a rhetorical one. Here, the Psalmist asks, "How long will the wicked triumph?" Some might wonder, "Isn't it wrong to doubt or question God?" Not necessarily – He already knows what is in our hearts and minds. He wants us to be honest with Him. It is important to remember that our present perception isn't always reality, but God's promises always are. His wisdom, power, and faithfulness are unending so He knows what is best for us and has the desire and ability to see it through. No matter how much the cares and concerns of our heart multiply, God's comfort and consolation are greater still. It is because of this we can take rest in the Rock of our refuge!

O God, You are the mighty judge of this world. Help me to remain focused on You as You rise up to put the proud in their place and render righteous vengeance. At times it seems the wicked go on unimpeded – it makes me wonder how long lawlessness will last? They boastfully brag about themselves while oppressing Your people, murdering widows, orphans and others they don't know. In their arrogance, they think You do not see or are paying attention. But it is they who should be attentive and come to their senses! Can they really think that You who designed and created the ear, eye, and mind of man cannot hear, see or know what they think? You will instruct and discipline the nations, for You, O LORD, know the thoughts of every person and that they are but a passing breath. Let me receive Your discipline with a joyful willing heart and instruction from Your Word, that I may find peace in my most distressful days. For I know You will never forsake me. When I see Your righteousness rendered in justice, let me follow obediently in loyal love. For only You are my shield and protection against evil and in Your mercy support my slipping foot. When worries grow and multiply in my mind, You come to me in comfort, bearing encouragement and providing peace within my soul. So when the worldly wicked come against me, You, O LORD, are my defender, my Rock and Refuge. Amen

Psalm 95

1 Oh come, let us sing to the Lord! Let us shout joyfully to the Rock of our salvation. 2 Let us come before His presence with thanksgiving; Let us shout joyfully to Him with psalms. 3 For the Lord is the great God, And the great King above all gods. 4 In His hand are the deep places of the earth; The heights of the hills are His also. 5 The sea is His, for He made it; And His hands formed the dry land. 6 Oh come, let us worship and bow down; Let us kneel before the Lord our Maker. 7 For He is our God, And we are the people of His pasture, And the sheep of His hand. Today, if you will hear His voice: 8 "Do not harden your hearts, as in the rebellion, As in the day of trial in the wilderness, 9 When your fathers tested Me; They tried Me, though they saw My work. 10 For forty years I was grieved with that generation, And said, 'It is a people who go astray in their hearts, And they do not know My ways.' 11 So I swore in My wrath, 'They shall not enter My rest.'" (NKJV)

Have you ever wondered what went wrong with the Israelites after being set free from 400 years of bondage? Despite witnessing the power of God firsthand – through ten plagues; escaping the army of Pharaoh at the Red Sea; miraculous gifts of food and water; and seeing His very presence day and night, that generation never entered God's rest. Why? This Psalm uses their plight to paint a picture of two hearts: one of worshipful obedience, the other hardened by disobedience. It was hardened hearts, refusing to believe God would provide for them in the Promised Land, that kept them in the wilderness. They didn't trust and obey. Ah, but lest we are too quick to point the finger, what about us? Do we consistently believe God and obey His Word? It was C. S. Lewis who said, "Obedience is the key that opens every door." Let us, therefore, be diligent to enter that rest, lest anyone fall according to the same example of disobedience. (Heb. 4:11)

O God, I come into Your presence with a thankful heart to joyfully sing praises to You, the Rock of my salvation. For You are a great God, reigning supreme – there is no one like You. The earth's deepest depth and highest heights are all hidden in Your hand. The vast oceans and all creation are Yours for You made them and You formed the dry land into its shape. I come O LORD, to bow down in worship, kneeling before You, my maker. For You are my God, shepherding me like a sheep in Your pasture. I pray that each day I will have eager ears and listen for Your voice; that my heart never hardens towards You, but rather it hungers to hastily hear You and promptly obey. Let me never doubt You but instead, daily live a life with a heart that faithfully follows Your ways so in the end, I may enter Your rest. Amen

Psalm 96

1 Sing to the LORD a new song; Sing to the LORD, all the earth. 2 Sing to the LORD, bless His name; Proclaim good tidings of His salvation from day to day. 3 Tell of His glory among the nations, His wonderful deeds among all the peoples. 4 For great is the LORD and greatly to be praised; He is to be feared above all gods. 5 For all the gods of the peoples are idols, But the LORD made the heavens. 6 Splendor and majesty are before Him, Strength and beauty are in His sanctuary. 7 Ascribe to the LORD, O families of the peoples, Ascribe to the LORD glory and strength. 8 Ascribe to the LORD the glory of His name; Bring an offering and come into His courts. 9 Worship the LORD in holy attire; Tremble before Him, all the earth. 10 Say among the nations, "The LORD reigns; Indeed, the world is firmly established, it will not be moved; He will judge the peoples with equity." 11 Let the heavens be glad, and let the earth rejoice; Let the sea roar, and all it contains; 12 Let the field exult, and all that is in it. Then all the trees of the forest will sing for joy 13 Before the LORD, for He is coming, For He is coming to judge the earth. He will judge the world in righteousness And the peoples in His faithfulness. (NASB)

This Psalm of wonderful worship is a beautiful blueprint for praise. It not only shows us how we should bless the Lord but highlights how all His creation does. And yet, even the beauty and majesty of nature has been marred by man's sin and disobedience. As the Apostle Paul said in Romans 8, even creation suffers under the slavery of sin and groans for the day of delivery. In anticipation of the Lord's return, the heavens will rejoice, the earth will be glad, the sea will roar and the trees will sing for joy. In the first book of the Bible (Genesis 3), we are told *Cursed is the ground for your sake; in toil you shall eat of it all the days of your life. Both thorns and thistles it shall bring forth to you…* " But in the last chapter of the Bible's final book (Revelation 22) we are told, "…*and the leaves of the tree were for the healing of the nations. And there shall no longer be any curse.* "This Psalm is a victory cry over Adam's curse which affects both man and creation. I wrote a poem to portray that triumph and how it was attained:

Adam's Curse Upon the Brow

While toiling in the garden, weeding out each thorn,
The flesh upon my fingers drips with blood as they are torn.
"This ground is foul" I mutter as I shovel, dig and plow,
Adam's curse is still upon us with sweat upon my brow.

The thistle and the briar soon entangle round my hoe,
Glancing down I'm taken back to a vision long ago.
Recalling that first garden devoid of any weed,
Amidst the crops of plenty, sin planted its first seed.

It could have been so different if Adam had obeyed.
The cost of his decision is a world become decayed.
God sent His Second Adam, all sin He did eschew,
To bring us hope eternal and right the world anew.

See Jesus in the garden known as Gethsemane,
The future weighs upon Him as He falls on bended knee.
He bows before the Father, to obey He does avow,
Blood and sweat are mingled, Adam's curse upon His brow.

Thistle, thorns, and briars are entwined to make a crown,
Mockingly it's placed upon then painfully pressed down.
Sin's suffering takes its full effect, the cost so clearly now,
From Eden up to Calvary, Adam's curse upon His brow.

Creation groans unwillingly subjected to that curse,
And cries out for its freedom as conditions just get worse.
The thorns are our reminder - what was... and soon will be,
When the Tree of Life is planted new and we are all set free.

O God, please give me a new song to sing unto You every day; let me join the entire earth to sing Your praise. May I bless Your name daily as I tell others about Your great salvation. Help me to be bold to declare Your glory and deeds of wonder to everyone I meet. For You, O LORD, are great and worthy to receive reverent praise. The insignificant idols of man are nothing compared to You for You made the heavens and all they contain. Your presence is one of majestic grandeur and strength and beauty surround You. Let my heart confess Your splendor and my lips bring You the glory You deserve. May my offering be given with a heart of thankful praise that has been sanctified by You. For I can only come into Your presence wrapped in Your holy attire. I kneel in awe of all You have done. For You, O God, reign in heaven and on earth and You will judge all in righteousness. Your created universe anticipates Your coming and all nature rejoices – from the happy heavens to surging seas to festive fields – even the trees of the forest will sing for joy. For You, O LORD, are faithful and true. Amen

Psalm 97

1 The LORD reigns, let the earth rejoice; let the many coastlands be glad! 2 Clouds and thick darkness are all around him; righteousness and justice are the foundation of his throne. 3 Fire goes before him and burns up his adversaries all around. 4 His lightnings light up the world; the earth sees and trembles. 5 The mountains melt like wax before the LORD, before the Lord of all the earth. 6 The heavens proclaim his righteousness, and all the peoples see his glory. 7 All worshipers of images are put to shame, who make their boast in worthless idols; worship him, all you gods! 8 Zion hears and is glad, and the daughters of Judah rejoice, because of your judgments, O LORD. 9 For you, O LORD, are most high over all the earth; you are exalted far above all gods. 10 O you who love the LORD, hate evil! He preserves the lives of his saints; he delivers them from the hand of the wicked. 11 Light is sown for the righteous, and joy for the upright in heart. 12 Rejoice in the LORD, O you righteous, and give thanks to his holy name! (ESV)

Having devoted most of my adult life in law enforcement, I've spent a fair amount of time in the courtroom. Some courtrooms are historically ornate with vaulted ceilings of carved wood, while others have an unadorned contemporary decorum, yet all have a common floor plan. I have pondered what the view is like when seated at the defendant's table instead of the prosecution. But both sides must look upward to the black robed judge, seated high on the bench. This Psalm harkens to such a setting. God is judge over all the earth, enveloped in a dark cloud like a black robe. His throne is the high bench, supported by righteousness and justice. Righteousness is the absolute ability to know right from wrong and justice is the capacity to perfectly execute judgment. When we face the Judge with Jesus as our advocate, we mustn't fear justice for in Him, the penalty has been paid in full.

O God, let everyone on earth – even in the most distant domains – rejoice that You reign as King. Your unapproachable holiness surrounds You like thick clouds in darkness and Your throne is secure in Your righteousness and justice. Your enemies and rebellious rivals are met by Your consuming fire. The world sees the fierce flash of Your lightning and trembles in fear. Even the greatest mountains melt like wax in Your presence, O LORD of all. The highest heavens proclaim Your righteousness and Your glory is plain for all to see. Those who unabashedly boast and bow down to their idols will become distraught with guilt and sheepish shame. For only You, O LORD, deserve devotion in our worship. Not only are You exalted above all the supernatural powers in the universe, they too will soon fall down and worship You, LORD God Most High. Preserve my soul, O LORD, as I demonstrate my love for You by putting You first and despise the evil of this world. Let Your Word be like little seeds of light sown within my soul, sprouting forth fulgent fruit of joy so my thankful heart may praise Your holy name. Amen

Psalm 98

A Psalm. **1** Oh, sing to the Lord a new song! For He has done marvelous things; His right hand and His holy arm have gained Him the victory. **2** The Lord has made known His salvation; His righteousness He has revealed in the sight of the nations. **3** He has remembered His mercy and His faithfulness to the house of Israel; All the ends of the earth have seen the salvation of our God. **4** Shout joyfully to the Lord, all the earth; Break forth in song, rejoice, and sing praises. **5** Sing to the Lord with the harp, With the harp and the sound of a psalm, **6** With trumpets and the sound of a horn; Shout joyfully before the Lord, the King. **7** Let the sea roar, and all its fullness, The world and those who dwell in it; **8** Let the rivers clap their hands; Let the hills be joyful together before the Lord, **9** For He is coming to judge the earth. With righteousness He shall judge the world, And the peoples with equity. (NKJV)

Each and every day, "guessing games" are being played. From children playing "I spy with my little eyes…" to adults on myriad television game shows, life is a constant game of "Clue." A key duty of law enforcement is to decipher the hints of evidence left behind by the criminal. The unlawful acts are nearly always carried out in secrecy or done with a determined effort by the culprit to remain unidentified. In this Psalm, we see that God's "holy arm" has worked out salvation and the great thing is it hasn't been done surreptitiously. It says the Lord has "made known" His salvation before the nations and He has revealed His righteousness. God has left clues in plain view for all to see. It is up to us to be inquisitive, ask the right questions, and closely listen to His responses. Praise God for giving us the answers to the guessing game of life.

O God, Because of all the wonderful and marvelous things You have done, my voice rises in song. With the supreme strength of Your omnipotent holy arm, You have triumphed! For the victory revealed is Your salvation which You demonstrated through the house of Israel and have shown to all mankind. When I think about that I stop what I am doing and break forth in joyful songs of praise. Let the sound of horns and harps join in flourishing fanfare before You. Let all nature join the joyful jubilation as the seas roar, the rivers applaud, and the mountains sing in unity. Let the entire earth and all its inhabitants join the communal concert before You, O LORD, for You are coming soon to judge the world with righteous justice for all. Amen

Psalm 99

1 The LORD reigns; let the peoples tremble! He sits enthroned upon the cherubim; let the earth quake! **2** The LORD is great in Zion; he is exalted over all the peoples. **3** Let them praise your great and awesome name! Holy is he! **4** The King in his might loves justice. You have established equity; you have executed justice and righteousness in Jacob. **5** Exalt the LORD our God; worship at his footstool! Holy is he! **6** Moses and Aaron were among his priests, Samuel also was among those who called upon his name. They called to the LORD, and he answered them. **7** In the pillar of the cloud he spoke to them; they kept his testimonies and the statute that he gave them. **8** O LORD our God, you answered them; you were a forgiving God to them, but an avenger of their wrongdoings. **9** Exalt the LORD our God, and worship at his holy mountain; for the LORD our God is holy! (ESV)

California is home to the infamous San Andreas Fault – habitat of earthquakes. I was born right on top of that fault line and have felt my fair share of earthquakes. After reading this Psalm one might ask, "What does God's holiness have to do with a quaking earth?" In the first verse the people "tremble" and the earth "quakes." The Hebrew word used for tremble (ragaz) has various meanings including to be disturbed, agitated or excited. The Hebrew word used for quake (nut) is found nowhere else in the Bible. In the presence of a holy God, the entire earth trembles and shakes, dangles and quakes - no one remains unaffected. When Isaiah saw God in His heavenly temple and the angels crying out, "Holy, Holy, Holy. The earth is full of His glory" his response sums it up: "Woe is me, for I am undone." Ponder God's holiness and praise Him with a trembling heart!

O God, People everywhere tremble before You for You reign as King, seated on Your throne high above the mightiest of angels. Let everyone bow before You in awe and wonder and praise Your exalted name, for You are holy! You are my mighty monarch who loves justice and embraces equity. I fall before Your footstool O God, for You are holy. Men of old witnessed Your wonder and called upon You and You answered from the cloudy column. Moses, Aaron, and Samuel heard Your teachings and kept Your testimonies. And even when they failed to follow, You forgave them and taught them the lessons of their disappointing deeds. I bow to worship and praise You, O God, for You are holy. Amen

Psalm 100

A Psalm of Thanksgiving. **1** Make a joyful shout to the Lord, all you lands! **2** Serve the Lord with gladness; Come before His presence with singing. **3** Know that the Lord, He is God; It is He who has made us, and not we ourselves; We are His people and the sheep of His pasture. **4** Enter into His gates with thanksgiving, And into His courts with praise. Be thankful to Him, and bless His name. **5** For the Lord is good; His mercy is everlasting, And His truth endures to all generations. (NKJV)

Have you ever left a pet dog at home and upon your return discovered it has done something destructive? Maybe it chewed up a slipper, pulled the stuffing out from a pillow, or dug a hole in the garden? So much for man's best friend. And yet, most dogs are incredibly smart, capable of complying with many a command, doing all kinds of tricks. It is clear to see why they are such a popular pet! But beyond being a "pet" they are often called upon to be a coworker in difficult tasks. While leading the FBI's Critical Incident Response Group, I authorized the use of specialized canines as part of the Hostage Rescue Team (HRT). These dogs truly were teammates to the Operators and in keeping with the HRT's motto (Servare Vitas) they too worked "to save lives" – not just their teammate's but in some cases, they actually saved the life of the "bad guys." Sheep, on the other hand are, well, let's just say they are not four-legged Einsteins wearing wool sweaters. They tend to wander, often get lost and can be exceedingly stubborn to the point of placing their life in peril. Sound familiar? It makes sense why the Bible so often refers to God's people as the sheep of His pasture. When we go astray needing protection and guidance, how good it is to hear God's voice calling, to recognize it and then obediently follow.

O God, You are LORD of all the earth and I joyfully shout before You. I come into Your presence with a happy heart. Let my worship be to serve You daily, not from a sense of duty but in a spirit of delight. For You, O LORD are God. You have made me and I am Yours and all my accomplishments are a result of Your bountiful blessings. Yes, I am Yours and like a sheep, You guide me from Your pleasant pastures through the grand gates into the courtyard of Your presence. I come with thankful praise and adoration to bless Your name because You are good. Your mercy is everlasting and Your faithfulness follows from one generation to the next. I praise You, O LORD! Amen

Psalm 101

A Psalm of David. **1** I will sing of lovingkindness and justice, To You, O LORD, I will sing praises. **2** I will give heed to the blameless way. When will You come to me? I will walk within my house in the integrity of my heart. **3** I will set no worthless thing before my eyes; I hate the work of those who fall away; It shall not fasten its grip on me. **4** A perverse heart shall depart from me; I will know no evil. **5** Whoever secretly slanders his neighbor, him I will destroy; No one who has a haughty look and an arrogant heart will I endure. **6** My eyes shall be upon the faithful of the land, that they may dwell with me; He who walks in a blameless way is the one who will minister to me. **7** He who practices deceit shall not dwell within my house; He who speaks falsehood shall not maintain his position before me. **8** Every morning I will destroy all the wicked of the land, So as to cut off from the city of the LORD all those who do iniquity. (NASB)

Which has the greater impact in your home: a thermometer or a thermostat? The former simply tells you what you already know – it's too hot or cold; the latter regulates it, causing the change you desire. One reads – the other remedies; one measures – the other moderates. In this Psalm, David devises a framework for fulfillment within his household, rules to regulate it. Some include: Sing praises to the Lord about His mercy. Behave wisely. Walk with a heart of integrity. Gaze not on worthless things to let them get a grip on you. Keep a heart that is pure. Remain a stranger to evil thoughts. Strive for humility and avoid the secret slanderer. While we may not have the courtly palace of a king, as Christians, we desire the King of the Universe to feel at home within our humble abode. Don't simply conform to your surroundings, but let God's Word transform you and your dwelling place - this should be our living sacrifice and our reasonable service of worship.

O God, I sing praises to You for Your lovingkindness and justice. Give me the desire and strength to willingly walk on Your perfect path with a heart of integrity. Let me put my praise into practice so the first steps of that journey begin in my own home. Do not let my eyes drift with the distractions of worthless worldly things, but rather, keep me focused firmly and only on that which is worthy of You. Keep my heart pure before You, to fleetly flee when evil approaches. Let me lovingly live with my neighbors and never display so much as a whiff of pride or aroma of arrogance. I pray for the leaders of my land, that they will walk blamelessly before You to serve their countrymen. May they persistently practice truth in all their proceedings and seek to root out evil morning by morning. In so doing, we as a people will live with integrity, not in iniquity, to the glory of Your name. Amen

Psalm 102

A Prayer of one afflicted, when he is faint and pours out his complaint before the Lord. **1** Hear my prayer, O LORD; let my cry come to you! **2** Do not hide your face from me in the day of my distress! Incline your ear to me; answer me speedily in the day when I call! **3** For my days pass away like smoke, and my bones burn like a furnace. **4** My heart is struck down like grass and has withered; I forget to eat my bread. **5** Because of my loud groaning my bones cling to my flesh. **6** I am like a desert owl of the wilderness, like an owl of the waste places; **7** I lie awake; I am like a lonely sparrow on the housetop. **8** All the day my enemies taunt me; those who deride me use my name for a curse. **9** For I eat ashes like bread and mingle tears with my drink, **10** because of your indignation and anger; for you have taken me up and thrown me down. **11** My days are like an evening shadow; I wither away like grass. **12** But you, O LORD, are enthroned forever; you are remembered throughout all generations. **13** You will arise and have pity on Zion; it is the time to favor her; the appointed time has come. **14** For your servants hold her stones dear and have pity on her dust. **15** Nations will fear the name of the LORD, and all the kings of the earth will fear your glory. **16** For the LORD builds up Zion; he appears in his glory; **17** he regards the prayer of the destitute and does not despise their prayer. **18** Let this be recorded for a generation to come, so that a people yet to be created may praise the LORD: **19** that he looked down from his holy height; from heaven the LORD looked at the earth, **20** to hear the groans of the prisoners, to set free those who were doomed to die, **21** that they may declare in Zion the name of the LORD, and in Jerusalem his praise, **22** when peoples gather together, and kingdoms, to worship the LORD. **23** He has broken my strength in midcourse; he has shortened my days. **24** "O my God," I say, "take me not away in the midst of my days— you whose years endure throughout all generations!" **25** Of old you laid the foundation of the earth, and the heavens are the work of your hands. **26** They will perish, but you will remain; they will all wear out like a garment. You will change them like a robe, and they will pass away, **27** but you are the same, and your years have no end. **28** The children of your servants shall dwell secure; their offspring shall be established before you. (ESV)

The best way to drive home a point is to contrast a spectrum's opposite ends. When I was a brand-new FBI Agent at age 26 I couldn't fathom what it would look like to spend more than half my life and an entire career as an Agent for 28 years. It was only at the end of that journey that I appreciated what that meant. As gratifying as it was, it paled in comparison to what is important in eternity. This Psalm shows the greatness of God compared to our feeble status. Upon seeing it, the Psalmist feels forlorn. We read word-pictures with which we can readily relate. Lives ending far too soon, fading away like smoke on the horizon; an evening shadow stretched too thin; grass withering away. Lives in isolation like an owl in the wilderness; a pelican without water; the lonely sparrow upon the housetop. And just when despair knocks on our heart's door, verse 12 arrives to brings us to our senses like a slap in the face: "BUT – You O Lord, sit enthroned <u>forever</u>!" The past praises of all mankind merge with the present and will join with those who are yet to come. Yes, our time here is short, but we serve a God who holds history, even all of time itself firmly in the palm of His hand.

O God, When I feel faint and afflicted… hear my prayer. May my supplication never become windy words or repetitive rhetoric but rather, uttered in earnest devotion, winding its way to Your discerning ear and into Your loving heart. On those days when my energy fails and life's purpose gives me pause, permit my petitions. When my heart hurts and feels wounded and withered, receive my requests. When sleep evades my eager eyes and I watch the night pass in seclusion, welcome my worship. When traitors taunt and attackers assail me, accept my appeals. And when my day seems like a roller coaster full of peaks and valleys and I come to the realization my life lingers like a lengthening shadow only to wane and wither away, listen to my longings. But You, O LORD, endure forever, eternally enthroned in glory and passed along in the minds and memories from one generation to the next. We cry out for Your kingdom to come but it all will happen in Your divine timing. We see the brief battles between good and evil but You already see the victorious outcome, when all the earth falls in fear at Your glory. In Your perfect plan, You provided a written record of Your sacred story of salvation so that even I, before my very existence, could become a member of Your chosen people to forever praise Your name. From Your holy height in heaven, you gaze upon the earth hearing the prayers of the poor and imprisoned, and delivering those doomed to death. And yet, in the end, death will come to all, like a worn-out garment we fade and vanish. But You, O LORD, remain forever, unchanged and eternal. May my children and children's children continue to find peace in their service to You. Amen

Psalm 103

A Psalm of David. **1** Bless the LORD, O my soul, And all that is within me, bless His holy name. **2** Bless the LORD, O my soul, And forget none of His benefits; **3** Who pardons all your iniquities, Who heals all your diseases; **4** Who redeems your life from the pit, Who crowns you with lovingkindness and compassion; **5** Who satisfies your years with good things, So that your youth is renewed like the eagle. **6** The LORD performs righteous deeds And judgments for all who are oppressed. **7** He made known His ways to Moses, His acts to the sons of Israel. **8** The LORD is compassionate and gracious, Slow to anger and abounding in lovingkindness. **9** He will not always strive with us, Nor will He keep His anger forever. **10** He has not dealt with us according to our sins, Nor rewarded us according to our iniquities. **11** For as high as the heavens are above the earth, So great is His lovingkindness toward those who fear Him. **12** As far as the east is from the west, So far has He removed our transgressions from us. **13** Just as a father has compassion on his children, So the LORD has compassion on those who fear Him. **14** For He Himself knows our frame; He is mindful that we are but dust. **15** As for man, his days are like grass; As a flower of the field, so he flourishes. **16** When the wind has passed over it, it is no more, And its place acknowledges it no longer. **17** But the lovingkindness of the LORD is from everlasting to everlasting on those who fear Him, And His righteousness to children's children, **18** To those who keep His covenant And remember His precepts to do them. **19** The LORD has established His throne in the heavens, And His sovereignty rules over all. **20** Bless the LORD, you His angels, Mighty in strength, who perform His word, Obeying the voice of His word! **21** Bless the LORD, all you His hosts, You who serve Him, doing His will. **22** Bless the LORD, all you works of His, In all places of His dominion; Bless the LORD, O my soul! (NASB)

It is easy sometimes to forget that each Psalm was composed as a hymn meant to be sung. But in this case, David's lyrics are abundantly clear that we have a song. In fact, many other songs of our faith, old and new, are based on these words. The vast majority of the Psalms contain some form of request or petition, but when you read this one you will note there is not a single supplication – it is all praise and worship. With our entire being, with everything we have and that which comprises our being, we are to bless the Lord. The Hebrew word for "bless" (barak) means to kneel. Three different times in this Psalm, we are told how great God's love, pity, and mercy is for those who do something. What is it? We are to "fear Him." By reverently kneeling in submission, we recognize how awesome He is and we bless Him. That, in turn, opens the door for the King of Universe to bless us.

O God, I bless You from my innermost being and praise Your holy name. My soul blesses You and remembers everything You have done for me. For You have healed me from the sickness of sin and bodily burden and redeemed my life from the grave. You have placed Your love and compassion on my head like a crown. You have satisfied my desires with the best of bountiful blessings and renewed my strength like an eagle ascending to new heights. It is You, O LORD, who performs perfect righteousness to vindicate the victim. You taught Moses Your ways and demonstrated Your might and power to Your people – let me see it also. For You are merciful, full of compassion and ever patient. You have forgiven my faults and have treated me so much better than I deserve. Heaven's heights cannot compare to Your mercy towards those who worship You in reverence. You have swept my sin so far away that even its memory melts in my mind. In Your tender compassion, You relate to those who rightly revere You because You know we are nothing more that dust destined to a life like a fleeting flower. The breeze blows over us and we are gone as if we were never there. But fortunately, Your everlasting lovingkindness endures forever, perpetually present to pass from one generation to the next to those who walk in Your ways. From Your throne in heaven, You rule, sovereign over Your universal dominion. Your angels bless You as they deliver Your message in might and in solemn service their duties discharge. I am but a single soul in the midst of creation's chorus to bless Your holy name, but I also join in with joy and gratitude. Amen

Psalm 104

1 My soul, bless the Lord! Lord my God, you are very great; you are clothed with majesty and splendor. 2 He wraps himself in light as if it were a robe, spreading out the sky like a canopy, 3 laying the beams of his palace on the waters above, making the clouds his chariot, walking on the wings of the wind, 4 and making the winds his messengers, flames of fire his servants. 5 He established the earth on its foundations; it will never be shaken. 6 You covered it with the deep as if it were a garment; the water stood above the mountains. 7 At your rebuke the water fled; at the sound of your thunder they hurried away— 8 mountains rose and valleys sank— to the place you established for them. 9 You set a boundary they cannot cross; they will never cover the earth again. 10 He causes the springs to gush into the valleys; they flow between the mountains. 11 They supply water for every wild beast; the wild donkeys quench their thirst. 12 The birds of the sky live beside the springs; they make their voices heard among the foliage. 13 He waters the mountains from his palace; the earth is satisfied by the fruit of your labor. 14 He causes grass to grow for the livestock and provides crops for man to cultivate, producing food from the earth, 15 wine that makes human hearts glad— making his face shine with oil— and bread that sustains human hearts. 16 The trees of the Lord flourish, the cedars of Lebanon that he planted. 17 There the birds make their nests; storks make their homes in the pine trees. 18 The high mountains are for the wild goats; the cliffs are a refuge for hyraxes. 19 He made the moon to mark the festivals; the sun knows when to set. 20 You bring darkness, and it becomes night, when all the forest animals stir. 21 The young lions roar for their prey and seek their food from God. 22 The sun rises; they go back and lie down in their dens. 23 Man goes out to his work and to his labor until evening. 24 How countless are your works, Lord! In wisdom you have made them all; the earth is full of your creatures. 25 Here is the sea, vast and wide, teeming with creatures beyond number— living things both large and small. 26 There the ships move about, and

Leviathan, which you formed to play there. **27** All of them wait for you to give them their food at the right time. **28** When you give it to them, they gather it; when you open your hand, they are satisfied with good things. **29** When you hide your face, they are terrified; when you take away their breath, they die and return to the dust. **30** When you send your breath, they are created, and you renew the surface of the ground. **31** May the glory of the Lord endure forever; may the Lord rejoice in his works. **32** He looks at the earth, and it trembles; he touches the mountains, and they pour out smoke. **33** I will sing to the Lord all my life; I will sing praise to my God while I live. **34** May my meditation be pleasing to him; I will rejoice in the Lord. **35** May sinners vanish from the earth and wicked people be no more. My soul, bless the Lord! Hallelujah! (CSB)

Light! We must have it; without it there is darkness and death. As a member of an FBI SWAT team, Night Vision Goggles (NVGs) were a very important tool for survival. Even in the pitch dark, when you looked through NVGs there was light. The invisible path became clear and the slithering snake crossing over it was evident, as well as the sudden precipice at the end of the trail. This regal Psalm paints a picture of God covering Himself in light like a cloak, harkening back to creation when God said: "let there be light." Other Psalms remind us that it is only through God's light that we can see light and when the Lord sends out His light and truth it can lead us into His presence. The Apostle John reminds us that God is light and in Him, there is no darkness at all. But he also chronicles Jesus telling us that He is the light of the world and if we follow Him we will no longer walk in darkness but have the light of life. So, what do we do with it? Jesus said we are to let our light shine in a way that glorifies God. The Apostle Paul reminds us that since we are the light of the Lord we are to walk as children of light, by bearing the fruit of light: goodness, righteousness, and truth.

O God, I bless You for You are my great God, clothed in glorious grandeur, might, and majesty. You have wrapped Yourself in light like a cloak and stretched out the heavens like the curtain of a tent. You dwell high above the heavens using clouds as Your chariot and walking on the wings of the wind. You made Your angelic messengers swift as the wind and blazing in fiery flames. You set the earth spinning on its axis perfectly balanced until You decide otherwise. At the earth's inception with a thundering voice You spoke and the waters waned, the mountains multiplied, and the valleys lay low in their proper place. Streams and springs flowed forth to restore and revive Your thirsting creation. Branches make the birds' abode as they sing their song of praise. The green grass grows for cattle and the fertile fields flourish with fruit, vines, and shrubs for mankind to bring forth food. Bread and wine and provisions so fine You have given. All Your creation takes refuge in Your handiwork. You have set the course of the sun and moon as our celestial clock and calendar. All Your creation marches to the rhythm of life. O LORD, the design, and diversity of Your creation displays Your wisdom and the richness of earth's abundant beauty. All creation depends on Your provision, for food and even the breath of life. The earth quakes from a mere glance of Your eyes and the slightest touch turns the mountains in smoldering smoke to rubble. O God, may my prayers please You for only then am I content. I look to that day when wickedness withdraws and sin is swept away. My soul blesses You and I praise You, O my LORD. Amen

Psalm 105

1 Oh give thanks to the LORD, call upon His name; Make known His deeds among the peoples. 2 Sing to Him, sing praises to Him; Speak of all His wonders. 3 Glory in His holy name; Let the heart of those who seek the LORD be glad. 4 Seek the LORD and His strength; Seek His face continually. 5 Remember His wonders which He has done, His marvels and the judgments uttered by His mouth, 6 O seed of Abraham, His servant, O sons of Jacob, His chosen ones! 7 He is the LORD our God; His judgments are in all the earth. 8 He has remembered His covenant forever, The word which He commanded to a thousand generations, 9 The covenant which He made with Abraham, And His oath to Isaac. 10 Then He confirmed it to Jacob for a statute, To Israel as an everlasting covenant, 11 Saying, "To you I will give the land of Canaan As the portion of your inheritance," 12 When they were only a few men in number, Very few, and strangers in it. 13 And they wandered about from nation to nation, From one kingdom to another people. 14 He permitted no man to oppress them, And He reproved kings for their sakes: 15 "Do not touch My anointed ones, And do My prophets no harm." 16 And He called for a famine upon the land; He broke the whole staff of bread. 17 He sent a man before them, Joseph, who was sold as a slave. 18 They afflicted his feet with fetters, He himself was laid in irons; 19 Until the time that his word came to pass, The word of the LORD tested him. 20 The king sent and released him, The ruler of peoples, and set him free. 21 He made him lord of his house And ruler over all his possessions, 22 To imprison his princes at will, That he might teach his elders wisdom. 23 Israel also came into Egypt; Thus Jacob sojourned in the land of Ham. 24 And He caused His people to be very fruitful, And made them stronger than their adversaries. 25 He turned their heart to hate His people, To deal craftily with His servants. 26 He sent Moses His servant, And Aaron, whom He had chosen. 27 They performed His wondrous acts among them, And miracles in the land of Ham. 28 He sent darkness and made it dark; And they did not rebel against His

words. **29** He turned their waters into blood And caused their fish to die. **30** Their land swarmed with frogs Even in the chambers of their kings. **31** He spoke, and there came a swarm of flies And gnats in all their territory. **32** He gave them hail for rain, And flaming fire in their land. **33** He struck down their vines also and their fig trees, And shattered the trees of their territory. **34** He spoke, and locusts came, And young locusts, even without number, **35** And ate up all vegetation in their land, And ate up the fruit of their ground. **36** He also struck down all the firstborn in their land, The first fruits of all their vigor. **37** Then He brought them out with silver and gold, And among His tribes there was not one who stumbled. **38** Egypt was glad when they departed, For the dread of them had fallen upon them. **39** He spread a cloud for a covering, And fire to illumine by night. **40** They asked, and He brought quail, And satisfied them with the bread of heaven. **41** He opened the rock and water flowed out; It ran in the dry places like a river. **42** For He remembered His holy word With Abraham His servant; **43** And He brought forth His people with joy, His chosen ones with a joyful shout. **44** He gave them also the lands of the nations, That they might take possession of the fruit of the peoples' labor, **45** So that they might keep His statutes And observe His laws, Praise the LORD! (NASB)

Each year, millions of us try to maintain a regular workout routine, a consistent set of exercises to keep in (or get us into) shape. In the FBI, while attending the Academy, we were required to complete physical exams in order to graduate. Once assigned to our field offices, we were encouraged to stay physically fit with weekly workout sessions and take annual fitness exams. The first five verses of this Psalm is a believer's checklist to exercise our walk with God. We are to (1) give thanks; (2) call upon Him; (3) make known His deeds; (4) sing to Him; (5) meditate upon all His past wondrous feats; (6) glory in His holy name; (7) rejoice in our heart; (8) seek Him and His strength and His face continually; and (9) remember His marvelous works and judgments. Sometimes the best way to anticipate how God will shape future events is to remember His grace and provision in the past. That's precisely what the Psalmist has done here – he provides a detailed history lesson by walking down the corridors of time to remind the Israelites who they are and how they got there. It also reminds us how great our God is who loves us so!

O God, I give thanks to You for all Your blessings. You hear me when I call, performing Your mighty deeds. I will praise You making melodies about Your marvelous miracles and meditate upon them. I will celebrate in Your holy name, O LORD, and seek You with a joyful heart. I will consistently look to You for my strength and purpose and worship You every day. I will maintain on the forefront of my memory Your wondrous deeds as I march down the halls of history – from Abraham to Isaac to Jacob, You established Your everlasting covenant with a promise of land and legacy, liberation and life. You saved Your people from famine and death by promoting Joseph from a prisoner to a prince. You sent Moses to rescue Your people from the clutches of Pharaoh's hand and with miracles and wonders, returned them to their promised land. Through Your chosen people You provided all mankind Your statutes and laws with a promise and plan for salvation. I praise You, O LORD, for making me a part of the story and for saving me! Amen

Psalm 106

1 Praise the Lord! Oh, give thanks to the Lord, for He is good! For His mercy endures forever. 2 Who can utter the mighty acts of the Lord? Who can declare all His praise? 3 Blessed are those who keep justice, And he who does righteousness at all times! 4 Remember me, O Lord, with the favor You have toward Your people; Oh, visit me with Your salvation, 5 That I may see the benefit of Your chosen ones, That I may rejoice in the gladness of Your nation, That I may glory with Your inheritance. 6 We have sinned with our fathers, We have committed iniquity, We have done wickedly. 7 Our fathers in Egypt did not understand Your wonders; They did not remember the multitude of Your mercies, But rebelled by the sea—the Red Sea. 8 Nevertheless He saved them for His name's sake, That He might make His mighty power known. 9 He rebuked the Red Sea also, and it dried up; So He led them through the depths, As through the wilderness. 10 He saved them from the hand of him who hated them, And redeemed them from the hand of the enemy. 11 The waters covered their enemies; There was not one of them left. 12 Then they believed His words; They sang His praise. 13 They soon forgot His works; They did not wait for His counsel, 14 But lusted exceedingly in the wilderness, And tested God in the desert. 15 And He gave them their request, But sent leanness into their soul. 16 When they envied Moses in the camp, And Aaron the saint of the Lord, 17 The earth opened up and swallowed Dathan, And covered the faction of Abiram. 18 A fire was kindled in their company; The flame burned up the wicked. 19 They made a calf in Horeb, And worshiped the molded image. 20 Thus they changed their glory Into the image of an ox that eats grass. 21 They forgot God their Savior, Who had done great things in Egypt, 22 Wondrous works in the land of Ham, Awesome things by the Red Sea. 23 Therefore He said that He would destroy them, Had not Moses His chosen one stood before Him in the breach, To turn away His wrath, lest He destroy them. 24 Then they despised the pleasant land; They did not believe His word, 25 But complained in their

tents, And did not heed the voice of the Lord. 26 Therefore He raised up His hand in an oath against them, To overthrow them in the wilderness, 27 To overthrow their descendants among the nations, And to scatter them in the lands. 28 They joined themselves also to Baal of Peor, And ate sacrifices made to the dead. 29 Thus they provoked Him to anger with their deeds, And the plague broke out among them. 30 Then Phinehas stood up and intervened, And the plague was stopped. 31 And that was accounted to him for righteousness To all generations forevermore. 32 They angered Him also at the waters of strife, So that it went ill with Moses on account of them; 33 Because they rebelled against His Spirit, So that he spoke rashly with his lips. 34 They did not destroy the peoples, Concerning whom the Lord had commanded them, 35 But they mingled with the Gentiles And learned their works; 36 They served their idols, Which became a snare to them. 37 They even sacrificed their sons And their daughters to demons, 38 And shed innocent blood, The blood of their sons and daughters, Whom they sacrificed to the idols of Canaan; And the land was polluted with blood. 39 Thus they were defiled by their own works, And played the harlot by their own deeds. 40 Therefore the wrath of the Lord was kindled against His people, So that He abhorred His own inheritance. 41 And He gave them into the hand of the Gentiles, And those who hated them ruled over them. 42 Their enemies also oppressed them, And they were brought into subjection under their hand. 43 Many times He delivered them; But they rebelled in their counsel, And were brought low for their iniquity. 44 Nevertheless He regarded their affliction, When He heard their cry; 45 And for their sake He remembered His covenant, And relented according to the multitude of His mercies. 46 He also made them to be pitied By all those who carried them away captive. 47 Save us, O Lord our God, And gather us from among the Gentiles, To give thanks to Your holy name, To triumph in Your praise. 48 Blessed be the Lord God of Israel From everlasting to everlasting! And let all the people say, "Amen!" Praise the Lord! (NKJV)

Do you at times, despite your best effort, feel like a flat-out failure? For those in that camp, this is a Psalm for us. The Psalmist provides example after example of how His people, individually and as a nation, disobeyed the Lord. And yet, God in His love remained faithful. We see how God delivered them from the yoke of their bondage in Egypt but upon arriving in the Promised Land, they didn't remove its inhabitants or their false gods. Verse 28 says they "joined" themselves to Baal – the Hebrew word (tsamad) likens it to a woman with two lovers, who chooses to bind, fasten or be yoked to one over the other. In effect, they go from the yoke of slavery to the yoke of idol worship. As believers, we have the yoke of sin taken away from us by Jesus who said, "Take my yoke upon you… and you will find rest for your souls." There is no burden we need to bear and there is no burden that He cannot bear.

O God, I praise and give You thanks for Your goodness and mercy of everlasting endurance. My words can neither express nor my praises rise up to match the level of Your greatness, but praise You I must. I can only be happy when I live in accordance with Your ways and persevere in pursuit of Your righteousness. Remember me when You bless Your people and bestow the salvation that only You can deliver. As I pray for myself I also pray for my nation that one day it would return to following You. For in our sin, we have drifted from You and in our pride pursued wickedness. As the children of Israel forgot Your awesome acts of deliverance, so has my country suppressed from its memory Your mighty hand of providence. Israel's record of rebellion is emulated in the hearts and minds of my people and their constant cries of defiance now echo in our courthouses and capitol corridors. But despite our unfaithfulness, You are ever faithful. Heal our eyes to once again see Your greatness. Restore our faith to once again believe Your Word. Reinstate our willingness to be patient for Your purpose. Replace our greed and lust for worldly wealth with a renewed love and longing for You. Hear our desperate cry and with Your loving hand draw our straying souls from this wilderness wandering and transform us into a people worthy of Your calling who forevermore praise Your name! Amen.

Psalm 107

1 Oh, give thanks to the Lord, for He is good! For His mercy endures forever. 2 Let the redeemed of the Lord say so, Whom He has redeemed from the hand of the enemy, 3 And gathered out of the lands, From the east and from the west, From the north and from the south. 4 They wandered in the wilderness in a desolate way; They found no city to dwell in. 5 Hungry and thirsty, Their soul fainted in them. 6 Then they cried out to the Lord in their trouble, And He delivered them out of their distresses. 7 And He led them forth by the right way, That they might go to a city for a dwelling place. 8 Oh, that men would give thanks to the Lord for His goodness, And for His wonderful works to the children of men! 9 For He satisfies the longing soul, And fills the hungry soul with goodness. 10 Those who sat in darkness and in the shadow of death, Bound in affliction and irons— 11 Because they rebelled against the words of God, And despised the counsel of the Most High, 12 Therefore He brought down their heart with labor; They fell down, and there was none to help. 13 Then they cried out to the Lord in their trouble, And He saved them out of their distresses. 14 He brought them out of darkness and the shadow of death, And broke their chains in pieces. 15 Oh, that men would give thanks to the Lord for His goodness, And for His wonderful works to the children of men! 16 For He has broken the gates of bronze, And cut the bars of iron in two. 17 Fools, because of their transgression, And because of their iniquities, were afflicted. 18 Their soul abhorred all manner of food, And they drew near to the gates of death. 19 Then they cried out to the Lord in their trouble, And He saved them out of their distresses. 20 He sent His word and healed them, And delivered them from their destructions. 21 Oh, that men would give thanks to the Lord for His goodness, And for His wonderful works to the children of men! 22 Let them sacrifice the sacrifices of thanksgiving, And declare His works with rejoicing. 23 Those who go down to the sea in ships, Who do business on great waters, 24 They see the works of the Lord, And His wonders in the

deep. **25** For He commands and raises the stormy wind, Which lifts up the waves of the sea. **26** They mount up to the heavens, They go down again to the depths; Their soul melts because of trouble. **27** They reel to and fro, and stagger like a drunken man, And are at their wits' end. **28** Then they cry out to the Lord in their trouble, And He brings them out of their distresses. **29** He calms the storm, So that its waves are still. **30** Then they are glad because they are quiet; So He guides them to their desired haven. **31** Oh, that men would give thanks to the Lord for His goodness, And for His wonderful works to the children of men! **32** Let them exalt Him also in the assembly of the people, And praise Him in the company of the elders. **33** He turns rivers into a wilderness, And the watersprings into dry ground; **34** A fruitful land into barrenness, For the wickedness of those who dwell in it. **35** He turns a wilderness into pools of water, And dry land into watersprings. **36** There He makes the hungry dwell, That they may establish a city for a dwelling place, **37** And sow fields and plant vineyards, That they may yield a fruitful harvest. **38** He also blesses them, and they multiply greatly; And He does not let their cattle decrease. **39** When they are diminished and brought low Through oppression, affliction and sorrow, **40** He pours contempt on princes, And causes them to wander in the wilderness where there is no way; **41** Yet He sets the poor on high, far from affliction, And makes their families like a flock. **42** The righteous see it and rejoice, And all iniquity stops its mouth. **43** Whoever is wise will observe these things, And they will understand the lovingkindness of the Lord. (NKJV)

Upon arriving at their first assignment in an FBI field office, new Agents are often told to go to "closed files" (completed and adjudicated investigations) to review a previous case and use it as a "pony" (an example). It was a great way to see how more experienced Agents proceeded in a similar type investigation and it was an excellent learning tool. Jesus didn't use ponies, but rather, taught His disciples with parables – stories that enabled them to see the point He was trying to get across. This Psalm uses a series of similes to demonstrate God's redemption to those who were once drifters – in His mercy, they finally arrive home. Some are wasteland wanderers without food or drink – just like when we are spiritually hungry or thirsty and can only be refreshed when we cry out to God. Some are padlocked in prison – just like when we are shackled in sin and can only be set free with the key of salvation in Christ. Some are fools feasting on their rebellious iniquities becoming feeble and frail – just like when God responds to our pleas by feeding us His holy Word to ease our suffering. Some are staggering sailors fearful of the raging sea – just like when we have lost our way and God calms life's storms to guide us home. When we recognize God's steadfast love we not only rejoice, but it also makes us wise.

O God, I give thanks unto You for Your everlasting goodness and mercy. You have rallied Your redeemed from the ends of the earth and rescued us from our wandering ways through the wilderness waste. When I was hungry you fed me the Bread of Life. You quenched my thirst with the Spring of Living Water. In my distress, You delivered me from the dire dilemmas of life. You set my path straight by showing me the way. Let everyone praise You for Your enduring love and wondrous works. When I defy Your Word and reject Your wise counsel, I make myself a prisoner of despair and stumble in gloomy misery. Upon seeing the folly of my decisions, I turn and cry out to You and You shatter my shackles of sorrow. When I stand on the ocean's stormy shores I see Your awesome power and realize my insignificance and helplessness. Like a drunken sailor staggering on a wave-tossed deck, I contemplate my doom. But in my peril, I cry out to You and the windswept waves withdraw and I find myself in a tranquil sea of serenity. When the world tempts and beckons me to come to its opulent oasis, let me see it for what it really is – a wasteland of wickedness, a quagmire of quicksand, a mirage in the middle of nowhere. Remind me that only You can transform the desert's parched plains into cool pools of refreshment and fill my hungry soul with the heavenly harvest of Your fruitful fields and vineyards. I rejoice in the blessing of my family's flock and ask that You give me the wisdom to heed Your Word, walk in Your ways, and continuously contemplate Your lovingkindness. Amen.

Psalm 108

A Song, a Psalm of David. **1** My heart is steadfast, O God; I will sing, I will sing praises, even with my soul. **2** Awake, harp and lyre; I will awaken the dawn! **3** I will give thanks to You, O LORD, among the peoples, And I will sing praises to You among the nations. **4** For Your lovingkindness is great above the heavens, And Your truth reaches to the skies. **5** Be exalted, O God, above the heavens, And Your glory above all the earth. **6** That Your beloved may be delivered, Save with Your right hand, and answer me! **7** God has spoken in His holiness: "I will exult, I will portion out Shechem And measure out the valley of Succoth. **8** Gilead is Mine, Manasseh is Mine; Ephraim also is the helmet of My head; Judah is My scepter. **9** Moab is My washbowl; Over Edom I shall throw My shoe; Over Philistia I will shout aloud." **10** Who will bring me into the besieged city? Who will lead me to Edom? **11** Have not You Yourself, O God, rejected us? And will You not go forth with our armies, O God? **12** Oh give us help against the adversary, For deliverance by man is in vain. **13** Through God we will do valiantly, And it is He who shall tread down our adversaries. (NASB)

Early in my FBI career, I was a member of a SWAT team. SWAT stands for "Special Weapons and Tactics" and team members were issued enhanced weapons and provided advanced training on their proper usage. My primary position on the SWAT team, Observer/Sniper, tends to be shortened to "sniper" but the reality is, in the five years I held that position I never took a single shot at a living person. I did, however, make many observations and conveyed those back to my team. That point is vital – while each member is trained in different areas and has distinctive duties, we all functioned as a team. The fine line between success and failure often depends on properly communicating the situation so everyone can operate in a unified manner. David understood the tactics of warfare. But he knew his most important weapons for success were songs of praise, clear communications in prayer, and total dependency on God!

O God, my soul awakens at day's dawning in songs of praise to You. Steady my heart in thankfulness throughout the day to remain resolute. For Your mercy extends above the heavens in greatness and Your faithfulness billows above the clouds. You are exalted above the heavens and Your glory the earth encircles. With Your love I am liberated and Your strength brings success. Your sacred promises prevail. With You, O LORD, I can conquer my enemies and I will not fear my foes for their faith is in their foolishness. Only You can save me in my time of need for human help is hopeless. For You will tread and trample my oppressors and through You, I can be valiant in Your victory! Amen.

Psalm 109

To the choirmaster. A Psalm of David. **1** Be not silent, O God of my praise! **2** For wicked and deceitful mouths are opened against me, speaking against me with lying tongues. **3** They encircle me with words of hate, and attack me without cause. **4** In return for my love they accuse me, but I give myself to prayer. **5** So they reward me evil for good, and hatred for my love. **6** Appoint a wicked man against him; let an accuser stand at his right hand. **7** When he is tried, let him come forth guilty; let his prayer be counted as sin! **8** May his days be few; may another take his office! **9** May his children be fatherless and his wife a widow! **10** May his children wander about and beg, seeking food far from the ruins they inhabit! **11** May the creditor seize all that he has; may strangers plunder the fruits of his toil! **12** Let there be none to extend kindness to him, nor any to pity his fatherless children! **13** May his posterity be cut off; may his name be blotted out in the second generation! **14** May the iniquity of his fathers be remembered before the LORD, and let not the sin of his mother be blotted out! **15** Let them be before the LORD continually, that he may cut off the memory of them from the earth! **16** For he did not remember to show kindness, but pursued the poor and needy and the brokenhearted, to put them to death. **17** He loved to curse; let curses come upon him! He did not delight in blessing; may it be far from him! **18** He clothed himself with cursing as his coat; may it soak into his body like water, like oil into his bones! **19** May it be like a garment that he wraps around him, like a belt that he puts on every day! **20** May this be the reward of my accusers from the LORD, of those who speak evil against my life! **21** But you, O GOD my Lord, deal on my behalf for your name's sake; because your steadfast love is good, deliver me! **22** For I am poor and needy, and my heart is stricken within me. **23** I am gone like a shadow at evening; I am shaken off like a locust. **24** My knees are weak through fasting; my body has become gaunt, with no fat. **25** I am an object of scorn to my accusers; when they see me, they wag their heads. **26** Help me, O LORD my God! Save me according to your steadfast love! **27**

Let them know that this is your hand; you, O LORD, have done it! **28** Let them curse, but you will bless! They arise and are put to shame, but your servant will be glad! **29** May my accusers be clothed with dishonor; may they be wrapped in their own shame as in a cloak! **30** With my mouth I will give great thanks to the LORD; I will praise him in the midst of the throng. **31** For he stands at the right hand of the needy one, to save him from those who condemn his soul to death. (ESV)

Despite being written over a period of 1,600 years by over 40 contributors, it is amazing to see how the entire Bible has a common theme, inseparably linked as a single book. At times, some passages seemingly come from different views – this Psalm may be one of them. At first, the words appear to echo from the Summit of Sinai rather than the Cross of Calvary. And yet, there is neither conflict nor contradiction, for God is just. The curses recorded are directed at the evil, wicked, haters of God. In the New Testament, the Apostle Paul says if anyone does not love the Lord Jesus Christ or if they preach a different gospel, let him be accursed. On the last day, even Jesus tells the workers of iniquity who didn't live out their faith in love, "Depart from me, you cursed…" Judgment goes awry when it is encased in our unjust, selfish, personal passions. God does not suffer from that problem. He is always just in His judgment!

O God in whom I praise, let me hear Your voice, especially when I am surrounded by those who speak their language of lies against me with heartless hatred. Even when I have acted in love they answer with unprovoked attacks. My response can only be to come to You in prayer. In the end, You O LORD, are the immortal judge of righteousness and will determine the destiny of all. You set forth their length of life and wages of wealth. You fix the fate of their family and fortune. And for those especially evil ones who pursue the poor, attack the afflicted, and distress the destitute, You will clothe them in their own curses with a cloak of calamity. But You, O LORD, are merciful and I will seek Your salvation. Reproached by many, I am poor and needy with a heavy heart. And when You save me, may it be clear for all to see that it was You alone in Your mercy Who accomplished it. May their curses be countered with Your bountiful blessings. With You standing by my side, let Your praises prevail in the private and public places. Amen.

Psalm 110

A Psalm of David. **1** The Lord said to my Lord, "Sit at My right hand, Till I make Your enemies Your footstool." **2** The Lord shall send the rod of Your strength out of Zion. Rule in the midst of Your enemies! **3** Your people shall be volunteers In the day of Your power; In the beauties of holiness, from the womb of the morning, You have the dew of Your youth. **4** The Lord has sworn And will not relent, "You are a priest forever According to the order of Melchizedek." **5** The Lord is at Your right hand; He shall execute kings in the day of His wrath. **6** He shall judge among the nations, He shall fill the places with dead bodies, He shall execute the heads of many countries. **7** He shall drink of the brook by the wayside; Therefore He shall lift up the head. (NKJV)

During my last five years in the FBI, I was privileged to carry a particular pistol: a Springfield Armory Professional Model 1911-A1. Its serial number was "CRG-1" which indicated it was the first .45 made by Springfield for the FBI's tactical teams. Although the pistol's design is now over a hundred years old, each "CRG" pistol was meticulously refined by going through the maker's custom shop to meet the FBI's stringent requirements. One of the features was an ambidextrous safety (a lock on either side of the slide) so no matter which hand you used to shoot, you could employ the safety. We often see scripture referring to God's strong right hand or Jesus sitting at His right hand as a place of honor. In reality and as a spirit, God doesn't have a hand like you or me. In any case, He is equally powerful with either hand. The fact of the matter is, God doesn't need to be ambidextrous when He is omnipotent!

O God, You have beckoned to my Lord Messiah to sit at Your right hand while You completely crush Your enemies. You have given Him Your sovereign scepter to rule in power. Your people will willingly join Your army as He leads it in strength, beautifully arrayed in holiness like a youthful mighty monarch. He is the princely priest who remains forever faithful to His calling in the line of Melchizedek's mission. In righteous wrath, He crushes kings and renders judgment over all the nations worldwide. His thirst is quenched at will and in victory He charges forth triumphantly. Amen

Psalm 111

1 Praise the LORD! I will give thanks to the LORD with all my heart, In the company of the upright and in the assembly. 2 Great are the works of the LORD; They are studied by all who delight in them. 3 Splendid and majestic is His work, And His righteousness endures forever. 4 He has made His wonders to be remembered; The LORD is gracious and compassionate. 5 He has given food to those who fear Him; He will remember His covenant forever. 6 He has made known to His people the power of His works, In giving them the heritage of the nations. 7 The works of His hands are truth and justice; All His precepts are sure. 8 They are upheld forever and ever; They are performed in truth and uprightness. 9 He has sent redemption to His people; He has ordained His covenant forever; Holy and awesome is His name. 10 The fear of the LORD is the beginning of wisdom; A good understanding have all those who do His commandments; His praise endures forever. (NASB)

We are told by the Apostle John that no one has seen God and yet, we certainly see His works. This Psalm tells us the works of God are great, full of splendor and majesty, to be remembered; they are powerful and have been demonstrated to His people; they are faithful and just, done in truth and uprightness and stand fast forever. With such input, you might ask, "what should I do about it?" The obvious answer is to praise and thank God with a reverential fear. Verse two sheds additional light telling us His works are "studied" by those who have pleasure in them. The Hebrew word used here for studied (darash) means to seek, repeatedly read, to tread or "beat a path." When hiking, you've likely seen well-worn trails over the terrain because they have been utilized by many people over and over again. It is the repetition of many feet over time that makes the trail. By pondering God's works often and deeply, our hardened hearts can be worn away, allowing us to thank, praise and love the Lord with our whole heart.

O God, to You I shout Hallelujah! From the depths of my heart, I give You thanks surrounded by Your people. How great are Your works O LORD, for I find the utmost joy when I pursue and purposely ponder them. Your righteous acts are full of glory. Timeless and unending Your marvels implant a memorial in my mind. My soul is saturated with Your grace and compassion and Your provision of plenty greets me as I fall at Your feet in reverence. I see Your powerful works on display and they are a lasting inheritance. Your fingers knit truth and justice into a faithful fabric of everlasting lessons of life. You have redeemed me and set me free with an enduring covenant underwritten by Your holy and awesome name. When I relegate my heart to You in reverence I take my first steps in the walk of wisdom, and each day I follow Your commandments I develop discernment. Let perpetual praise rise in song before You, now and forever more! Amen.

Psalm 112

1 Praise the LORD! Blessed is the man who fears the LORD, who greatly delights in his commandments! **2** His offspring will be mighty in the land; the generation of the upright will be blessed. **3** Wealth and riches are in his house, and his righteousness endures forever. **4** Light dawns in the darkness for the upright; he is gracious, merciful, and righteous. **5** It is well with the man who deals generously and lends; who conducts his affairs with justice. **6** For the righteous will never be moved; he will be remembered forever. **7** He is not afraid of bad news; his heart is firm, trusting in the LORD. **8** His heart is steady; he will not be afraid, until he looks in triumph on his adversaries. **9** He has distributed freely; he has given to the poor; his righteousness endures forever; his horn is exalted in honor. **10** The wicked man sees it and is angry; he gnashes his teeth and melts away; the desire of the wicked will perish! (ESV)

In many ways, this Psalm is a continuation of the previous one. Whereas the former focuses on God's righteousness, this one highlights the righteousness of a godly person. And yet, we know as humans we really don't have any virtue or uprightness in and of ourselves. Whatever goodness we have is because of the Lord when we reflect His light and love. The deeds of goodness done for those in need are like beams of light shining in a dark world. The prophet Isaiah said it this way: "Feed the hungry, and help those in trouble. Then your light will shine out from the darkness, and the darkness around you will be as bright as noon." (Isaiah 58:10, NLT). Jesus told us we are the light of the world and we are to let our light shine before men so that they will see our good works and glorify our Father in heaven. Good works may be "good" but good works done to glorify God are great and in the end, give them true meaning and purpose.

O God, I praise You, for I am truly blessed when I come before You with a reverent heart and joyfully keep Your commandments. May my children and grandchildren be honored with the heritage of faith You have bestowed upon me. For the greatest wealth and prosperity I may possess is a passionate piety for You. Despite the darkness that dwells around me may I be a bright beacon of light that points to Your grace and compassion. In response, may I graciously give to others and be honest in all my dealings. May my heart remain steadfast and secure and because my trust is in You, let me be firm and fearless even amidst the torrential tidings that life often brings. May I persevere in Your power so that all who see me, especially the wayward and wicked, will feel the folly of futile frustration of following a path apart from You. Amen.

Psalm 113

1 Praise the Lord! Praise, O servants of the Lord, Praise the name of the Lord! 2 Blessed be the name of the Lord From this time forth and forevermore! 3 From the rising of the sun to its going down The Lord's name is to be praised. 4 The Lord is high above all nations, His glory above the heavens. 5 Who is like the Lord our God, Who dwells on high, 6 Who humbles Himself to behold The things that are in the heavens and in the earth? 7 He raises the poor out of the dust, And lifts the needy out of the ash heap, 8 That He may seat him with princes— With the princes of His people. 9 He grants the barren woman a home, Like a joyful mother of children. Praise the Lord! (NKJV)

During my time in the FBI, I had the unique privilege to witness and participate in some very interesting "behind the scenes" discussions with the FBI Director, deliberations that lead to decisions on policies, procedures, and investigations. Have you read a scripture passage and wondered what the full discussion was between those involved; what it would be like to overhear all the details of such Biblical colloquies, to become eternity's proverbial "fly on the wall?" There's Lazarus and his sisters chatting after Jesus raised him from the dead? O to hear Jesus' complete discourse to the two disciples on the road to Emmaus. What did God and Adam discuss in the Garden of Eden before the fall? And finally, the real mind-blower, what if we could go all the way to eternity past and enter into the discussion of our Triune God prior to the universe's creation? Wow! While we will likely never know such things, that is when we must remember that God, through His holy Word, has given us everything we do need to know unto salvation and to live life here on earth to its fullest!

O God, I praise Your name. Let my earnest endeavor be to come before You with a humble heart of admiring adoration. Long after my speech is stilled may my praise unto You echo through eternity, for You, O LORD, are worthy of worship without end. The veracity of man's voice is only measured in the context of its relationship to You. As the sun swings through the sky, from its rising to setting, let Your name be praised. There is no one like You, O LORD, for Your glory is above the heavens. In fact, You are so high and exalted You must stoop to place Your downward gaze on the sky and earth. You lift the poor from their poverty and provide the needy with their necessities. You bring life to the lifeless and joy flowers forth in Your family. Hallelujah! Amen.

Psalm 114

1 When the Israelites escaped from Egypt— when the family of Jacob left that foreign land— 2 the land of Judah became God's sanctuary, and Israel became his kingdom. 3 The Red Sea saw them coming and hurried out of their way! The water of the Jordan River turned away. 4 The mountains skipped like rams, the hills like lambs! 5 What's wrong, Red Sea, that made you hurry out of their way? What happened, Jordan River, that you turned away? 6 Why, mountains, did you skip like rams? Why, hills, like lambs? 7 Tremble, O earth, at the presence of the Lord, at the presence of the God of Jacob. 8 He turned the rock into a pool of water; yes, a spring of water flowed from solid rock. (NLT)

As a child, did you ever experience the dread of encountering that neighborhood or school bully? Despite the extra effort to avoid the ruffian, he always found a way to find you. I recall such a person in elementary school, but fortunately, there was also another person persistently present. He was someone who was somewhat bigger and stronger, with a good heart and understood the situation. Best of all, this rescuer-in-waiting took a particular delight in impeding the would-be oppressor from carrying out his despicable doings. There was no physical or even verbal altercation, just a very real presence to send the antagonist slithering back into the shadows. This Psalm demonstrates God's omnipotence over land and sea, as it trembles and flees before Him. Today, let the Lord be your deliverer. He is willing and able to take on any and all of life's problems!

O God, You are so great! You led Your people out of bondage in a faraway foreign land and took them as Your own to dwell among them. As You marched Your people home, the seas separated and rivers retreated. Even the mountains danced in delight and the hills jumped for joy. And why did this happen? Because all creation trembles before You, Creator and Master of the universe. May I daily let You be the Master of my life. Amen.

Psalm 115

1 Not to us, O LORD, not to us, But to Your name give glory Because of Your lovingkindness, because of Your truth. 2 Why should the nations say, "Where, now, is their God?" 3 But our God is in the heavens; He does whatever He pleases. 4 Their idols are silver and gold, The work of man's hands. 5 They have mouths, but they cannot speak; They have eyes, but they cannot see; 6 They have ears, but they cannot hear; They have noses, but they cannot smell; 7 They have hands, but they cannot feel; They have feet, but they cannot walk; They cannot make a sound with their throat. 8 Those who make them will become like them, Everyone who trusts in them. 9 O Israel, trust in the LORD; He is their help and their shield. 10 O house of Aaron, trust in the LORD; He is their help and their shield. 11 You who fear the LORD, trust in the LORD; He is their help and their shield. 12 The LORD has been mindful of us; He will bless us; He will bless the house of Israel; He will bless the house of Aaron. 13 He will bless those who fear the LORD, The small together with the great. 14 May the LORD give you increase, You and your children. 15 May you be blessed of the LORD, Maker of heaven and earth. 16 The heavens are the heavens of the LORD, But the earth He has given to the sons of men. 17 The dead do not praise the LORD, Nor do any who go down into silence; 18 But as for us, we will bless the LORD From this time forth and forever. Praise the LORD! (NASB)

What's in a name? One of the first things you are taught as a new FBI agent is to conduct an "indices search" on the subject of the investigation. Checking a person's name lets you know if any previous information exists on that individual. Your name is part of who you are and defines you as an individual. Have you noticed in the Psalms how often it is to God's "name" that we are to focus upon? His <u>name</u> is majestic, protects us, saves us, is blessed, is awesome, is great, is our help, and endures forever. We are to love, sing praises to, trust in, exalt, give glory to, give thanks to, remind others of, wait on, fear, call upon, seek, and know His <u>name</u>. We are to not forget His name, not use it as a curse, or not take it in vain. So much is wrapped up in God's name and who He is. It isn't any wonder when Moses asked God for His name, the response was "I AM WHO I AM." Let us never let our own name get in the way of placing God's name first and foremost in our hearts and minds.

O God, nothing noble or praiseworthy comes from my hand – only You deserve all glory and honor because of Your mercy and faithfulness. For I live among people who have put their hope only in what is visible and demonstrate disdain for You who reigns in heaven on high, doing whatever You please. In their pride, they place their worldly workmanship on a pedestal and call it their god. The idols of their heart may sound good but are silent of the truth; they are deaf to the cries of the heart and lack the sweet fragrance of life. They sit idly by offering nothing of value for they are the work of man's hands. Those who put their trust in these dull dead idols soon become like them, lacking life's luster and joy. But I will put my trust in You, O LORD, for You are my shield and salvation who created the heavens and earth and bestows blessings beyond measure. The muted mouths of the dead cannot sing Your praise. Let my living lips forevermore bless Your name. Amen.

Psalm 116

1 I love the LORD, because He hears My voice and my supplications. 2 Because He has inclined His ear to me, Therefore I shall call upon Him as long as I live. 3 The cords of death encompassed me And the terrors of Sheol came upon me; I found distress and sorrow. 4 Then I called upon the name of the LORD: "O LORD, I beseech You, save my life!" 5 Gracious is the LORD, and righteous; Yes, our God is compassionate. 6 The LORD preserves the simple; I was brought low, and He saved me. 7 Return to your rest, O my soul, For the LORD has dealt bountifully with you. 8 For You have rescued my soul from death, My eyes from tears, My feet from stumbling. 9 I shall walk before the LORD In the land of the living. 10 I believed when I said, "I am greatly afflicted." 11 I said in my alarm, "All men are liars." 12 What shall I render to the LORD For all His benefits toward me? 13 I shall lift up the cup of salvation And call upon the name of the LORD. 14 I shall pay my vows to the LORD, Oh may it be in the presence of all His people. 15 Precious in the sight of the LORD Is the death of His godly ones. 16 O LORD, surely I am Your servant, I am Your servant, the son of Your handmaid, You have loosed my bonds. 17 To You I shall offer a sacrifice of thanksgiving, And call upon the name of the LORD. 18 I shall pay my vows to the LORD, Oh may it be in the presence of all His people, 19 In the courts of the LORD'S house, In the midst of you, O Jerusalem. Praise the LORD (NASB)

Death. As humans, we must all share in its reality. Although it is usually a word surrounded by dread and sorrow, verse 15 of this Psalm tells us that the death of a godly person is precious in the Lord's sight. In June 1849, the great American evangelist C.G. Finney used this Psalm in a sermon at a friend's funeral. In his closing remarks, he said, "Since I came here to reside, you know I have buried my father, my mother, and a sister; a little daughter; my son-in-law—and my dear wife. These repeated deaths have made me familiar with the thoughts of heaven, and with all that appertains to death as the passage thither. My experience has thoroughly taught me the value of such influences, drawing the mind away from earth and constraining it to hold communion with the eternal world. This deep communion with heaven and heavenly things disrobes death of all terror, and makes it look in every aspect of it, glorious." How can we disrobe death of all its terror? The Apostle Paul hinted at that same question when he wrote to the church of Corinth, "O death, where is thy sting? O grave, where is thy victory?" Fortunately, he also gave us the answer a couple verses later, reminding us to be thankful to God who has given us the victory over death through the saving power of our Lord Jesus Christ!

O God, I love You so, for You hear my prayers and answer them. Because You listen, as long as air fills my lungs I will call out to You. If left alone to contemplate the constricting cords of death, distress and sorrow would soon encircle me. But then I call on Your name to deliver me and in Your grace and mercy, I am saved. For on my own, I am helpless but in Your goodness, O LORD, my satisfied soul finds rest. You have liberated my life, wiping away my tears and steadying my steps so I can walk worthily in the land of the living. My affection is answered with Your assurance; my trials with trust in You, for faith in the flesh is futile. What can I do to possibly pay back Your kindness? I have nothing to give except gratitude for Your gift, the precious gift that cost You everything to save me. You have broken the bonds of my soul so when the time comes, I am fearlessly free to boldly bang on death's door. Whether public or private, let my praise unto You be pure and always performed with a thankful heart. Amen.

Psalm 117

1 Praise the LORD, all nations! Extol him, all peoples! **2** For great is his steadfast love toward us, and the faithfulness of the LORD endures forever. Praise the LORD! (ESV)

Despite its size, this Psalm is a standout! Not only is it the Bible's middle chapter, it is also its shortest. But as Shakespeare said, "Brevity is the soul of wit." Packed into these two short verses are some crucial truths: (1) Not only is Israel to praise the Lord but ALL nations and peoples should; (2) our only ability to approach God is due to His merciful kindness (steadfast love) and faithfulness (truth); and (3) His love and truth are eternal. How privileged we are to partake in worshiping our God. As if to emphasize universal worship, two distinct words are used to "praise" Him: the more common Hebrew "halal" meaning to shine upon, celebrate or bring attention to; and "shabach," a word with a root more common to Aramaic/Arabic which means to commend, bring glory, extol, triumph. No matter what language is used, let us all praise the Lord!

O God, I praise You just as all nations will one day praise You. Through Abraham all people have been blessed and as such all people should give glory to You in worship. Even when we resist You, Your limitless love prevails and tenacious truth overcomes. I praise You, my everlasting LORD. Amen.

Psalm 118

1 Give thanks to the LORD, for he is good! His faithful love endures forever. 2 Let all Israel repeat: "His faithful love endures forever." 3 Let Aaron's descendants, the priests, repeat: "His faithful love endures forever." 4 Let all who fear the LORD repeat: "His faithful love endures forever." 5 In my distress I prayed to the LORD, and the LORD answered me and set me free. 6 The LORD is for me, so I will have no fear. What can mere people do to me? 7 Yes, the LORD is for me; he will help me. I will look in triumph at those who hate me. 8 It is better to take refuge in the LORD than to trust in people. 9 It is better to take refuge in the LORD than to trust in princes. 10 Though hostile nations surrounded me, I destroyed them all with the authority of the LORD. 11 Yes, they surrounded and attacked me, but I destroyed them all with the authority of the LORD. 12 They swarmed around me like bees; they blazed against me like a crackling fire. But I destroyed them all with the authority of the LORD. 13 My enemies did their best to kill me, but the LORD rescued me. 14 The LORD is my strength and my song; he has given me victory. 15 Songs of joy and victory are sung in the camp of the godly. The strong right arm of the LORD has done glorious things! 16 The strong right arm of the LORD is raised in triumph. The strong right arm of the LORD has done glorious things! 17 I will not die; instead, I will live to tell what the LORD has done. 18 The LORD has punished me severely, but he did not let me die. 19 Open for me the gates where the righteous enter, and I will go in and thank the LORD. 20 These gates lead to the presence of the LORD, and the godly enter there. 21 I thank you for answering my prayer and giving me victory! 22 The stone that the builders rejected has now become the cornerstone. 23 This is the LORD's doing, and it is wonderful to see. 24 This is the day the LORD has made. We will rejoice and be glad in it. 25 Please, LORD, please save us. Please, LORD, please give us success. 26 Bless the one who comes in the name of the LORD. We bless you from the house of the LORD. 27 The LORD is God, shining upon us.

Take the sacrifice and bind it with cords on the altar. **28** You are my God, and I will praise you! You are my God, and I will exalt you! **29** Give thanks to the LORD, for he is good! His faithful love endures forever. (NLT)

Many Bible verses have been put to song and this Psalm has one such verse: "This is the day that the Lord has made, I will rejoice and be glad in it." Surely, this is a declaration we can use each morning we awaken, but we should also look at the verse in context. The writer is seeking God's gate to salvation and prophetically proclaims that the stone in that foundation (once rejected) has become the cornerstone. While modern buildings may not have an actual cornerstone, the concept continues – the placement of the first stone is vital to a firm foundation. It is the reference point to bring into line every other stone. The Psalmist recognizes only God could have accomplished such a marvelous thing. Jesus is both our gateway to God as well as the cornerstone of our faith. Let us rejoice because of that glorious day and daily align our lives with Him.

O God, I give You thanks for Your great goodness and limitless love. When I find myself in distress Your help is timely and Your mercy is timeless. I call upon You and I am set free. What should I fear from anyone when You, the eternal God, are at my side? My trust is in You, O LORD, not man. Even when my enemies surround me like a swarm of bees I will persevere and prevail; with one Holy Hand You hold me up and with the other, You assail my adversaries. For You are my strength and song, my battle-cry of victory. In triumph, I will shout Your joyful song of salvation. When I stray, Your firm hand sets me straight in love and righteousness. Because You have shown me the light of Your way, bind my heart to Yours as I kneel at Your altar. For You are my God whom I praise and exalt and I thank You for Your everlasting mercy. Amen.

Psalm 119 – Aleph (1-8)

1 Blessed are the undefiled in the way, Who walk in the law of the Lord! 2 Blessed are those who keep His testimonies, Who seek Him with the whole heart! 3 They also do no iniquity; They walk in His ways. 4 You have commanded us To keep Your precepts diligently. 5 Oh, that my ways were directed To keep Your statutes! 6 Then I would not be ashamed, When I look into all Your commandments. 7 I will praise You with uprightness of heart, When I learn Your righteous judgments. 8 I will keep Your statutes; Oh, do not forsake me utterly! (NKJV)

Thus begins the longest Psalm (and chapter) in the Bible. As mentioned in the introduction, using seven different words to describe God's Word, this Psalm focuses on our relationship with it and the impact it will have on our life. It is apropos that this Psalm starts with a double "blessed" for they go hand-in-hand. True contentment comes when you walk blamelessly (completely and with integrity) in accordance with God's Word. Absolute fulfillment comes when you stay true to the Lord's testimonies (Word) and seek Him with your <u>whole</u> heart. Notice the emphasis on whole – we are to diligently desire that our top priority is seeking Him. How can such a victory be attained? Time spent in God's Word will change our hearts - softening, sharpening, and shaping it to be more aligned with Him and His ways. Then we can seek God with ALL of our heart.

O God, I am so happy when walking in accordance with Your law, for it makes my life complete, transforming me into a person of integrity. How blessed I am when I seek You with my whole heart and let Your testimonies be the witness for my soul. It is only then, I can walk in Your ways without worry and on Your path stay straight. You have commanded me to be diligently devoted to the details You have set forth. I want my ways to be Your ways so Your statutes are engraved upon my heart. Your commandments are of the utmost authority, not merely persuasive words of purpose. With a sincere heart, I will thank You as I live according to Your Word. I know You will not forsake me as I follow You in obedience. Amen.

Psalm 119 – Beth (9-16)

9 How can a young man keep his way pure? By keeping it according to Your word. **10** With all my heart I have sought You; Do not let me wander from Your commandments. **11** Your word I have treasured in my heart, That I may not sin against You. **12** Blessed are You, O LORD; Teach me Your statutes. **13** With my lips I have told of All the ordinances of Your mouth. **14** I have rejoiced in the way of Your testimonies, As much as in all riches. **15** I will meditate on Your precepts And regard Your ways. **16** I shall delight in Your statutes; I shall not forget Your word. (NASB)

Have you ever wandered off the beaten path without a map or compass? In today's world with GPS devices on our phones and at our fingertips it seems so improbable that we might get lost. And yet, in life, so many of us are more lost than we would like to admit. We see our surroundings but do we really know where we are or where we are going? The message of this Psalm is that the unfailing satellite by which we set our bearings and mark our course is God's Word. And here is the profound promise: we can have access to that power anytime and anywhere, even when we go astray! There is no fear of loss of signal or dead batteries. For here is the sublime secret of success: by hiding God's Word deep in your heart it not only will provide perfect direction, it will become part of your very being – something ever available that you will never forget.

O God, whether I'm young or old, the sure way to stay on the pure path of life is by walking in Your Word. Let me not become distracted with worldly wanderings of life's diverging detours but to focus on You with my whole heart. Make Your Word a buried treasure deep within my soul so I might not sin against You. Teach me Your statutes that I may openly speak them to others. May I rejoice in Your testimonies, recognizing them as righteous riches. Your precepts give me purpose as I meditate upon them. Lock them into my memory so I never forget Your Word. Amen.

Psalm 119 – Gimel (17-24)

17 Deal bountifully with your servant, that I may live and keep your word. 18 Open my eyes, that I may behold wondrous things out of your law. 19 I am a sojourner on the earth; hide not your commandments from me! 20 My soul is consumed with longing for your rules at all times. 21 You rebuke the insolent, accursed ones, who wander from your commandments. 22 Take away from me scorn and contempt, for I have kept your testimonies. 23 Even though princes sit plotting against me, your servant will meditate on your statutes. 24 Your testimonies are my delight; they are my counselors. (ESV)

The first word of this group of verses (gimel) from which it derives its name, means to "deal bountifully" or "show favor." We must not mistakenly interpret that to mean to "deal fairly" for it is only by God's grace and abundant mercy, and not out of our merit, that we can even begin to live out our life and keep God's Word. I find it interesting that in other places in the Old Testament the word gimel also means to "wean a child" (complete one's nursing) and in another case, "to ripen." The truth is, only with God's vision can we even see His Word and thereby act upon it. I think of what the Apostle Paul said to the Corinthians (as well as the author of Hebrews) that neither had matured to eat solid food and still needed milk. Let us grow in grace and mature so that we may wean ourselves from the milk of God's Word and feast upon its solid meat. Then our souls will ripen to bear much fruit unto the Lord.

O God, it is only through Your bountiful grace that I may serve You. It is only through Your work in me that I may perform any good works for You. In my daily life let me obey Your Word. Give me spiritual eyes to see the hidden truths of Your law. In my journey as a stranger here on earth, place Your commandments in plain sight to guide me. The desperate yearning I have for Your ordinances constantly crushes my soul. Keep me close to Your commandments so pride does not rear its ugly head within me. With a prayerful heart, I will follow Your true testimonies to stop the stinging scorn of man. While others sit around and conspire against me let me sit with You in meditation on Your statutes. Your testimonies trace a path before me to be my guide and counselor. Help me to always follow and obey. Amen.

Psalm 119 – Daleth (25-32)

25 My soul clings to the dust; Revive me according to Your word. **26** I have declared my ways, and You answered me; Teach me Your statutes. **27** Make me understand the way of Your precepts; So shall I meditate on Your wondrous works. **28** My soul melts from heaviness; Strengthen me according to Your word. **29** Remove from me the way of lying, And grant me Your law graciously. **30** I have chosen the way of truth; Your judgments I have laid before me. **31** I cling to Your testimonies; O Lord, do not put me to shame! **32** I will run the course of Your commandments, For You shall enlarge my heart. (NKJV)

These verses highlight the letter "D" and I'd like to focus on three Hebrew words: The first is "dabaq" which means to cling to. We begin this section with an image of our soul sunk low, our belly dragging in the dust. The second word is "dalaph" meaning to melt, weep or leak. I picture our soul leaking joy when we let the sorrows of life overcome us. The third word, "derek" appears five times in this section and means "the way." There is a real comparison here, almost a battle going on, between our way and God's way. The Psalmist, however, is always returning to the right way, the proper path, by allowing God's Word to guide him. I especially like the end verse which says we don't just follow the way/path, but we run it. It is with vigor and energy we run it for God has enlarged our heart. Yes, let us open our hearts to God's Word and His ways.

O God, my soul strains in the dust of this earth – revive me through Your holy Word. When I confess my wanton ways before You in humility, You hear and answer. In Your pardoning process of my transgressions, teach me Your statutes. Reveal the innermost meaning of Your precepts so I may meditate on Your wondrous works. When my sorrowful soul weeps under grief's grip let Your Word strengthen my heavy heart. Loosen the longing of my lying lips and through Your grace grant me the desire to live by Your law. Give me a willing heart to choose the way of truth because I know Your ordinances are worthy. I shall not be disappointed as I cling to Your testimonies. With eager enthusiasm let me run life's race following Your commandments and with each step enlarge my heart to gladly glorify Your name. Amen.

Psalm 119 – He (33-40)

33 Teach me, O LORD, the way of Your statutes, And I shall observe it to the end. **34** Give me understanding, that I may observe Your law And keep it with all my heart. **35** Make me walk in the path of Your commandments, For I delight in it. **36** Incline my heart to Your testimonies And not to dishonest gain. **37** Turn away my eyes from looking at vanity, And revive me in Your ways. **38** Establish Your word to Your servant, As that which produces reverence for You. **39** Turn away my reproach which I dread, For Your ordinances are good. **40** Behold, I long for Your precepts; Revive me through Your righteousness. (NASB)

Today, our world emphasizes our right to choose, the "freedom of choice." This part of the Psalm is a prayer asking to be taught God's Word. In order to achieve that, notice how quickly the Psalmist gives away that right. His request is not to be led down a path, but rather "make me walk" it. His request is not to ignore the world's worthless things but for his eyes to "turn away" from them. His request is not to be attracted to God's Word but for his heart to "incline" to it. The Hebrew words used here are helpful: "abar" (turn away) means to cross over or alienate; "natah" (incline) means to bend, stretch, extend, spread out. It can also be used when someone pitches their tent. In order to truly learn God's Word and make it a part of us, we must long for it. We need to alienate our eyes to worldly vanity and firmly pitch the tent of our heart squarely upon it.

O God, teach me the meaning of Your statutes so that I may follow them to the very end. Give me discernment and insight to obey Your law not out of duty but out of dauntless devotion. Guide my steps in the path of Your commandments so I don't merely mull over them but willingly walk them in delight. Mold my mind and fashion my heart to fit within Your testimonies and not devise money-making motives. Revive me so my eyes always remain the gateway to behold You as I focus on Your ways and not the futile vanities of this world. Plant the promise of Your Word deep within me so my reverence for You increases. Let me never fear the world's reproach as it rails against Your ways, for I know that Your ordinances are safe, solid and sound. O LORD, I long for Your precepts for through Your righteousness I am revived. Amen.

Psalm 119 – Vav (41-48)

41 Let your faithful love come to me, Lord, your salvation, as you promised. **42** Then I can answer the one who taunts me, for I trust in your word. **43** Never take the word of truth from my mouth, for I hope in your judgments. **44** I will always obey your instruction, forever and ever. **45** I will walk freely in an open place because I study your precepts. **46** I will speak of your decrees before kings and not be ashamed. **47** I delight in your commands, which I love. **48** I will lift up my hands to your commands, which I love, and will meditate on your statutes. (CSB)

It was one of our founding fathers, John Adams, who said, "We are a government of laws, not men." This is the basis for the phrase "rule of law." Rulers, whether elected officials or monarchs, have personal agendas and desires which at times can obfuscate fairness and justice. A well-written law that is clearly defined and equitably enforced is not a constraint. Within the FBI, I was given clear guidance as to what was allowed and what was not. I liked that clarity for there was no doubt about what was permitted. The chalk lines on a football field may seem to be a nuisance, but they are measurements of progress and boundaries of containment. Picture the confusion of trying to play a game without those lines. Within bounds, there is freedom. As humans, we tend to feel inhibited by the law but in reality, following the law gives liberty. Our Psalmist twice says how much he loves God's commandments. Why? Because when we let them guide our steps, our path is straight and wide.

O God, I come to You as a sinner saved through Your lovingkindness and because Your Word first came to me. When I trust in Your Word Your peaceful pardon empowers me to refute those who castigate and curse me. At the very least, let me maintain in my mouth a morsel of truth from Your Word that I might savor it, for I constantly crave Your ordinances. Obedience to Your law brings heavenly happiness here on earth and Your precepts pursued imparts freedom. As I walk in Your liberty I am not ashamed to proclaim Your testimonies, even among the high and mighty on earth. I love Your commandments for they are my delight. I will raise them in reverence before You, O LORD, and perpetually ponder Your statutes. Amen.

Psalm 119 –Zayin (49-56)

49 Remember your word to your servant, in which you have made me hope. 50 This is my comfort in my affliction, that your promise gives me life. 51 The insolent utterly deride me, but I do not turn away from your law. 52 When I think of your rules from of old, I take comfort, O LORD. 53 Hot indignation seizes me because of the wicked, who forsake your law. 54 Your statutes have been my songs in the house of my sojourning. 55 I remember your name in the night, O LORD, and keep your law. 56 This blessing has fallen to me, that I have kept your precepts. (ESV)

Do you recall as a child, riding in the car or being on a long bus trip, singing songs to pass the time? Songs like "The Wheels on the Bus Go Round and Round" or "The Ants Go Marching" may come to mind – but be careful, they may get stuck in your head! For millennia, songs have brought comfort and cheer to the weary traveler. Ah, but what song to sing? Surely, something more important than spinning tires or marching ants. In truth, this Psalm is all about that message. In verse 54 we are told that God's statutes (or His Word) have become the sure sojourner's song, the traveler's tune, the pilgrim's poem. It can be difficult at times to remember that our life on earth is not the main act or final destination. We are passing through and while we must certainly make the most of our time here, our primary purpose is the safe landing on the runway to eternity. Let God's Word become your supporting song in life to guide you home.

O God, I thank you for being forever faithful to remember the promises pronounced in Your Word. In faith, I make them my only hope. Your Word does not exempt me from times of trial and tribulation but when encountered, Your Word confirms and comforts me, keeping me alive through troubles. When the vexing voices of the arrogant deride me, I will stand steadfast in Your law. May Your everlasting ordinances remain embedded in my memory, a deep and unwavering well of comfort. When the wicked walk the path of destruction because they have forsaken Your law, I feel the heat rise in me. While plodding the pilgrim's path of life, Your statutes guide me – my soul's sustaining song. As each day ends I will meditate on Your law and think of You throughout the night. By keeping Your precepts, I do not earn Your blessings, but rather, I am transformed to turn and receive them. Amen.

Psalm 119 – Heth (57-64)

57 LORD, you are mine! I promise to obey your words! **58** With all my heart I want your blessings. Be merciful as you promised. **59** I pondered the direction of my life, and I turned to follow your laws. **60** I will hurry, without delay, to obey your commands. **61** Evil people try to drag me into sin, but I am firmly anchored to your instructions. **62** I rise at midnight to thank you for your just regulations. **63** I am a friend to anyone who fears you— anyone who obeys your commandments. **64** O LORD, your unfailing love fills the earth; teach me your decrees. (NLT)

Have you ever been taught a life-lesson which at the time seemed bothersome but in hindsight, you now see its value? I recall the time my Dad first taught me how to change a flat tire: the proper sequence; where to safely place the jack; and how to loosen the nuts before jacking the car off the ground. Step-by-step, I conducted each task as instructed. With the spare tire on, I came to the final step of replacing the nuts. Each nut was carefully threaded and securely tightened. I removed the jack and triumphantly thought, "mission accomplished!" It was only then that my Dad said, "great, you did everything perfect except the last step…you put all the nuts on backward." I said, "Great, why didn't you explain that to me BEFORE I tightened the first nut?" Over fifty years later, his answer still resonates today: "Because now you will never forget it." This Psalm emphasizes the value of remembering God's Word. Let us carefully learn and never forget it.

O God, while others look to the world's gimmicks and gadgets or trifles and trinkets, I will remember that You are my entire portion, my all-in-all, and I will keep Your words. With my whole heart, I have sought You and Your favor and plead Your promise to be gracious to me. When I ponder my performance and consider my conduct, I respond and turn my feet toward Your testimonies. Let me not lazily linger but rapidly return to keeping Your commandments. Though the wicked try to secure me to their sin, I will remain safely secure in Your law. In the deep night Your righteous ordinances call out to me and I rise and give You thanks. Those who rightly revere You and keep Your precepts are those whose company I keep. The earth cries forth full of Your lovingkindness. O LORD, let me longingly listen and learn Your statutes. Amen.

Psalm 119 – Teth (65-72)

65 You have dealt well with Your servant, O Lord, according to Your word. **66** Teach me good judgment and knowledge, For I believe Your commandments. **67** Before I was afflicted I went astray, But now I keep Your word. **68** You are good, and do good; Teach me Your statutes. **69** The proud have forged a lie against me, But I will keep Your precepts with my whole heart. **70** Their heart is as fat as grease, But I delight in Your law. **71** It is good for me that I have been afflicted, That I may learn Your statutes. **72** The law of Your mouth is better to me Than thousands of coins of gold and silver. (NKJV)

Have you ever looked back over your life and in retrospect seen God's hand at work? Most of my FBI promotions were for positions I either didn't initially request or for ones to which I had been "strongly encouraged" to apply. There was only one promotion I really wanted and for which I applied that I didn't get. In that case, I was told by everyone, you are "perfect for the job!" As the process went along, I was told "the job is yours" and those who were in the initial decision-making positions said it was a "done deal." But in the end, the Director chose someone else. I wouldn't say I felt "afflicted" but I was disappointed. Incredibly, a couple years later, the Director transferred the majority of the myriad mission responsibilities, personnel, and budget from the division and position I didn't get to the section in the division of which I was already the chief. I didn't go to the desired job but the job came to me. As always, God's timing was perfect. When you seek the Lord and His will, He will direct your path.

O God, it is a wonder You have taken the time to deal with me and moreover, dealt well with me according to Your Word. Your commandments lie before me like a banquet; give me a discerning taste to partake in confidence and acquire knowledge and good judgment. It is only in hindsight that I get a glimpse into Your foresight and realize the twisted turns and bumps in the road were there to guide me back to You and Your Word. For You are so good and consistently carry out goodness – teach me Your statutes. The wicked have woven words of deceit around me but I will hold Your precepts close to my heart. Their hardened hearts are encased by the fashionable fat of this world but I will delight in Your law. Let me be a sterling student in the school of suffering so that I might learn Your statutes. The law from Your mouth is of unspeakable value. Let me delightfully dine on its seasoned samples and treasure them in my heart. Amen.

Psalm 119 – Yod (73-80)

73 Your hands made me and fashioned me; Give me understanding, that I may learn Your commandments. 74 May those who fear You see me and be glad, Because I wait for Your word. 75 I know, O LORD, that Your judgments are righteous, And that in faithfulness You have afflicted me. 76 O may Your lovingkindness comfort me, According to Your word to Your servant. 77 May Your compassion come to me that I may live, For Your law is my delight. 78 May the arrogant be ashamed, for they subvert me with a lie; But I shall meditate on Your precepts. 79 May those who fear You turn to me, Even those who know Your testimonies. 80 May my heart be blameless in Your statutes, So that I will not be ashamed. (NASB)

Have you ever created a work of art or constructed a device of necessity, and upon completion, looked it over with a sense of satisfaction? When done well, we want to protect and care for it but no matter how great our effort or the marvelousness of our masterpiece, it is still an inanimate object that one day will be tossed into the trash bin of history. It is not so with God. In this Psalm we are reminded of our relationship with the Lord – He is the creator, we are the created ones. He has taken the time to form us, to conform us in His image with a spirit, to inform us with minds of intellect, and transform us with heartfelt desires. And although our bodies will eventually fail and return to dust, our souls – the real "us" – will last forever. When we delight in God's Word and make it an integral part of our lives, we develop the proper perspective. We realize that in this life we are to serve the Lord – for He has created us.

O God, You have fashioned and formed me; mold my mind to receive understanding so I may learn Your commandments. May those who hold You in reverence rejoice to see me because in Your Word I wait in hope. I know my life is not a series of accidental affairs or chance circumstances. In Your love, Your decisions are fair and just no matter how they impact my life. I will wrap Your love around me like a cozy comforter, confidently content in Your promises. As Your mercy moves towards me I feel life leap into my soul for Your law is my delight. Let shame squeeze the proud as they twist the truth against me, but I will remain resolute and meditate on Your precepts. Let those of us who treasure You turn together toward one another to delve deeper into learning Your testimonies. Let my heart remain brazenly bold and constantly true to Your statutes that I might maintain an undivided love for You. Amen.

Psalm 119 – Kaph (81-88)

81 I am worn out waiting for your rescue, but I have put my hope in your word. **82** My eyes are straining to see your promises come true. When will you comfort me? **83** I am shriveled like a wineskin in the smoke, but I have not forgotten to obey your decrees. **84** How long must I wait? When will you punish those who persecute me? **85** These arrogant people who hate your instructions have dug deep pits to trap me. **86** All your commands are trustworthy. Protect me from those who hunt me down without cause. **87** They almost finished me off, but I refused to abandon your commandments. **88** In your unfailing love, spare my life; then I can continue to obey your laws. (NLT)

Have you ever worked so hard at something, given so much effort that you felt you didn't have an ounce of energy left? For most of us, this occurs when we have physically overdone ourselves. But it isn't the Psalmist's body that is spent, finished, utterly exhausted and about to faint, but his soul by longing for God's salvation. Using another description of physical exertion, he says his eyes are pushed to the point of failure from longingly looking for God's Word. For most of us, spiritual cravings seldom exceed physical ones, leaving us feeling lost, sunk in desperation and despair. Far too often we feel failure worming its way toward our heart, delving deeply into our soul, attempting to drain all hope. But true hope prevails when we stand on God's Word, for no matter how bad things appear, we have a footing that remains faithful, stable, steady and true. It is our energy bar to fend off fatigue, allowing us to expectantly endure.

O God, I thank You when my soul sighs at the edge of exhaustion that I can wait for Your Word, my sure salvation. My eyes strain with expectancy to peer at Your promises and in wonder watch for Your coming comfort. Even when worn and withered and I seem so dry, Your statutes remain fresh in my mind, able to renew me. I pray my patience prevails as I await Your intervention against those who persecute me. For the proud sow seeds of suspicion and quarry deep in the mines of worldly pleasures to distract me and defy Your law. But I will seek Your help from their tangled lies for all Your commandments are faithful and true. When faced with failure and on the precipice about to fall, I will stand fast on Your precepts and be saved. When I keep Your testimonies I am not only saved, but life anew runs through me according to Your lovingkindness. Amen.

Psalm 119 – Lamedh (89-96)

89 Forever, O LORD, Your word is settled in heaven. 90 Your faithfulness continues throughout all generations; You established the earth, and it stands. 91 They stand this day according to Your ordinances, For all things are Your servants. 92 If Your law had not been my delight, Then I would have perished in my affliction. 93 I will never forget Your precepts, For by them You have revived me. 94 I am Yours, save me; For I have sought Your precepts. 95 The wicked wait for me to destroy me; I shall diligently consider Your testimonies. 96 I have seen a limit to all perfection; Your commandment is exceedingly broad. (NASB)

We live in a world ever changing. Even our daily routine of rising each morning has an air of predictability, but we know that no two days are exactly the same. But our Psalmist reminds us at least two things are constant and never change – God's Word and His faithfulness. They reflect two of God's attributes: He is eternal and unchangeable. The first word of this section, (le'olam) means forever. It not only means from ancient days past but also an indefinite futurity. Every token this world has to offer is fleeting, but not so with God. The section's final verse can be confusing but I think what the Psalmist meant was this: "I have lived to see the very best things this world has to offer, but even they have an end. But Your Word continues on, forever and far beyond what we can see or imagine." When you stand on God's Word, you will stand stable and firm.

O God, Your Word stands firmly fixed in heaven and lasts forever. Your faithfulness remains constant and available from one generation to the next, recurring like the regular rotation of the earth. Every earthly element and hint of heaven stands fast in service to You according to Your ordinances. I thank You for the comfort of Your law, O LORD, for without it I would melt in misery. I will readily remember and respect Your precepts for through them my life is revived and restored. And as I have sought them You have saved me, for I am Yours. Though the wicked wait to waylay me I will fervently focus on Your testimonies. All good things eventually end except You and Your commandments for Your Word endures forever. Amen.

Psalm 119 – Mem (97-104)

97 O how I love Your law! It is my meditation all the day. **98** Your commandments make me wiser than my enemies, For they are ever mine. **99** I have more insight than all my teachers, For Your testimonies are my meditation. **100** I understand more than the aged, Because I have observed Your precepts. **101** I have restrained my feet from every evil way, That I may keep Your word. **102** I have not turned aside from Your ordinances, For You Yourself have taught me. **103** How sweet are Your words to my taste! Yes, sweeter than honey to my mouth! **104** From Your precepts I get understanding; Therefore I hate every false way. (NASB)

How often do you read your Bible? Only on Sundays? Daily? And when you do read it, does it sometimes feel more like a duty, a chore? Here, our Psalmist emphatically exclaims how much he loves God's Word! It means so much to him that he ponders it throughout the day. He also realizes the great benefits that come from studying scripture: understanding and wisdom. The Hebrew word for understanding (sakal) means to have comprehension or insight – the ability to see which choice is correct. The Hebrew word for "makes me wiser" (chakam) has one definition as: "to be free from defect by the exercise of skill." When we spend quality time in scripture we acquire the insight to see the proper path ahead and we develop the wisdom that enables us to actually walk it. Let us delve deeply into God's Word and restrain our feet from wandering ways.

O God, I thank You for Your law and how I have come to love it. Throughout the day may it be my focal point. When I commit Your commandments deep within me I gain wisdom without worries about my enemies. When I take Your testimonies as my mental meditation I gain insights that no teacher ever taught. When I perform Your precepts as my daily deeds of obedience I gain understanding well beyond my years. Your Word, O LORD, brings perfect freedom, and so I beg You to fetter my feet to it; hold my heart to it; shackle my soul to it, that I may always keep it close within me. When I let Your Spirit teach me Your ordinances, I will not wander from the proper path. Your promises are my palate's pleasure and my tongue's treasure – sweeter than the finest honey. As Your precepts become the manual for my mind I gain understanding. As my heart grows in love with You and Your Word, may my eyes foresee falsehoods so I may stop, turn, and walk away in disdain from them. Amen.

Psalm 119 – Nun (105-112)

105 Your word is a lamp to guide my feet and a light for my path. **106** I've promised it once, and I'll promise it again: I will obey your righteous regulations. **107** I have suffered much, O LORD; restore my life again as you promised. **108** LORD, accept my offering of praise, and teach me your regulations. **109** My life constantly hangs in the balance, but I will not stop obeying your instructions. **110** The wicked have set their traps for me, but I will not turn from your commandments. **111** Your laws are my treasure; they are my heart's delight. **112** I am determined to keep your decrees to the very end. (ESV)

Although the word doesn't appear in this segment of Psalm 119, to me it is all about <u>worship</u> – through God's Word, through obedience, through prayer. I tend to use acronyms to form words that help me remember certain lessons of life. I believe in this case, the word "WORSHIP" is a good example:

<u>W</u>: **W**ithstand **W**orldly **W**ickedness by **W**earing the **W**hole armor of God
<u>O</u>: **O**bey the Lord in all things
<u>R</u>: **R**outinely **R**ead, **R**esearch, **R**eview and **R**etain the Bible
<u>S</u>: **S**erve the Lord by **S**erving others
<u>H</u>: **H**ave a **H**umble **H**eart
<u>I</u>: **I**ncorporate God's Word and **I**ntegrate Jesus' love by the **I**nspiration of the Holy Spirit **I**n all you say and do
<u>P</u>: **P**ray **P**erpetually

Let God's Word daily light your path, in worship and praise!

O God, Your Word is my life's lamp and the pointer on the path ahead. Let me not simply read Your righteous ordinances but to daily live them in outright obedience. When burdens beset me and all looks lost, Your Word is my life support. As Your ordinances delve deep into my heart may I respond with offerings of praise, acceptable to You. Despite the dangers of daily living, I will press on and not forget Your law. Even when wicked people set a snare to trap me I will stay the course holding fast to Your precepts. I have taken Your testimonies as my trusted treasure for they are my heart's hope and joy. Let my love for You become the affection of my heart that drives my hands and feet to perform Your statutes and to carry them to completion for as long as life's journey lasts. Amen.

Psalm 119 – Samekh (113-120)

113 I hate those who are double-minded, but I love your instruction. **114** You are my shelter and my shield; I put my hope in your word. **115** Depart from me, you evil ones, so that I may obey my God's commands. **116** Sustain me as you promised, and I will live; do not let me be ashamed of my hope. **117** Sustain me so that I can be safe and always be concerned about your statutes. **118** You reject all who stray from your statutes, for their deceit is a lie. **119** You remove all the wicked on earth as if they were dross from metal; therefore, I love your decrees. **120** I tremble in awe of you; I fear your judgments. (CSB)

This part of the Psalm seems to be a study about value, contrasting between useful and useless. But a closer look shows it has more to do with the stance one chooses to take. The Psalmist despises those who are "double-minded" or have "vain thoughts." The Hebrew word is seeph and is used only here in all the O.T. It means to be divided or half-hearted on a position. It is that wishy-washy person who struggles inside, unable to make up their mind, stopping halfway between two opposite opinions. In the N.T. James describes those doubting God's Word as "double-minded" and unstable. It harkens to where Jesus tells the church of Laodicea they are neither hot or cold but because they are lukewarm He will spit them out of His mouth. By knowing God's Word, we can place our trust and hope in it, and with that foundation, firmly take a stand!

O God, how I detest double-minded people. Their loyalties lie like the shifting sand, basing their beliefs on the popular position of the day. Let my love for Your law only grow and remain my true standard. For in Your Word I place my total trust, for You are my haven of hope and my shield of protection. Let me not keep company with those who in their vanity place their desires over Yours and would hinder me from obeying You and Your commandments. Because You have promised to sustain me I will unashamedly keep the faith and my hope in You will remain unshaken. For it is only through Your strength I remain secure and am able to relentlessly respect Your statutes. Those who wander from them are only fooling themselves. What a waste the wicked are, for one day You will remove them like trash tossed into a heap. How can I not love Your testimonies? Who is able to stand before You, my holy God? Keep me humble to remember that Your judgments are certain and that only through Your provision I can pass through the proper portal to come into Your presence. Amen.

Psalm 119 – Ayin (121-128)

121 Don't leave me to the mercy of my enemies, for I have done what is just and right. **122** Please guarantee a blessing for me. Don't let the arrogant oppress me! **123** My eyes strain to see your rescue, to see the truth of your promise fulfilled. **124** I am your servant; deal with me in unfailing love, and teach me your decrees. **125** Give discernment to me, your servant; then I will understand your laws. **126** LORD, it is time for you to act, for these evil people have violated your instructions. **127** Truly, I love your commands more than gold, even the finest gold. **128** Each of your commandments is right. That is why I hate every false way. (NLT)

There is a long history of the master-servant relationship and because of our nation's dark past with slavery, we tend to paint all such dealings in a bad light. But here, in three of the eight verses, the Psalmist makes reference to being God's servant. First, he asks God to "be surety" for him. The Hebrew word (arab) means to associate, to interweave – it infers an intermingling of interests wherein the Master becomes the servant's guardian. He not only seeks protection but also looks to the Lord to treat him with love and mercy. This is demonstrated by God teaching His servant His statutes and giving him understanding to fully comprehend His Word. The Psalmist's straightforward statement, "I am your servant" is a humble confession conferring his love, loyalty, dependence, and obedience to God and His Word. It is recognition of our subservient position to the Lord. It is an example we too can follow!

O God, as I daily devote myself to do deeds that are right and just, I pray your protection from my ever-present oppressors. Confer upon me Your comforting assurance and grant me the grace to carry on. May Your righteous promises bring relief as my straining eyes longingly look for Your salvation. Let Your marvelous mercy be displayed as I grasp the privilege of Your divine teaching. As I seek to be Your servant, O LORD, impart to me the understanding needed to know Your testimonies. As the world displays its contempt and disdain for Your law I naturally want to cry out for Your just response to take action. But remind me to do my part to work for You to improve the situation. Because I love Your commandments let me dig deep into them to gather the gleaming golden nuggets of truth. Once found, may I never squander their value in vain exploits but put their worth to work to glorify Your name. Because I know Your precepts are right and true, I will use them to guide my way and keep me off the twisted trail of deceit. Amen.

Psalm 119 – Pe (129-136)

129 Your testimonies are wonderful; Therefore my soul observes them. **130** The unfolding of Your words gives light; It gives understanding to the simple. **131** I opened my mouth wide and panted, For I longed for Your commandments. **132** Turn to me and be gracious to me, After Your manner with those who love Your name. **133** Establish my footsteps in Your word, And do not let any iniquity have dominion over me. **134** Redeem me from the oppression of man, That I may keep Your precepts. **135** Make Your face shine upon Your servant, And teach me Your statutes. **136** My eyes shed streams of water, Because they do not keep Your law. (NASB)

In this portion of the chapter, we once again see the linkage between God's written Word and the Living Word, Jesus. The Psalmist says God's testimonies are wonderful. The same Hebrew word (pele) literally means "wonders" and is often used as a revelation of God's miraculous power. It is the same word used in Isaiah to refer to the Messiah as the Wonderful Counselor. Next, we see the "unfolding" of the Word. The Hebrew word (pethach) is used only once in the Bible and means to open and enter as through a doorway. In John 10 Jesus said, "I am the door." By unfolding the Word, we are given light. John's Gospel also tells us that Jesus said He is the light of the world. Finally, our Psalmist opens wide his mouth, as if eager to feed on the Word. Jesus said He is the Bread of Life – whoever comes to Him will never hunger or thirst. Let us hunger and pant for God's Word as we walk life's journey, satisfied in the company of Jesus.

O God, because Your testimonies are such a marvelous miracle how can my soul not obey them? As Your words unfold before me, light leaps forth and understanding bids the dull dim darkness of my feeble mind to flee. I will open my mouth and deeply drink from Your commandments for they quench the thirst of my soul. I love You LORD and Your holy name and longingly look to see You turn to me in Your love and mercy. Make my footsteps firmly fixed in Your Word so that no single sin has dominion over me. Loosen the shackles of man's oppression so I will keep Your precepts. Your smile upon me is the radiance of genuine joy as You teach me Your statutes. When I see how mankind has turned from You, no longer keeping Your law, my heart breaks and the flood of woe becomes a torrent of tears. O God, I pray we make an about-face to seek You and turn from our wicked ways. Amen.

Psalm 119 – Tsadhe (137-144)

137 Righteous are You, O Lord, And upright are Your judgments. **138** Your testimonies, which You have commanded, Are righteous and very faithful. **139** My zeal has consumed me, Because my enemies have forgotten Your words. **140** Your word is very pure; Therefore Your servant loves it. **141** I am small and despised, Yet I do not forget Your precepts. **142** Your righteousness is an everlasting righteousness, And Your law is truth. **143** Trouble and anguish have overtaken me, Yet Your commandments are my delights. **144** The righteousness of Your testimonies is everlasting; Give me understanding, and I shall live. (NKJV)

In my later years in the FBI, once I had reached positions of higher authority within the Senior Executive Service, I always tried to remember what it was like when I was a brand-new Agent. There are sayings that resonated with me like, "Practice what you preach;" or "What's good for the goose is good for the gander;" or the one I tried to avoid, "Do as I say, not as I do." The Apostle Paul put it this way in his letter to the Romans: Don't think more highly of yourself than you should; instead, evaluate yourself with sound judgment. This Psalm reminds us that God's law is perfect. It is powerfully applicable to everyone, no matter what their status is in life. If you think too highly of yourself, God's Word has a way of knocking you down a peg or two and remind you that you are not God; if you see yourself too lowly, it can elevate you to new heights, reminding you that you are created in God's image and He cares for you.

O God, as I progress in my pursuit of You, I'm in awe and adore Your perfect righteousness and fair judgments. Your testimonies are consistently carried out in faultless faithfulness. May my zeal for You become so firmly focused and completely consuming that nothing else distracts me, including any adversarial attacks. May the pureness of Your Word refine my soul and increase my love for it and You. From the greatest general to the paltry private, Your precepts prevail over all – let me never forget them. From time out of mind, Your righteousness reigns for Your law is faultless and final. When trouble and woe worm their way into my life, Your commandments console and delight me. Your testimonies remain forever and give me the understanding I need to live. Amen.

Psalm 119 – Qoph (145-152)

145 I cried with all my heart; answer me, O LORD! I will observe Your statutes. **146** I cried to You; save me And I shall keep Your testimonies. **147** I rise before dawn and cry for help; I wait for Your words. **148** My eyes anticipate the night watches, That I may meditate on Your word. **149** Hear my voice according to Your lovingkindness; Revive me, O LORD, according to Your ordinances. **150** Those who follow after wickedness draw near; They are far from Your law. **151** You are near, O LORD, And all Your commandments are truth. **152** Of old I have known from Your testimonies That You have founded them forever. (NASB)

It wasn't until more recently in my Christian faith, that I began attending a church with liturgical leanings. One prayer I look forward to each Sunday morning is the one we pray at the very beginning of the worship service, the Collect for Purity. It has a well-documented history, with roots going back over a thousand years. To me, it helps quiet my mind and heart, to displace distractions, and reminds me why I am at church. It goes like this:

"Almighty God, to You all hearts are open, all desires known, and from You no secrets are hid: Cleanse the thoughts of our hearts by the inspiration of Your Holy Spirit, that we may perfectly love You, and worthily magnify Your Holy Name; through Christ our Lord. Amen."

This Psalm also is about a worshiper's open heart, desiring to commune with the Living God. We meditate and hope in God's Word, with the expectation He will hear and answer the words of our prayer!

O God, I call out to You with my whole heart, listening for Your attentive answer. Let me commit myself daily to obey Your statutes. When I call out for You to save me, let me seek and keep Your testimonies. Before the sun's rays rise of the day's first fresh hour, I will seek You and expectantly await Your words of promise. During the solitary hours of the night with ardent anticipation, I will meditate on Your Word. In Your great love hear my voice, O LORD, and awaken within me the spark of life according to your Word. Those who delve deep into depravity are far from Your law, but You, O LORD, are near me with all Your true commandments. For as long as I can remember, Your testimonies have spoken to me, reminding me You have established them as mankind's firm foundation. Let me forever follow them. Amen.

Psalm 119 – Resh (153-160)

153 Look on my affliction and deliver me, for I do not forget your law. **154** Plead my cause and redeem me; give me life according to your promise! **155** Salvation is far from the wicked, for they do not seek your statutes. **156** Great is your mercy, O LORD; give me life according to your rules. **157** Many are my persecutors and my adversaries, but I do not swerve from your testimonies. **158** I look at the faithless with disgust, because they do not keep your commands. **159** Consider how I love your precepts! Give me life according to your steadfast love. **160** The sum of your word is truth, and every one of your righteous rules endures forever. (ESV)

Truth. It is the foundation of our legal system. Before testifying in a court of law, every witness swears to tell the truth, the whole truth and nothing but the truth. But for many, the truth is not clearly defined, not a yes or no, black or white circumstance. Far too many live their lives in various shades of gray and see truth according to the situation they are in. Even Pontius Pilate asked Jesus that all important question two thousand years ago, "What is truth?" In this segment, our Psalmist says that no matter how bad the situation appears, he will not swerve or deviate from the testimonies of the Lord. Why is that? Because the sum of God's Word is truth! In its totality, from beginning to end, top to bottom, we can depend on it to provide us the lessons of life we need. It isn't a one-time "get out of jail free" card, but an enduring guide to keep us out of trouble in first place.

O God, consider the state of my weakness and in Your wisdom, rescue me, for I hold Your law fast in the forefront of my mind. You, O LORD, are my one true advocate who has redeemed me and given me life anew according to Your Word. Shameless sinners seek not Your statutes and thus, salvation remains shrouded from their sight. Because of Your many mercies, You infuse new life in me according to Your ordinances. Despite those who oppress and oppose me, I will not stray or turn from Your testimonies. The faithless foment feelings of displeasure within me for they defiantly fly in the face of Your Word. Reinforce my love for Your precepts so it will revive my life to reflect Your love and better serve You. Truth is the tally and total sum of Your Word and all of Your ordinances are eternally righteous. Amen

Psalm 119 – Shin (161-168)

161 Powerful people harass me without cause, but my heart trembles only at your word. **162** I rejoice in your word like one who discovers a great treasure. **163** I hate and abhor all falsehood, but I love your instructions. **164** I will praise you seven times a day because all your regulations are just. **165** Those who love your instructions have great peace and do not stumble. **166** I long for your rescue, LORD, so I have obeyed your commands. **167** I have obeyed your laws, for I love them very much. **168** Yes, I obey your commandments and laws because you know everything I do. (NLT)

Upon my arrival at the academy as a new Agent trainee, I was issued two revolvers: my duty weapon (a Smith & Wesson Model 13, .357 magnum) and a handgun called a "red handle" (the color signified its incapacity to fire real bullets). Those who had never worn a gun became accustomed to the extra weight on their hip. But at the range, we wore our real guns. Over the next 16 weeks we each shot thousands of rounds. Our firearms instructors performed critical training watching each shooter's form and technique, providing guidance along the way. In this Psalm, we are told that loving God's law brings peace. The Hebrew word "torah" is usually translated "law" in English Bibles and we tend to associate it with the five books Moses wrote. But the literal meaning of the word torah is "instruction," originating from the idea of an archer or javelin thrower aiming at a target and hitting it. God's Word is our instruction for living life. Following God's word not only improves our marksmanship to hit the target, but it allows us to experience God's peace in the process.

O God, when peers persecute and I must consume contempt's cup without cause, Your words speak to my heart shaking sensibility into it. Your promises produce more joy in me than finding a long-lost treasure. Falsehoods flourish around me which I despise and disdain, but I will focus on Your law which I love. As I fixate on Your faithful ordinances let them form the foundation of my constant praise throughout the day. Because I love Your law I'm at perfect peace and the stumbling blocks of life become stepping stones on the path around its pitfalls. May my faith's fruit flower into the hope of my salvation and in response to Your faithfulness I will obey You and Your commandments. Let me demonstrate the practical proof of my love for You by taking in Your testimonies and practicing Your precepts, for all my life lies before You, from dawn to dusk and beginning to end. You know my heart, O LORD, and may it always be pleasing to You. Amen.

Psalm 119 – Tav (169-176)

169 Let my cry come before you, O LORD; give me understanding according to your word! **170** Let my plea come before you; deliver me according to your word. **171** My lips will pour forth praise, for you teach me your statutes. **172** My tongue will sing of your word, for all your commandments are right. **173** Let your hand be ready to help me, for I have chosen your precepts. **174** I long for your salvation, O LORD, and your law is my delight. **175** Let my soul live and praise you, and let your rules help me. **176** I have gone astray like a lost sheep; seek your servant, for I do not forget your commandments. (ESV)

We now come to the final verse of the longest chapter in the Bible, and what a climax it is! In the preceding 175 verses, our Psalmist has continuously mentioned the greatness of God's Word and how he loves it, follows it, will never forget it, has hidden it in his heart, declared it, delighted in it, and meditated on it. Does this result in an attitude of self-righteous pride? No. He recognizes that despite all this, he still comes up short and tends to wander. In 1757, at the age of 22, English pastor Robert Robinson penned one of my favorite hymns "Come Thou Fount of Every Blessing." The final verse of this Psalm certainly influenced these lyrics: "O to grace how great a debtor, Daily I'm constrained to be! Let Thy goodness like a fetter, Bind my wandering heart to Thee. Prone to wander, Lord, I feel it, Prone to leave the God I love; Here's my heart, O take and seal it, Seal it for Thy courts above." That the God of the universe would take the time to seek out a single lost sheep, is truly one of life's mysteries. And here is a great irony to remember: It is only when we handcuff our heart and shackle our soul to God's Word, that we can truly experience the freedom we desire.

O God, let my heart's cry come near You and illuminate my mind with Your Word. Let my prayers and petitions find favor in Your presence and deliver me in keeping with Your Word. Let my lips proclaim Your promises as You teach me Your statutes. Let my daily anthem be based solely on Your Word so that neither my sinful silence nor my personal pleas impede a worthy song of praise of Your righteous commandments. Let Your able arm assist me as I hold fast to Your precepts. Let my hunger for Your salvation be satisfied as I delightfully dine on Your law. Let Your ordinances help sustain my soul so I can ever praise You. Without You, O LORD, I am like a lost sheep straying every which way but You have sought and saved me. Help me to remember, respect and respond in obedience to Your commandments. Amen.

Psalm 120

A Song of Ascents. **1** In my distress I cried to the Lord, And He heard me. **2** Deliver my soul, O Lord, from lying lips And from a deceitful tongue. **3** What shall be given to you, Or what shall be done to you, You false tongue? **4** Sharp arrows of the warrior, With coals of the broom tree! **5** Woe is me, that I dwell in Meshech, That I dwell among the tents of Kedar! **6** My soul has dwelt too long With one who hates peace. **7** I am for peace; But when I speak, they are for war. (NKJV)

This is the first of fifteen individual Psalms referred to as "A Song of Ascents." No one knows precisely its meaning, but some think it refers to sojourners marching up to Jerusalem or the fifteen steps taken up to the temple itself. Others think it may relate to the stages of singing, with ever rising voices in degrees. At any rate, in this life's journey, we should be in the consistent mindset of progressing forward. As my dad used to always say, "onward and upward." One barrier we must overcome in our vertical voyage is dealing with the insidiously invective liars in our life. The old saying, "sticks and stones may break my bones but words will never hurt me" may literally be true in a physical sense, yet we all have tasted deception's deep discomfort. The pointed barbs of fiery words will surely come, but our Heavenly Father is always there to soothe our souls as we overcome obstacles in our upward walk.

O God, I thank You that when troubling times transpire You hear my cry for help. My soul seeks Your deliverance, O LORD, from lying lips and a treacherous tongue. First and foremost, keep me from being the offender for I would rather receive the slander than author it. But when subjected to such suffering, remind me of the dreadful doom of the deceitful. For while their words cut like a warrior's weapon and burn like crimson coals aglow, Your love shields me and Your Word is a balm to my wounds. In the end, You will bend their blades, dull their daggers and the consuming fire of Your justice will prevail. As I journey in this world of woe and dwell among those who hate harmony, give me the power to be Your peacemaker, an instrument for You, O Jehovah Shalom. Amen.

Psalm 121

A Song of Ascents. **1** I will lift up my eyes to the mountains; From where shall my help come? **2** My help comes from the LORD, Who made heaven and earth. **3** He will not allow your foot to slip; He who keeps you will not slumber. **4** Behold, He who keeps Israel Will neither slumber nor sleep. **5** The LORD is your keeper; The LORD is your shade on your right hand. **6** The sun will not smite you by day, Nor the moon by night. **7** The LORD will protect you from all evil; He will keep your soul. **8** The LORD will guard your going out and your coming in From this time forth and forever. (NASB)

One of the first motion pictures I can remember seeing at the movie theater was "The Sound of Music." With its panoramic vistas of majestic mountains, it is a must-see on the big screen. In one of its final scenes, the von Trapp family is trying to escape the Nazis by hiding inside the abbey. In a word of guidance and encouragement, the Mother Abbess tells Maria, "You will not be alone. Remember, 'I will lift up mine eyes unto the hills, from whence cometh my help.'" Although this might have been good advice as an avenue of escape, the hills really can't save us. In truth, the verse she quoted (Ps. 121:1) isn't a statement, but rather, as you can see above, it is a question. The next verse actually answers it: "My help comes from the Lord, who made heaven and earth." Amazingly, the God of all creation is available to help us – all we need to do is to call upon Him!

O God, as I travel the trail of life I will encounter hardship's hills and mountainous obstacles. Upon seeing them I will pause and ponder, "Who will help me?" The answer is crystal clear – it is You, O LORD, who created the heavens and earth. Nothing distracts You as You keep watch over me for You do not sleep and therefore, I will not slip. For You are Jehovah Shamar, the LORD My Keeper and Guardian. You are my shade against the scorching sun and when winter's nippy nights fall You warm me. You, O LORD, protect me from evil for You are the keeper of my soul. Whether I am coming or going, You keep me in Your care. Looking back I see Your hand at work and know I am safely in Your protective love, now and forevermore. Amen.

Psalm 122

A Song of Ascents. Of David. **1** I was glad when they said to me, "Let us go to the house of the LORD!" **2** Our feet have been standing within your gates, O Jerusalem! **3** Jerusalem—built as a city that is bound firmly together, **4** to which the tribes go up, the tribes of the LORD, as was decreed for Israel, to give thanks to the name of the LORD. **5** There thrones for judgment were set, the thrones of the house of David. **6** Pray for the peace of Jerusalem! "May they be secure who love you! **7** Peace be within your walls and security within your towers!" **8** For my brothers and companions' sake I will say, "Peace be within you!" **9** For the sake of the house of the LORD our God, I will seek your good. (ESV)

How long have you lived in your house? It is not uncommon for FBI Agents to be transferred often and many times throughout their careers. My wife and I have now lived in the same house for over 20 years, longer than any other abode. The walls of our home not only have photos hanging on them, but they also house our family's shared memories. When we discuss the prospect of selling and moving on, our children (and now grandchildren) pause in deep thought and say, "but we have so many memories there..." David's joy was not in his palace but rather, to be called into the house of the Lord. His deep-seated gladness was not in the building but in the sharing of a community (let us go...) to enter God's presence. Jerusalem, the City of David, had walls around it, but notice that David prays for peace "within" its walls. While the walls of our homes might bring security from the external elements, let us pray for God's peace to reside within them.

O God, I am a stranger on this earth so there is great gladness to enter Your holy house. Someday I will stand within the gates of Jerusalem, whether it is during the present pilgrimage of this lifetime or the one to come in the new Jerusalem, I know not when but You do. For Jerusalem has been built as a gathering place for the tribes of the earth, for Israel and all Your people worldwide. Let all Your people give You thanks. Justice will be established from Your throne and the people will see peace and prosperity prevail for those who love You. I pray for Your peace, O LORD, for Jerusalem and the earth; for friends and family, and indeed within me. Amen.

Psalm 123

A Song of Ascents. **1** To You I lift up my eyes, O You who are enthroned in the heavens! **2** Behold, as the eyes of servants look to the hand of their master, As the eyes of a maid to the hand of her mistress, So our eyes look to the LORD our God, Until He is gracious to us. **3** Be gracious to us, O LORD, be gracious to us, For we are greatly filled with contempt. **4** Our soul is greatly filled With the scoffing of those who are at ease, And with the contempt of the proud. (NASB)

After resigning from the sheriff's department and en route to the FBI Academy, I didn't know what to expect. Although I had already attended a police academy four years earlier, things were different. I now had two children as well as my wife who were being left behind nearly 3000 miles away. Failure was not an available option. Two characteristics seemed to exemplify those who excelled during my time at the Academy: focus and heart. Paying attention to instructions without succumbing to distractions and then following through with perseverance and humility were keys to success. In this Psalm, we see someone who recognizes their proper place before the Lord – with humility, their focus is only on God. The Psalmist gazes upon the Lord until he receives mercy. A humble heart that patiently perseveres is something the Lord desires and that we must endeavor to attain.

O God, You are enthroned in the heavens above and as my eyes elevate upward and focus on You, let them be evidence of a humble heart hoping for the tranquil touch of Your hand; an obedient heart devotedly doing my duty to serve You; a thankful heart knowing You are a gracious, gentle and good God. May my eyes look to You and no one else. I am surrounded by those who hold You in disdain and as I follow Your ways, they deride me. As the cleaving cuts of contempt dig deep within my soul I will find refuge and relief remembering You know best of all the scorn and scoffing of this world, being despised and rejected by men. So when the mighty mock me and the self-satisfied sneer, I will still look to You, my Master and LORD of all. Amen.

Psalm 124

A Song of Ascents. Of David. **1** If it had not been the LORD who was on our side— let Israel now say—**2** if it had not been the LORD who was on our side when people rose up against us, **3** then they would have swallowed us up alive, when their anger was kindled against us; **4** then the flood would have swept us away, the torrent would have gone over us; **5** then over us would have gone the raging waters. **6** Blessed be the LORD, who has not given us as prey to their teeth! **7** We have escaped like a bird from the snare of the fowlers; the snare is broken, and we have escaped! **8** Our help is in the name of the LORD, who made heaven and earth. (ESV)

Being on an FBI SWAT team, I learned there are common ingredients in order to have a successful tactical resolution: proper planning, real-world rehearsal, and effective execution of that plan. During the execution phase, what makes a SWAT team unique is the concept you can engage the "bad guy" with speed, surprise, and overwhelming force. Quite often, an unexpected entry quickly carried out (sometimes using a distraction) by a large number of well-trained operators is enough to keep an armed hostage-taker from even getting a shot off and thus rescue the hostage. In this Psalm, we see the luxury of going into an armed conflict with the Lord on your side. Talk about "overwhelming force!" Our help comes not from other men and women but the Maker of heaven and earth. Despite the enormity of our enemy, our God is greater still!

O God, I look to You for help because You are Jehovah Shammah, the LORD Ever Present at my side. When my enemies rise to strike me, You are close at hand to close their hand; when they become like lions longing to consume me alive, You step in to shut their massive mouths; when their anger flickers into a flaming furnace about to incinerate me, You intervene to save me; and when their waves of malice wash over me like a raging river to surround and swallow my soul, You recover and rescue me. I praise You LORD for sheltering my soul from Satan's seducing snares, for You have set me free. My help is found in You, O LORD, creator of heaven and earth, and in Your name, I will call for comfort and aid. Amen.

Psalm 125

A song for pilgrims ascending to Jerusalem. **1** Those who trust in the LORD are as secure as Mount Zion; they will not be defeated but will endure forever. **2** Just as the mountains surround Jerusalem, so the LORD surrounds his people, both now and forever. **3** The wicked will not rule the land of the godly, for then the godly might be tempted to do wrong. **4** O LORD, do good to those who are good, whose hearts are in tune with you. **5** But banish those who turn to crooked ways, O LORD. Take them away with those who do evil. May Israel have peace! (NLT)

As we read the Bible, it is easy to forget that the various writers of the different books presumed their readers knew the geography of the places they described. When the Psalmist wrote, "As the mountains surround Jerusalem…" he expected that his audience not only knew there were mountains encircling Mount Zion, but they probably had seen them. The topography of Jerusalem is unique as it sits on several hills separated by distinct valleys, providing it a plateau of protection. The surrounding mountains that envelop Jerusalem contributed additional security. Our Psalmist is trying to convey a picture of safety, shelter, sureness, and stability for those who place their trust in the Lord. It is God who dependably protects us and gives us the footing we need in this life when we depend on Him. It is only when we fail to let Him lead that our path meanders through the valley of uncertainty.

O God, take the trust I have in You and let it gradually grow so my faith flourishes, firm and resolute like a towering mountain that cannot be moved. As the hills encircle Jerusalem, so You, O LORD, envelop Your people in love and Your hand of protection enfolds them. By Your grace, the ruling rod of the ruthless will not rest upon Your righteous; keep my hands busy doing Your work, O LORD, and to not meddle with mischief or tamper with transgressions. Impart Your pleasure and prosperity to those who obediently walk in Your ways and follow with a faithful heart, for that is the pathway to peace and the highway to happiness. But those who deviate from Your perfect plan to choose their own crooked course will find it is a detour to destruction. O LORD, keep my feet firmly fixed on You and Your passageway to peace. Amen.

Psalm 126

A Song of Ascents. **1** When the LORD brought back the captive ones of Zion, We were like those who dream. **2** Then our mouth was filled with laughter And our tongue with joyful shouting; Then they said among the nations, "The LORD has done great things for them." **3** The LORD has done great things for us; We are glad. **4** Restore our captivity, O LORD, As the streams in the South. **5** Those who sow in tears shall reap with joyful shouting. **6** He who goes to and fro weeping, carrying his bag of seed, Shall indeed come again with a shout of joy, bringing his sheaves with him. (NASB)

Those blessed with perfect vision may not relate to this, but for us who require corrective lenses to see properly, it is easy to remember the first time we stepped out of the eye doctor's office wearing our new glasses or contact lenses. Everything was so bright and clear. I remember thinking, "Wow! I had no idea this is what the world looked like." Those who have been long-imprisoned must surely feel the same way upon their release, uttering "I forgot what freedom felt like." All of us have experienced spiritual blindness and imprisonment and this Psalm is a song, prayer, and promise of when our sacred eyes are given sight and our captive souls are set free. We depart the dull dream-like state of this world and enter into the joyful realm of reality. Only God can take tears of woe that distort our vision and transform them into crops of contentment and joy.

O God, when dismal days and doldrums want to barricade my spirit from its joy, it is You who awakens my soul from a dreamlike state and sets my captive heart free. It is then I can no longer contain my laughter or shouts of joy. Let everyone who witnesses Your wondrous works stand in awe and proclaim Your glory. Let everyone who is released and rescued, recognize You as their redeemer. Keep me from holding on to those things that would hamper me from possessing the full-fledged freedom You have provided. Let me never try to limit the love You have for me, for it is greater than surging streams in a dry desert bringing life anew. Only You can heal those who sow seeds of sorrow and transform trial's tears into sheaves of solace, bundles of bliss, and bouquets of blessings, for You are Jehovah Rophe, the LORD My Healer. Amen.

Psalm 127

A Song of Ascents. Of Solomon. **1** Unless the Lord builds the house, They labor in vain who build it; Unless the Lord guards the city, The watchman stays awake in vain. **2** It is vain for you to rise up early, To sit up late, To eat the bread of sorrows; For so He gives His beloved sleep. **3** Behold, children are a heritage from the Lord, The fruit of the womb is a reward. **4** Like arrows in the hand of a warrior, So are the children of one's youth. **5** Happy is the man who has his quiver full of them; They shall not be ashamed, But shall speak with their enemies in the gate. (NKJV)

If Solomon is the author of this Psalm it seems most appropriate. Coming from the king of wisdom and wealth, he reminds us the importance of putting things into perspective. But he was also subject to excesses and it is the latter that taught him the vanity of the labors of life unless it is overseen by the Lord. But then he shifts gears and notes that children are a heritage, a gift, an inheritance from God. In other words, we can work our fingers to the bone in an effort to accumulate wealth and possessions, but in the end, it will be fruitless. The true fruit of life is what we receive from God. No matter what, only God determines those gifts we receive to include our children. As I write this, I'm at a beach house surrounded by my four daughters, their husbands and my six grandchildren. God has been gracious to give me children and allowed me to have the joy of knowing my children's children. Let us always be grateful for God's gifts!

O God, so often we ponder the past and persist in the present instead of fixing our focus on the future. All our life we strive to build a hardy home, safe and secure, full of family and fortune. And yet, all is in vain unless You, the Master Builder, Jehovah Bara, the LORD Creator of all, build that house. Dead-bolted doors, garrisoned gates, and watchful wardens are all employed to shield and shelter that house, but it is all for naught unless You, Jehovah Sabaoth, the LORD of Hosts, place Your protection over it. Rooms remain empty, vacant and void of voices unless You, Jehovah Jireh, the LORD My Provider, fill that house with family. All life's desires are delusional, hopeless and hollow, futile, fruitless and doomed to failure, unless You, O LORD, are the guiding hand to govern my life. Help me daily to let loose my close-fisted fingers so I can be firmly fortified in the grip of Your grace. Amen.

Psalm 128

A Song of Ascents. **1** Blessed is every one who fears the Lord, Who walks in His ways. **2** When you eat the labor of your hands, You shall be happy, and it shall be well with you. **3** Your wife shall be like a fruitful vine In the very heart of your house, Your children like olive plants All around your table. **4** Behold, thus shall the man be blessed Who fears the Lord. **5** The Lord bless you out of Zion, And may you see the good of Jerusalem All the days of your life. **6** Yes, may you see your children's children. Peace be upon Israel! (NKJV)

Family. We are all part of one – some large, some quite small. Families are a blessing from God. The word "wife" only appears twice in the Psalms – once as part of a curse (against the wicked man) and here as part of a blessing (upon the one who fears God). In Peter's first letter, he describes what the real beauty of a wife should be: "but let your adorning be the hidden person of the heart with the imperishable beauty of a gentle and quiet spirit, which in God's sight is very precious." I am fast approaching my fourth decade being with my wife and I can truly say, the Lord has blessed me greatly in allowing me to share the majority of my life with such a person. She is not only a fruitful vine, but she tends to make everything and everyone around her grow and flourish. I wrote a poem to capture that sentiment:

A Wife, Precious in the Sight of God

From your youth, you've maintained both beauty and charm,
A delicate hand and a strong, graceful arm.
Married younger than most, decades pass, married still;
Staying true to your vow, to the end you fulfill.

The kids are all grown, there remains just us two.
But that doesn't mean there's not plenty to do.
The family extended all over the earth,
Having left far behind their places of birth.

You've chosen to stand by your man from the start,
Remaining as one, until death we do part.
The world says you've taken a stance incorrect,
It's just one more view that we choose to reject.

Inward beauty aglow, with respect you impart,
Hidden within, your true person and heart,
Outward beauty remains for all to behold,
Hair turning silver, but a heart that is gold.

O God, true happiness can only come to those who form the right relationship with You and in reverence and obedience walk in Your ways. Through Your eyes, I can revel and rejoice in the rewards of my labor for You are the one who makes it fruitful. I am thankful and humbled You have given me a wife who is the heart of my home, who through the fruit of her labor lavished upon me four delightful daughters. How can I not cease to hold You in awe and reverence? I thank You LORD for Your provision of peace and prosperity, not as the world reckons riches, but with a treasured inheritance money can't buy. How blessed I am that You have let me see my children's children. One day, may they all live and prosper in a world of peace, from Israel to the ends of the earth. Amen.

Psalm 129

A Song of Ascents. **1** "Greatly have they afflicted me from my youth"— let Israel now say—**2** "Greatly have they afflicted me from my youth, yet they have not prevailed against me. **3** The plowers plowed upon my back; they made long their furrows." **4** The LORD is righteous; he has cut the cords of the wicked. **5** May all who hate Zion be put to shame and turned backward! **6** Let them be like the grass on the housetops, which withers before it grows up, **7** with which the reaper does not fill his hand nor the binder of sheaves his arms, **8** nor do those who pass by say, "The blessing of the LORD be upon you! We bless you in the name of the LORD!" (ESV)

Have you ever read a scripture passage and found yourself drawn to a particular word or phrase? It is as if, no matter what, your eye seems captivated, ever returning to it. Reading this Psalm, we recall Israel's toils, its past affliction and ultimate victory over its enemies. But my eyes keep returning to verse 3: "The plowers plowed on my back; They made their furrows long." I don't want to get too graphic, but all I can picture are the long, deep wounds "ploughed" into Jesus' back before His crucifixion. The Hebrew word used for furrow (maanah) appears only twice in the Bible and its root origin means "a place for doing a task." Jesus' task was to bear our sins and His back bore the brunt of it. As Isaiah 53 says, "Surely, He has borne our griefs...and by His stripes (wounds) we are healed." Yes, indeed – through Him we are truly healed and redeemed!

O God, when those with hateful hearts pursue me, I know their persecution will not prevail for You are my LORD Preserver. You cut the cords and break the bonds of the back-biters and back-stabbers. For You, O LORD, are righteous and will send the wicked to wither away in the wind. They are like a farmer whose harvest is an empty hand, nothing more than a venture in vanity. How can those who hold You in contempt, O LORD, expect to hear "God bless you." But as for me, I will praise Your name forevermore, for You bore the punishment I deserved and through it, have set me free! Amen.

Psalm 130

A Song of Ascents. **1** Out of the depths I have cried to You, O LORD. **2** Lord, hear my voice! Let Your ears be attentive To the voice of my supplications. **3** If You, LORD, should mark iniquities, O Lord, who could stand? **4** But there is forgiveness with You, That You may be feared. **5** I wait for the LORD, my soul does wait, And in His word do I hope. **6** My soul waits for the Lord More than the watchmen for the morning; Indeed, more than the watchmen for the morning. **7** O Israel, hope in the LORD; For with the LORD there is lovingkindness, And with Him is abundant redemption. **8** And He will redeem Israel From all his iniquities. (NASB)

As a deputy sheriff in northern California, there were chiefly three shifts I worked: the day shift, which was usually more "business" like (e.g., taking theft reports); the swing shift which went from late afternoon to past midnight and tended to see the most action; and finally, the graveyard shift. It too could see its fair share of activity, but once the bars shut down at 2:00 am and everyone arrived home, safely "tucked into bed," the night watch began. No matter how much sleep I got the day before, the hours between 4:00 am and 6:00 am could often drag as I struggled to remain vigilant, looking for the sunrise and the end of my shift. How much does our Psalmist long for God? More than the night watchman eagerly looks for the coming dawn. May we each seek the Lord with such desire and anticipation as He turns our darkness into daybreak.

O God, it is only from the darkest depths of despair that my prayers proceed from my heart and not simply from my lips. It is enough to know You hear my deepest desires and will respond in accordance with Your infinite wisdom and love and not based on my merit. For You know all my sins and were You to justly place them on my back, how could I stand? The truth is I couldn't! But because of Your great mercy and righteous redemption, I receive the forgiveness You provide. It gives me pause to ponder and revel in reverential awe and dutiful devotion. And as I wait, I know it is not in vain, for my hope is in Your unfailing promise. Yes, my soul longs for You with great anticipation, O LORD, for I have been ransomed, rescued and redeemed and in Your love, set free. Amen.

Psalm 131

A song for pilgrims ascending to Jerusalem. A psalm of David. 1 LORD, my heart is not proud; my eyes are not haughty. I don't concern myself with matters too great or too awesome for me to grasp. 2 Instead, I have calmed and quieted myself, like a weaned child who no longer cries for its mother's milk. Yes, like a weaned child is my soul within me. 3 O Israel, put your hope in the LORD — now and always. (NLT)

We now come to a series of Psalms within the Songs of Ascents that are quite short. While some are only three verses long, they are not short on message. Here, David tells the Lord that he has remained humble of heart and doesn't have lofty or haughty eyes. We have all seen that kind of person, the one with the superior air of conceit looking down at others. The Bible is full of verses that mention how God disdains those who have that haughty look and they are usually mentioned in context with a proud heart. In fact, in the list of seven things God hates in Proverbs 6, the first thing mentioned is haughty eyes. So what is the basis for David's humble state? It is his calm, composed and quiet soul. He has become weaned of selfish desires and self-sufficiency and put his complete trust in the Lord alone. O that we may do likewise!

O God, don't let me have a haughty heart or egotistical eyes. I don't want an arrogant attitude. Don't let me meddle in matters my mind cannot conceive for I know my place in life. May I manifest my heart with a childlike countenance and maintain a calm and quiet spirit. I should only feel contentment close to You. My hope remains in You, O LORD, now and forevermore. Amen.

Psalm 132

A Song of Ascents. **1** Remember, O LORD, on David's behalf, All his affliction; **2** How he swore to the LORD And vowed to the Mighty One of Jacob, **3** "Surely I will not enter my house, Nor lie on my bed; **4** I will not give sleep to my eyes Or slumber to my eyelids, **5** Until I find a place for the LORD, A dwelling place for the Mighty One of Jacob." **6** Behold, we heard of it in Ephrathah, We found it in the field of Jaar. **7** Let us go into His dwelling place; Let us worship at His footstool. **8** Arise, O LORD, to Your resting place, You and the ark of Your strength. **9** Let Your priests be clothed with righteousness, And let Your godly ones sing for joy. **10** For the sake of David Your servant, Do not turn away the face of Your anointed. **11** The LORD has sworn to David A truth from which He will not turn back: "Of the fruit of your body I will set upon your throne. **12** If your sons will keep My covenant And My testimony which I will teach them, Their sons also shall sit upon your throne forever." **13** For the LORD has chosen Zion; He has desired it for His habitation. **14** "This is My resting place forever; Here I will dwell, for I have desired it. **15** I will abundantly bless her provision; I will satisfy her needy with bread. **16** Her priests also I will clothe with salvation, And her godly ones will sing aloud for joy. **17** There I will cause the horn of David to spring forth; I have prepared a lamp for Mine anointed. **18** His enemies I will clothe with shame, But upon himself his crown shall shine." (NASB)

In the FBI, as in any organization that seeks to sustain effective long-term management, I was always looking for the right people to "move up the ranks" to be the future leaders. Succession planning is a key to structural success. When it comes to a monarchy, determining who is the next in line can get a bit tricky. An heirless king often results in a chaotic situation. In this Psalm, David refers to a promise from God that if he and his heirs follow God's laws and keep their covenant with the Lord, then an heir of David will be on the throne forever. There are only two ways to accomplish this: an unending and unbroken line of succession or to have a single person who lives forever. God's promise was realized in the latter in the person of His Son, Jesus Christ. Jesus is our shining lamp in the darkness to whom we should always look.

O God, no matter what afflictions I face give me the deepest desire to make my heart a dwelling place for You. Let me not rest until it is prepared as a sanctuary, suitably sanctified so I may then worship in Your presence. Remove the ragged robes and grubby garments that I wear and clothe me in Your righteousness so I may sing and shout for joy! As You made the horn of David spring forth, renew my strength daily. As You have prepared a lamp for Your anointed, give me the clarity to see the truth. And as You have placed a shining crown on Your king, help me to remember that in Your gracious love You have called me to be an heir unto Your royal and eternal kingdom. Let me walk in a manner worthy of that calling. Amen.

Psalm 133

A Song of Ascents. Of David. **1** Behold, how good and pleasant it is when brothers dwell in unity! **2** It is like the precious oil on the head, running down on the beard, on the beard of Aaron, running down on the collar of his robes! **3** It is like the dew of Hermon, which falls on the mountains of Zion! For there the LORD has commanded the blessing, life forevermore. (ESV)

When I first read this Psalm, admittedly, the idea of oil running down my hair (and into my beard when I had one), was not particularly enticing. I spend enough time trying to keep my hair clean! But that isn't the message here. My wife has recently taken an interest in the benefits of essential oils. The "essential" moniker means it comes from the pure oil of the plant from which it is extracted. Some of my favorites are clove, frankincense, and myrrh. I now better appreciate the gifts of the wise men to baby Jesus! Oils were a symbol of joy and demonstrate David's desire. He knew firsthand how domestic discord drains one's joy. But "brothers" mentioned here goes beyond family ties. Our unity comes in the "essential" truths we share with fellow-believers in the Lord. May we live each and every day to joyfully emit the sweet fragrance of Christ in all we say and do!

O God, what a blessing it is to have household harmony and to enjoy family unity in You. Let Your peace extend, far beyond to the union I share with my brothers and sisters in You. Such peace is better than the most precious perfume or having my head anointed abundantly with the finest oil. Your blessings are like the morning dew glistening from the highest mountain tops. For only in You and Your promises is there life eternal. Amen.

Psalm 134

A Song of Ascents. **1** Behold, bless the LORD, all servants of the LORD, Who serve by night in the house of the LORD! **2** Lift up your hands to the sanctuary And bless the LORD. **3** May the LORD bless you from Zion, He who made heaven and earth. (NASB)

Although this Psalm has only three verses, much may be learned from it. It is the final of the fifteen listed as a "Song of Ascents." We can envision the traveler completing his sojourn up to the temple and is now ready to depart. The main message here has to do with those whose job it was to keep watch over God's house during the night. Having secured and cleansed it from the day's activities, they ensure it has been properly prepared for the next day's worship. Today, most churches have cleaning crews who perform janitorial services after hours before the building is locked up for the night. Our pastors, ministers, and priests must also tarry, performing pastoral care for their flock, preparing for the upcoming sermons, praying for their parishioners. Let us regularly pray for all who care for our church, from the clergy to the custodian!

O God, let my service be acceptable unto You. Watch over those whom You have given responsibility to watch over Your people. Give me a servant's heart as I bless Your name. Give me holy hands to lift up to You in blessing – not because of anything I've done, but in Your grace and love. I will continue to seek Your blessing, O LORD, maker of heaven and earth. Amen.

Psalm 135

1 Praise the LORD! Praise the name of the LORD! Praise him, you who serve the LORD, 2 you who serve in the house of the LORD, in the courts of the house of our God. 3 Praise the LORD, for the LORD is good; celebrate his lovely name with music. 4 For the LORD has chosen Jacob for himself, Israel for his own special treasure. 5 I know the greatness of the LORD — that our Lord is greater than any other god. 6 The LORD does whatever pleases him throughout all heaven and earth, and on the seas and in their depths. 7 He causes the clouds to rise over the whole earth. He sends the lightning with the rain and releases the wind from his storehouses. 8 He destroyed the firstborn in each Egyptian home, both people and animals. 9 He performed miraculous signs and wonders in Egypt against Pharaoh and all his people. 10 He struck down great nations and slaughtered mighty kings—11 Sihon king of the Amorites, Og king of Bashan, and all the kings of Canaan. 12 He gave their land as an inheritance, a special possession to his people Israel. 13 Your name, O LORD, endures forever; your fame, O LORD, is known to every generation. 14 For the LORD will give justice to his people and have compassion on his servants. 15 The idols of the nations are merely things of silver and gold, shaped by human hands. 16 They have mouths but cannot speak, and eyes but cannot see. 17 They have ears but cannot hear, and mouths but cannot breathe. 18 And those who make idols are just like them, as are all who trust in them. 19 O Israel, praise the LORD! O priests— descendants of Aaron—praise the LORD! 20 O Levites, praise the LORD! All you who fear the LORD, praise the LORD! 21 The LORD be praised from Zion, for he lives here in Jerusalem. Praise the LORD! (NLT)

If the verses of this Psalm sound familiar there is a reason why. It is a montage of many verses, a patchwork of passages found elsewhere in the Bible. And yet, they are woven together to create a common theme of the greatness of God, over creation, over man, over any other gods that man tries to create.

Verse 4 is a hinge pin because it reminds us that it is the Lord who chose Jacob, not the other way around. As it says in Deuteronomy, God didn't choose Israel because they were such a great people but in fact, they were the least of the nations. But despite that, God chose them to be His prized possession. Likewise, it is God who chooses us. Certainly, we must make a decision whether or not to follow the Lord, but as Jesus said in John's gospel, no one can come to Him unless God draws them to Him. We do not do great spiritual works and suddenly catch God's attention wherein He says, "O, I must get so-and-so to become a part of my family!" No, it is God in His perfect love and grace who draws us to Him. How great is our God!

O God, I praise You and Your holy noble name. Whether in or out of Your house let me serve You with a heart of praise. Let me sing praises to You, O LORD, for You are good and Your name brings comfort and joy. In Your wisdom and love, You chose Jacob as Your own; Israel to be Your treasured possession. You selected him not because he was superior to all other people but out of Your surpassing sovereign grace. Remind me daily that You chose me first not the other way around and Your choice was not based on my merit but in Your infinite love. How great You are, O LORD, for there is no one above You! You do whatever pleases You for all time and space are firmly held in the grasp of Your hand. You cause clouds to ascend their lofty heights and let loose lightning to dart across the sky. You bestow breath of life to all, man and beast alike, and extinguish earth's high and mighty as You deem best, for You are Jehovah Naheh, the LORD Who Smites. Mankind's mightiest mortals erect memorials to maintain their fame but death and decay eventually erase the memory of all. But You, O LORD, remain forever, like a gift granted and passed along from one generation to the next. Despite the marvelous mind You have given man, his ignorance is on display for all to see as he fashions and forms his false gods. Even if made of silver and gold they are worthless – muted mouths, blind eyes, deaf ears, breathless bodies of death. And that is what man becomes when he places the works of his hands as lord of his heart instead of worshiping You, the LORD of life and rightful ruler of all. Let all the earth bless You LORD and praise Your holy name. Amen.

Psalm 136

1 Give thanks to the LORD, for he is good! His faithful love endures forever. 2 Give thanks to the God of gods. His faithful love endures forever. 3 Give thanks to the Lord of lords. His faithful love endures forever. 4 Give thanks to him who alone does mighty miracles. His faithful love endures forever. 5 Give thanks to him who made the heavens so skillfully. His faithful love endures forever. 6 Give thanks to him who placed the earth among the waters. His faithful love endures forever. 7 Give thanks to him who made the heavenly lights— His faithful love endures forever. 8 the sun to rule the day, His faithful love endures forever. 9 and the moon and stars to rule the night. His faithful love endures forever. 10 Give thanks to him who killed the firstborn of Egypt. His faithful love endures forever. 11 He brought Israel out of Egypt. His faithful love endures forever. 12 He acted with a strong hand and powerful arm. His faithful love endures forever. 13 Give thanks to him who parted the Red Sea. His faithful love endures forever. 14 He led Israel safely through, His faithful love endures forever. 15 but he hurled Pharaoh and his army into the Red Sea. His faithful love endures forever. 16 Give thanks to him who led his people through the wilderness. His faithful love endures forever. 17 Give thanks to him who struck down mighty kings. His faithful love endures forever. 18 He killed powerful kings— His faithful love endures forever. 19 Sihon king of the Amorites, His faithful love endures forever. 20 and Og king of Bashan. His faithful love endures forever. 21 God gave the land of these kings as an inheritance— His faithful love endures forever. 22 a special possession to his servant Israel. His faithful love endures forever. 23 He remembered us in our weakness. His faithful love endures forever. 24 He saved us from our enemies. His faithful love endures forever. 25 He gives food to every living thing. His faithful love endures forever. 26 Give thanks to the God of heaven. His faithful love endures forever. (NLT)

This Psalm provides a long litany of reasons to thank God. Myriad examples of historical events provide the rationale for praise. And yet, we hear the same refrain in each of the twenty-six verses as the true basis of praise: God's steadfast love (or lovingkindness or mercy) endures forever (is everlasting)! The Hebrew word used for "steadfast love" (hasdow) is often defined as covenant loyalty. This harkens back to God's promise to His people in Deuteronomy 7 where He says he didn't love them because of who they were or what they did, but rather, He loves them in keeping with the oath He gave their forefathers. He loves us because He chooses to love us. That is the true meaning of mercy. As humans, our love falters and fluctuates depending on deeds done or a moment's mood. Praise God, <u>His</u> love endures forever!

O God, I give You thanks for You are so good and Your lovingkindness is everlasting. I confess You as LORD God, the ruler of all for Your love has no end. I acknowledge You as the One alone who performs marvelous deeds and wonders. You made the world with wisdom and skill and Your mercy endures forever. You parted the seas to safely shepherd Your people and then guide them through the wilderness. Your kindness never fails. In Your steadfast love, You sought me out, even while I was in a lowly bankrupt state, saving me from my enemies and redeemed me from my greatest enemy – sin. O God of heaven, I give You thanks for Your constant love never fails. Amen.

Psalm 137

1 By the waters of Babylon, there we sat down and wept, when we remembered Zion. 2 On the willows there we hung up our lyres. 3 For there our captors required of us songs, and our tormentors, mirth, saying, "Sing us one of the songs of Zion!" 4 How shall we sing the LORD's song in a foreign land? 5 If I forget you, O Jerusalem, let my right hand forget its skill! 6 Let my tongue stick to the roof of my mouth, if I do not remember you, if I do not set Jerusalem above my highest joy! 7 Remember, O LORD, against the Edomites the day of Jerusalem, how they said, "Lay it bare, lay it bare, down to its foundations!" 8 O daughter of Babylon, doomed to be destroyed, blessed shall he be who repays you with what you have done to us! 9 Blessed shall he be who takes your little ones and dashes them against the rock! (ESV)

Do you ever have difficulty when someone asks you the question, "Where are you from?" My wife and I were both born in southern California but raised in the Sierra foothills of northern California. Even after leaving there over 30 years ago, living in Texas over a decade and Virginia over two decades, it is still the place we call "home." And yet, is that really where we are from? Each place we have lived and spent time has had an impact in shaping us into who we are. Looking in the rearview mirror can be interesting but looking through the windshield is probably more important. In the end, isn't the better question to ask, "Where are you going?" Where do you aspire to make your final home, your permanent place of residence? Our life on earth is a fleeting moment compared to what lies ahead in eternity.

O God, there are times when we must leave our homeland, even against our wishes. It may cause us to mourn as memories mingle with our tears. Our heads hang in dismay and with hushed harps hung on the wall we no longer sing our song unto You for we are in a strange land. Even today, I feel like a stranger in this world. And yet, You, O LORD, still remain in our midst. Let me remember my true home lies in heaven and not any place on earth. Silence my lips against any angst if I fail to remember You or if I appoint any abode above my heavenly home. Make my foremost desire be to remain content as I devotedly dwell in Your presence. Amen.

Psalm 138

Of David. **1** I will give you thanks with all my heart; I will sing your praise before the heavenly beings. **2** I will bow down toward your holy temple and give thanks to your name for your constant love and truth. You have exalted your name and your promise above everything else. **3** On the day I called, you answered me; you increased strength within me. **4** All the kings on earth will give you thanks, Lord, when they hear what you have promised. **5** They will sing of the Lord's ways, for the Lord's glory is great. **6** Though the Lord is exalted, he takes note of the humble; but he knows the haughty from a distance. **7** If I walk into the thick of danger, you will preserve my life from the anger of my enemies. You will extend your hand; your right hand will save me. **8** The Lord will fulfill his purpose for me. Lord, your faithful love endures forever; do not abandon the work of your hands. (CSB)

What is your purpose in life? More importantly, what is God's purpose for your life? I'm not talking about which profession you should pursue or discerning a desirable decision. Even as a child I knew I wanted to be an FBI Agent. Not many of us say "when I grow up I'm going to be a (fill in the blank)" and actually get to do it. But a profession and a purpose are two different things. David gives us a clear answer to his purpose: to praise and worship the Lord! You may be thinking that response obvious or a bit simplistic but don't forget, although David was a king, that was the true quest for his life. He praises God for hearing his calls; for answering his prayers; for His great glory; for His steadfast love and faithfulness. Even as king, David recognized the supremacy of the ultimate King of the universe and where he stood in life's pecking order. David gives us an answer for success: Remember, God is God and you are not. The Lord knows each heart and carefully considers humility over haughtiness. Worship God with a humble heart and you will know true success in life.

O God, I give You thanks with my whole heart, healed by Your loving hand. I sing Your praises to boldly confess You above all which You have created for there is no other God but You. I will bow before You with a humble heart to give You thanks for Your everlasting love and faithfulness. You make promises only You can keep and are able to answer me whenever I call upon You. You strengthen my soul with boldness. The high and mighty of the earth will kneel in thankfulness when they hear You speak Your Word. They will sing of Your glorious ways for You are El Kabowd, the God of Glory. Even from Your heavenly heights, You hear the humble, but the haughty are left to their own happenings. Though walking through troublesome times, You are there to save and sustain me, placing Your powerful arm around me to provide protection and vanquish violent enemies. Help me remain patient in Your perfect peace for I know You will complete the job You began in me – absolutely accomplished in full for the works of Your hands are never done in vain. Amen.

Psalm 139

For the choir director. A Psalm of David. **1** O LORD, You have searched me and known me. **2** You know when I sit down and when I rise up; You understand my thought from afar. **3** You scrutinize my path and my lying down, And are intimately acquainted with all my ways. **4** Even before there is a word on my tongue, Behold, O LORD, You know it all. **5** You have enclosed me behind and before, And laid Your hand upon me. **6** Such knowledge is too wonderful for me; It is too high, I cannot attain to it. **7** Where can I go from Your Spirit? Or where can I flee from Your presence? **8** If I ascend to heaven, You are there; If I make my bed in Sheol, behold, You are there. **9** If I take the wings of the dawn, If I dwell in the remotest part of the sea, **10** Even there Your hand will lead me, And Your right hand will lay hold of me. **11** If I say, "Surely the darkness will overwhelm me, And the light around me will be night," **12** Even the darkness is not dark to You, And the night is as bright as the day. Darkness and light are alike to You. **13** For You formed my inward parts; You wove me in my mother's womb. **14** I will give thanks to You, for I am fearfully and wonderfully made; Wonderful are Your works, And my soul knows it very well. **15** My frame was not hidden from You, When I was made in secret, And skillfully wrought in the depths of the earth; **16** Your eyes have seen my unformed substance; And in Your book were all written The days that were ordained for me, When as yet there was not one of them. **17** How precious also are Your thoughts to me, O God! How vast is the sum of them! **18** If I should count them, they would outnumber the sand. When I awake, I am still with You. **19** O that You would slay the wicked, O God; Depart from me, therefore, men of bloodshed. **20** For they speak against You wickedly, And Your enemies take Your name in vain. **21** Do I not hate those who hate You, O LORD? And do I not loathe those who rise up against You? **22** I hate them with the utmost hatred; They have become my enemies. **23** Search me, O God, and know my heart; Try me and know my anxious thoughts; **24** And see if there be any hurtful way in me, And lead me in the everlasting way. (NASB)

Many Psalms proclaim the majesty of God's universe, but here David turns his attention inward and reminds us of some of God's attributes: He knows and sees all (omniscient), He is everywhere (omnipresent), and He is all-powerful (omnipotent). How silly we must appear when we think, "Will God see me do this?" or "No one including God will know what I just did." David's acknowledgment of the absurdity of such thoughts goes beyond a statement of fact but is a call for action. When we see God as all-knowing, it demands an openness, loyalty, and love before Him. This Psalm harkens to another wherein the question is asked, "What is man that You are mindful of him?" The fact that the all-powerful God of the Universe knows us and cares for us is both mind-blowing and humbling. Let the Lord Almighty lead us in His everlasting way!

O God, You are El Roi – the God Who Sees all! You know me inside out. You know every action I take and have discerned my deepest motivation behind each deed. You know my innermost intentions. My habits and behaviors are laid bare before You. Nothing I say surprises You, for before my mind molds a single word, forms a phrase, or it leaves my lips, You already knew it. The thought that You not only see me doing everything in the here and now, but saw and knew it before the creation of all things is a concept I cannot comprehend; it is beyond the grasp of my meager mind. If I think I can run and hide from Your eternal eye I am dining on a delusional dish. No matter where I go, You are there for You truly are heaven's hound, persistently pursuing with a panoptic reach. Even if I skimmed the sea's surface at the speed of light to reach the rays of the rising sun, I would still remain in the palm of Your hand; Your loving hand to guide my wandering ways and support me in perfect power. If I plunge into the depths of the deepest dungeon in total darkness – there You are and Your glowing gleam of light makes all the darkness flee. Before my birth, You wondrously wove me in my mother's womb, fashioning me with skill I cannot fathom. Before the first word was written in my life's story, you had already finished my final chapter. While I'm left living life one page at a time, I take solace in the knowledge that my concluding sentence is part of Your perfect plan. When I contemplate and consider Your countless concepts and immeasurable thoughts I am once again struck by awe and wonder of who You are – an infinite God allowing, nay, imploring me, a finite feeble man, to form a relationship to walk humbly with You, now and through eternity. With that thought in mind, delve deep into my heart, O God, and show me those areas in my life that raise roadblocks between us. For You have already built the bridge beckoning me to follow You on the path of Your everlasting way. Amen.

Psalm 140

To the choirmaster. A Psalm of David. **1** Deliver me, O LORD, from evil men; preserve me from violent men, **2** who plan evil things in their heart and stir up wars continually. **3** They make their tongue sharp as a serpent's, and under their lips is the venom of asps. Selah **4** Guard me, O LORD, from the hands of the wicked; preserve me from violent men, who have planned to trip up my feet. **5** The arrogant have hidden a trap for me, and with cords they have spread a net; beside the way they have set snares for me. Selah **6** I say to the LORD, You are my God; give ear to the voice of my pleas for mercy, O LORD! **7** O LORD, my Lord, the strength of my salvation, you have covered my head in the day of battle. **8** Grant not, O LORD, the desires of the wicked; do not further their evil plot, or they will be exalted! Selah **9** As for the head of those who surround me, let the mischief of their lips overwhelm them! **10** Let burning coals fall upon them! Let them be cast into fire, into miry pits, no more to rise! **11** Let not the slanderer be established in the land; let evil hunt down the violent man speedily! **12** I know that the LORD will maintain the cause of the afflicted, and will execute justice for the needy. **13** Surely the righteous shall give thanks to your name; the upright shall dwell in your presence. (ESV)

From the beginning of time, an ever-continuing conflict between good and evil has been fought – amidst those trying to follow God and those who are against Him. In this Psalm, as David cries out to the Lord to protect and deliver him, there seem to be two threats posed by evil people: He not only mentions violent men who want to physically harm him, but he also notes their verbal attacks by describing the sharpened tongues and poisonous words of a slanderer. Verse 5 tells how the proud are trying to trip him up with a trap and snare. In Hebrew, the word "pach" (trap) is the hidden net, but the word "moqesh" (snare) infers a lure or bait. Both can easily cause our steps to stumble. I think the latter can be the more lethal. If we will allow it to, God's

Word will light our path to give us the vision we need to see the hidden traps. It will also cleanse our hearts so we are not easily enticed to take the enemy's bait.

O God, rescue me from malicious men who are devoted to depravity, devising evil in their hearts and waging wars with delight. Like a serpent's sharpened tongue, poison presses from their fangs. Preserve me, O LORD, in the palm of Your hand and protect me from the pitfalls of the proud. O LORD, because You are the strength of my salvation hear my plea for help. In Your justice do not grant the devilish desires of the depraved. So often they become engulfed by their own mischievous musings and their lie-tipped tongues of slandering slits their own throats. It is You, O LORD, who brings blessings to the beggar, prosperity to the poor and affluence to the afflicted, not in worldly wealth but in Your justice and righteousness. Let me always seek Your face with a thankful and humble heart. Amen.

Psalm 141

A Psalm of David. **1** O LORD, I call upon You; hasten to me! Give ear to my voice when I call to You! **2** May my prayer be counted as incense before You; The lifting up of my hands as the evening offering. **3** Set a guard, O LORD, over my mouth; Keep watch over the door of my lips. **4** Do not incline my heart to any evil thing, To practice deeds of wickedness With men who do iniquity; And do not let me eat of their delicacies. **5** Let the righteous smite me in kindness and reprove me; It is oil upon the head; Do not let my head refuse it, For still my prayer is against their wicked deeds. **6** Their judges are thrown down by the sides of the rock, And they hear my words, for they are pleasant. **7** As when one plows and breaks open the earth, Our bones have been scattered at the mouth of Sheol. **8** For my eyes are toward You, O GOD, the Lord; In You I take refuge; do not leave me defenseless. **9** Keep me from the jaws of the trap which they have set for me, And from the snares of those who do iniquity. **10** Let the wicked fall into their own nets, While I pass by safely. (NASB)

In this Psalm, we hear David's cry for God's help. He has choices to make and it is his ardent desire that he chooses wisely. He pleads, "Do not let my heart incline to any evil, to busy myself with wicked deeds." It may have been the basis for the line in the Lord's Prayer, "Lead us not into temptation, but deliver us from evil." It reminds me of the failed choices that were made in the Garden of Eden. I sometimes wonder why didn't Eve or Adam cry out to the Lord when they were first confronted by the devil. I wrote a poem that depicts the journey from Eden to today and the choices that we also face on a daily basis:

Choices: From Eden to the Eve of Destruction

Strolling each day in the garden, in the cool of the evening breeze,
Heaven-on-earth to be certain, allowed whatever they please...
Except for that one lone denial from which they must never partake,
Thus far they seemed to avoid it but soon came the slithering snake.

"Oh, why can't you eat of this fruit here? There must be a reason for sure."
"It's shiny and looks so delightful; it is probably sweet and so pure!"
So Eve took a glance at the tree there, and doubt crept into her mind,
Not knowing her upcoming action would corrupt and alter mankind.

Walking closer she gazed at its beauty, for food it must surely be good.
No longer safe in the garden, Eve's foot on the precipice stood.
Stretching her arm out to grasp it, that fruit of the enemy's lies,
And licking her lips as she pondered this craving to now become wise.

Our choices today are no different, for we know what it means to obey;
Right and wrong are still there before us, our cravings we must daily slay.
Carnal desires surround us, like sirens ensnaring their prize;
All-out attempts to impound us with beckoning calls for our eyes.

The lust of the flesh, the lust of the eyes, but the worst is the pride of life;
If we think we have all the answers, we slide into sin's certain strife.
In a world once made in perfection but now shows the signs of decay,
From results we never intended, of the choices we chose not to weigh.

Love not this world any longer nor the things to which they belong,
If you do God's love is not in you, and your life will be empty and wrong.
For this world and all that it offers, each day is passing away,
But he who obeys the Father, lives in Him and will not go astray.

O God, in haste, hear my cry for help and pleas for pardon. As the day ends and evening approaches, let my prayer start as a flickering flame, enkindled by Your Holy Spirit and ascend to You as ignited incense of praise and worship. Like a sentinel unwaveringly watching from the castle keep, keep watch over my mouth, for You are Jehovah Misqabbi, the LORD My High Tower. Halt my heart from sliding down the slippery slope of sin so I don't practice the wrongful works of the wicked. May I dine on the delicacies of Your Word and not the deceitful deeds of worldly men. If I stray, use those who walk before You in righteousness to reprimand me in love and let me willingly receive it. Keep my eyes entirely focused on You in whom I take my refuge. Let me firmly grasp Your hand as You guide my steps to safely stride around the snares set before me. Amen.

Psalm 142

A Contemplation of David. A Prayer when he was in the cave. **1** I cry out to the Lord with my voice; With my voice to the Lord I make my supplication. **2** I pour out my complaint before Him; I declare before Him my trouble. **3** When my spirit was overwhelmed within me, Then You knew my path. In the way in which I walk They have secretly set a snare for me. **4** Look on my right hand and see, For there is no one who acknowledges me; Refuge has failed me; No one cares for my soul. **5** I cried out to You, O Lord: I said, "You are my refuge, My portion in the land of the living. **6** Attend to my cry, For I am brought very low; Deliver me from my persecutors, For they are stronger than I. **7** Bring my soul out of prison, That I may praise Your name; The righteous shall surround me, For You shall deal bountifully with me." (NKJV)

The primary focus of this book has been on prayer and in this Psalm, David gives us an excellent example of how he prays to the Lord. He prays with his voice. Sometimes silent prayer is appropriate but other times the words we convey to God need to be cried out above the din and distractions of this world to ascend into the heavenly throne room. He pours out his complaint. The word "complaint" can be tricky to define as we tend to think of a whining, ungrateful attitude. But it has a much richer meaning to include those things that often occupy our thoughts, that make us anxious or gives us concern. David pleads for mercy. In the courtroom, the plaintiff is the one approaching the judge with a case to plead. As the Apostle Peter wrote in his first letter, we need to cast all our cares and anxieties before the Lord because He deeply cares for us.

O God, my voice cries out and pleads Your pity, pouring my troubled thoughts before You. I tell them to You not to make You aware of the situation because You know everything, but rather, I make mention to motivate my mind and memory to always seek You first in all aspects of life. When my spirit staggers, stunned and straying, surrounded by uncertainty, You, O LORD, know my path, guiding me amongst the hidden traps of life. When all seems lost and there is no one left to help me, I turn to You, my refuge and all I have in the land of the living. Deliver me, O LORD, when I feel powerless from those who pursue me. Break the bars of despair's dungeon and release me from the prison of pessimism's pain, and then I can turn to You in the company of the righteous to thank Your Holy Name. Amen.

Psalm 143

A Psalm of David. **1** Hear my prayer, O LORD; listen to my plea! Answer me because you are faithful and righteous. **2** Don't put your servant on trial, for no one is innocent before you. **3** My enemy has chased me. He has knocked me to the ground and forces me to live in darkness like those in the grave. **4** I am losing all hope; I am paralyzed with fear. **5** I remember the days of old. I ponder all your great works and think about what you have done. **6** I lift my hands to you in prayer. I thirst for you as parched land thirsts for rain. Interlude **7** Come quickly, LORD, and answer me, for my depression deepens. Don't turn away from me, or I will die. **8** Let me hear of your unfailing love each morning, for I am trusting you. Show me where to walk, for I give myself to you. **9** Rescue me from my enemies, LORD; I run to you to hide me. **10** Teach me to do your will, for you are my God. May your gracious Spirit lead me forward on a firm footing. **11** For the glory of your name, O LORD, preserve my life. Because of your faithfulness, bring me out of this distress. **12** In your unfailing love, silence all my enemies and destroy all my foes, for I am your servant. (NLT)

In this Psalm, David reminds us that our struggles in life are against two types of enemies: the physical and the spiritual. And yet, his emphasis seems to be on the spiritual battles we encounter. Although David does request rescue from his physical foes, his primary prayer is a plea for mercy, for he recognizes that like everyone else, on his own he cannot attain a suitable righteousness before God. While he prays for the Lord's deliverance from his physical enemies, it is his nameless spiritual enemy, sin, that has pursued his soul and crushed his life to the ground. This reminds me where Jesus tells His disciples in Matthew 10 that they should not fear those who can only kill the body and not touch the soul. Rather, they should fear God who can destroy both. And yet, it is the Lord's desire to save our souls. He has provided us that pathway through His Son, Jesus.

O God, I ask You to hear my prayer and consider my supplications. Because I seek Your forgiveness, You are faithful to answer in justice. For my trust is not on the basis of my own doing or deeds, but subject to Your sustaining salvation. Apart from Your perfect provision I would stand judged, not justified. When my enemies bring the crushing weight of doom upon me and in despair's darkness I dwell, let me not be dismayed. I will hand You my hopeless heart and consider all Your past works of greatness and meditate on Your marvelous feats. Right before my fortitude falters I will stretch out my hand to receive Your lovingkindness. Because I trust in You I will receive Your new morning's mercy and Your dawning day's love. As I lift my soul to You, let me distinctly discern the direction You want me to walk. As I run to You as my refuge, rescue me from my rivals. Because You are my God, teach me how to best obey You. Let Your sanctifying Spirit lead me unto the level land of righteousness, for You are Jehovah M'Kaddesh, the LORD Who Sanctifies. As You save and sustain me, let Your great salvation honor and glorify Your Holy Name. Amen.

Psalm 144

Of David. **1** Blessed be the LORD, my rock, who trains my hands for war, and my fingers for battle; **2** he is my steadfast love and my fortress, my stronghold and my deliverer, my shield and he in whom I take refuge, who subdues peoples under me. **3** O LORD, what is man that you regard him, or the son of man that you think of him? **4** Man is like a breath; his days are like a passing shadow. **5** Bow your heavens, O LORD, and come down! Touch the mountains so that they smoke! **6** Flash forth the lightning and scatter them; send out your arrows and rout them! **7** Stretch out your hand from on high; rescue me and deliver me from the many waters, from the hand of foreigners, **8** whose mouths speak lies and whose right hand is a right hand of falsehood. **9** I will sing a new song to you, O God; upon a ten-stringed harp I will play to you, **10** who gives victory to kings, who rescues David his servant from the cruel sword. **11** Rescue me and deliver me from the hand of foreigners, whose mouths speak lies and whose right hand is a right hand of falsehood. **12** May our sons in their youth be like plants full grown, our daughters like corner pillars cut for the structure of a palace; **13** may our granaries be full, providing all kinds of produce; may our sheep bring forth thousands and ten thousands in our fields; **14** may our cattle be heavy with young, suffering no mishap or failure in bearing; may there be no cry of distress in our streets! **15** Blessed are the people to whom such blessings fall! Blessed are the people whose God is the LORD! (ESV)

Do you ever feel like you are living in the midst of a war? David did, encountering battles from friends, foes, and family. As an FBI Agent, I had to be prepared every day for a potential armed conflict and even though I regularly trained for such a possibility, I never had to fire my weapon in a real-world armed confrontation. Battles come in many forms and foes, but our greatest fight is one of spiritual warfare. In those situations, it is not only the Lord who trains us but He protects us. In his letter to the Ephesians, the

Apostle Paul gave us a list of tactical gear we need to utilize in order to succeed in battle. I wrote this poem as a reminder of what that armor is and to put it on daily:

Daily Armor

I thank Thee Lord for morning new, awaken from my bed;
For bringing me through evening past, give strength the day ahead.
So as I rise to face this day, in power let me stand;
To greet it not upon my own, but by Thy strong right hand.

Sin crouches now at my heart's door, prepared to pounce anew;
To draw me off Your chosen path so I will not stay true.
I place Your armor 'round about to guard against those plots,
From powers of this world of woe who try to seize my thoughts.

Firmly cinch Your *Belt of Truth* around my waist so tight,
To see the devil's lying schemes with Your unfailing sight.
A *Breastplate of Your Righteousness* now bind around my heart,
To keep it strong and pure for You that we shall never part.

Now shod my feet securely with the *Gospel of Your Peace*,
To swiftly do Your bidding and let all striving cease.
I now hold fast Your *Shield of Faith* to quench each flaming dart
My foe will launch throughout the day directed at my heart.

I place *Salvation's Helmet* like a crown upon my head,
The mind of Christ I carry so protect it as I tread.
Thy *Word* is mine to firmly grasp, the *Spirit's Sword of power*,
So strengthen now my hand I pray to use it every hour.

And now I plead Your Spirit come to keep my mind alert,
Preserved in *prayer* throughout the day so sin I might avert.

O God, blessed are You, Jehovah Sel'i, the LORD My Rock, for You have trained my hand to wage war with fighting fingers for You. May my battles only carry out Your justice and solely be done in Your strength. Your steadfast love never fails me for You are Jehovah Ma'oz, the LORD My Fortress, my stronghold, my deliver. You are my sacred shield to Whom I run for refuge. When I pause and ponder Your power and consider the greatness of Your glorious grandeur, I stand still and ask, "What is mortal man that You would even notice him?" Like a shifting shadow, we are but a mere mirage melting into nothing. Shake us to our senses and let Your kingdom come. With smoking mountains and lightning flashing forth, stretch forward Your hand, reach out and rescue me, for I am surrounded by strangers singing their songs of lies and deceit. But I will sing a new song to You, O God, to praise You for the salvation You have provided. You have graciously granted me many children and grandchildren, like tall towering trees and polished palace pillars let them always stand strong for You. May our barns burst forth with Your blessings and peace prevail in our streets. For true blessings come only to those who put their trust in You, to those who make You LORD of all. Amen.

Psalm 145

A Psalm of Praise, of David. **1** I will extol You, my God, O King, And I will bless Your name forever and ever. **2** Every day I will bless You, And I will praise Your name forever and ever. **3** Great is the LORD, and highly to be praised, And His greatness is unsearchable. **4** One generation shall praise Your works to another, And shall declare Your mighty acts. **5** On the glorious splendor of Your majesty And on Your wonderful works, I will meditate. **6** Men shall speak of the power of Your awesome acts, And I will tell of Your greatness. **7** They shall eagerly utter the memory of Your abundant goodness And will shout joyfully of Your righteousness. **8** The LORD is gracious and merciful; Slow to anger and great in lovingkindness. **9** The LORD is good to all, And His mercies are over all His works. **10** All Your works shall give thanks to You, O LORD, And Your godly ones shall bless You. **11** They shall speak of the glory of Your kingdom And talk of Your power; **12** To make known to the sons of men Your mighty acts And the glory of the majesty of Your kingdom. **13** Your kingdom is an everlasting kingdom, And Your dominion endures throughout all generations. **14** The LORD sustains all who fall And raises up all who are bowed down. **15** The eyes of all look to You, And You give them their food in due time. **16** You open Your hand And satisfy the desire of every living thing. **17** The LORD is righteous in all His ways And kind in all His deeds. **18** The LORD is near to all who call upon Him, To all who call upon Him in truth. **19** He will fulfill the desire of those who fear Him; He will also hear their cry and will save them. **20** The LORD keeps all who love Him, But all the wicked He will destroy. **21** My mouth will speak the praise of the LORD, And all flesh will bless His holy name forever and ever. (NASB)

This is the final Psalm specifically attributed to David and is sometimes referred to as his personal Psalm of praise. The consistency of his praise is daily and the duration of his praise is forever. There are many reasons why

David praises the Lord, but the first is because of God's greatness. There is no need to try and identify just how great He is because all the searching in the world will come up short. God also merits our praise for His goodness – He treats us so much better than we deserve. The Lord is to be praised for His glorious and everlasting kingdom. David says all should praise God for all the provisions of life, especially by those who look to the Lord in their time of need. Finally, we praise God because only in Him mercy and righteousness can perfectly coexist. It is His pure and complete provision that saves us for which He is to be praised.

O God, I bless You and perpetually praise Your name, for You are Jehovah Helech 'Olam, my LORD King Forever. Let Your royal nature awaken within me a loyal spirit of service to You. Each and every day provides a reason to praise You, for Your greatness is boundless and You are worthy of all praise. You are eternal, O God, and span the ages of time. Man must, therefore, move the message of Your praise from one generation to the next; a delegated duty for each descendant to declare Your dynamic deeds. On Your wondrous works and majestic might, I will meditate and all will declare the strength of Your awesome acts of power. With eager enthusiasm let acclamations recall Your abundant goodness. For You, O LORD, are so gracious, full of love and mercy and slow to anger. Your compassion covers creation and calls it to respond with gratitude for Your grace and glory. Let my praise be seasoned with a deep abiding love for You. Your kingdom endures forever and Your reign reaches through all time and space. In love, You lift the lowly and lay low those who live with a lofty view of themselves. All eyes expectantly look to Your open hand for survival and in response, You provide in Your perfect wisdom. Only You can fill the desires of my heart so let my heart grow in love and reverence for You. Let my voice join creation's chorus in forever praising Your Holy Name. Amen.

Psalm 146

1 Praise the Lord! Praise the Lord, O my soul! 2 While I live I will praise the Lord; I will sing praises to my God while I have my being. 3 Do not put your trust in princes, Nor in a son of man, in whom there is no help. 4 His spirit departs, he returns to his earth; In that very day his plans perish. 5 Happy is he who has the God of Jacob for his help, Whose hope is in the Lord his God, 6 Who made heaven and earth, The sea, and all that is in them; Who keeps truth forever, 7 Who executes justice for the oppressed, Who gives food to the hungry. The Lord gives freedom to the prisoners. 8 The Lord opens the eyes of the blind; The Lord raises those who are bowed down; The Lord loves the righteous. 9 The Lord watches over the strangers; He relieves the fatherless and widow; But the way of the wicked He turns upside down. 10 The Lord shall reign forever— Your God, O Zion, to all generations. Praise the Lord! (NKJV)

The last five Psalms each begin and end with the exclamation: "Praise the Lord" and are sometimes called the "Hallelujah Psalms." Hallelujah is a compound word, formed by transliterating the Hebrew word "Hallelu" (meaning praise) and Yah (the shortened name of YHVH or Yahweh). Hence, we get "Praise God" or "Praise the Lord." This Psalm reminds us that it is the Lord who saves us and no one else. During the last five years of my tenure in the FBI, one of the components I oversaw was the FBI's Hostage Rescue Team (HRT). The HRT's motto is a Latin phrase "Servare Vitas" ("to save lives"). Good men doing valiant deeds can save lives in a crisis situation, but any such rescue is temporary, for there is no everlasting deliverance from death or eternal hope of salvation provided by man. It only comes from God and by His provision. That is reason enough to Praise the Lord!

O God, with my entire being I say Hallelujah! I will praise You as long as I live until my last breath leaves my lungs and upon my lips lingers. I will not put my trust in mortal men, princes or politicians, for all are powerless to save me. In the end, they will each deliver their souls to dust, their plans perish, designs die and their spirits slip away. No, I will place my hope on You, O LORD, for You made the heavens, earth, and sea and everything in them. You keep Your crowded creation completely intact. You provide protection to the poor and nourishment to the needy. You set the captive free. You sustain strangers and relieve the burden of the blind. For You, O LORD will reign forever. Hallelujah, Amen.

Psalm 147

1 Praise the LORD! How good to sing praises to our God! How delightful and how fitting! 2 The LORD is rebuilding Jerusalem and bringing the exiles back to Israel. 3 He heals the brokenhearted and bandages their wounds. 4 He counts the stars and calls them all by name. 5 How great is our Lord! His power is absolute! His understanding is beyond comprehension! 6 The LORD supports the humble, but he brings the wicked down into the dust. 7 Sing out your thanks to the LORD; sing praises to our God with a harp. 8 He covers the heavens with clouds, provides rain for the earth, and makes the grass grow in mountain pastures. 9 He gives food to the wild animals and feeds the young ravens when they cry. 10 He takes no pleasure in the strength of a horse or in human might. 11 No, the LORD's delight is in those who fear him, those who put their hope in his unfailing love. 12 Glorify the LORD, O Jerusalem! Praise your God, O Zion! 13 For he has strengthened the bars of your gates and blessed your children within your walls. 14 He sends peace across your nation and satisfies your hunger with the finest wheat. 15 He sends his orders to the world— how swiftly his word flies! 16 He sends the snow like white wool; he scatters frost upon the ground like ashes. 17 He hurls the hail like stones. Who can stand against his freezing cold? 18 Then, at his command, it all melts. He sends his winds, and the ice thaws. 19 He has revealed his words to Jacob, his decrees and regulations to Israel. 20 He has not done this for any other nation; they do not know his regulations. Praise the LORD! (NLT)

As humans, when it comes to our own creative abilities, we tend to give ourselves much more credit than we deserve. Sure, as a race we have accomplished much: we have split the atom, traveled to the moon, developed vaccines to combat diseases, and yet, all those successes are more of a tribute to the capabilities God has instilled in mankind, rather than our own exploits. My wife is a master gardener. She has one of the greenest thumbs I've ever seen, creating verdant layers of a bucolic paradise in our backyard. And yet, despite all her horticulture ability, she doesn't make the grass grow. She didn't develop the fifty shades of green that adorn the painter's pastoral palette. Her creative spirit is merely a trace of our great Creator's skill displayed in this Psalm. Pause to ponder how great our God is and marvel at His creation.

O God, it is good to give glory to You and make melody in a song of praise! You patch holes in my broken heart and bandage bruises of my soul. How could I ever doubt that You are more than able to cure all of mankind's maladies? For You formed each and every star across the vast universe and You know each one by name. Your abundant ability to know everything and powerful provision to remedy all is infinite. Your understanding of all things is too great for my understanding to comprehend. And yet, You look lovingly upon the lowly and lift them up and put the ungodly in their proper place. Let me answer Your call with praises of thanksgiving. Your clouds cover the sky, rain falls, and the green grass springs forth. You provide for all creation, beasts and birds, cattle and crows, catering to all their needs. You are not impressed with the stallion's strength or man's might; both are feeble compared to You. What interests You is a hopeful heart longing for Your love and mercy. You are worthy, O LORD, to be praised for Your protection, provision, and peace. Your Word rules the world, both commanding and communicating with Your creation. You scatter snow, send forth frost, and issue ice with a word – who can withstand such cold? But then, with a word You send the warm whirling winds and misery melts into fresh flowing waters. Through Your Word, statutes, and ordinances You have reached out to the world and yet, we are heedless, so hard of hearing and hard-hearted. You are not seeking our programmed praise pronounced in an impassionate process. You want a relationship, not out of duty but devotion. In the end, You want all of me. That is my greatest gift of praise. Let it be so. Amen

Psalm 148

1 Hallelujah! Praise the Lord from the heavens; praise him in the heights. 2 Praise him, all his angels; praise him, all his heavenly armies. 3 Praise him, sun and moon; praise him, all you shining stars. 4 Praise him, highest heavens, and you waters above the heavens. 5 Let them praise the name of the Lord, for he commanded, and they were created. 6 He set them in position forever and ever; he gave an order that will never pass away. 7 Praise the Lord from the earth, all sea monsters and ocean depths, 8 lightning and hail, snow and cloud, stormy wind that executes his command, 9 mountains and all hills, fruit trees and all cedars, 10 wild animals and all cattle, creatures that crawl and flying birds, 11 kings of the earth and all peoples, princes and all judges of the earth, 12 young men as well as young women, old and young together. 13 Let them praise the name of the Lord, for his name alone is exalted. His majesty covers heaven and earth. 14 He has raised up a horn for his people, resulting in praise to all his faithful ones, to the Israelites, the people close to him. Hallelujah! (CSB)

Each Sunday, millions of Christians of all denominations sing a song of praise which is generally called "The Doxology." Written by Anglican Bishop Thomas Ken and published in 1709, it would appear to have been greatly influenced by the words of this Psalm:

> Praise God from whom all Blessings flow,
> Praise Him all Creatures here below,
> Praise Him above, ye Heavenly Host.
> Praise Father, Son, and Holy Ghost.

I love that song and this Psalm. The "heavenly host" can refer to the Angels in heaven or the stars. Scientists have discovered that each star in the universe emits a unique sound-wave based on its size. Were we to hear all of them at the same time, imagine the galactic chorus. As creatures here below, let us lift our praise to join with the heavenly host!

O God, let this be a prayer of praise, my alleluia anthem of adoration to join creation's chorus of commendation. From Heaven's highest heights to earth's deepest depths and everywhere in between let the song of praise be raised unto You. With a word, You spoke and Your controlling command created the cosmos and all celestial beings – let the angelic host of heaven praise You. Some contemplate constellations and use them to chart their lives and determine their destiny, but the stars are Yours. With a word, they were formed by Your unending utterance and eternal edict. Let all the earth and its inhabitants praise You. Brutish beasts and behemoths, dwellers of the deep, let all praise You. Let all the elements of nature and climate cry out in praise – fire's fierce flames, hammering hailstones, blinding blizzards of snow, and the vagrant vapors of frosty fog as it drifts through valleys and over mountains meander. Orchards of flowering fruit trees and the expansive reach of far-flung forests full of flying fowl, beasts and cattle and all creeping critters praise You. All mankind, regardless of rank or status: rulers, subjects, and servants; judges, juries, and jailbirds; mature men, tender teens, and merry maidens; let everyone praise Your name. There is no other name under heaven or earth full of glory and worthy to be exalted and praised. Amen.

Psalm 149

1 Praise the LORD! Sing to the LORD a new song, And His praise in the congregation of the godly ones. 2 Let Israel be glad in his Maker; Let the sons of Zion rejoice in their King. 3 Let them praise His name with dancing; Let them sing praises to Him with timbrel and lyre. 4 For the LORD takes pleasure in His people; He will beautify the afflicted ones with salvation. 5 Let the godly ones exult in glory; Let them sing for joy on their beds. 6 Let the high praises of God be in their mouth, And a two-edged sword in their hand, 7 To execute vengeance on the nations And punishment on the peoples, 8 To bind their kings with chains And their nobles with fetters of iron, 9 To execute on them the judgment written; This is an honor for all His godly ones. Praise the LORD! (NASB)

Do you have a favorite hymn of old; one that you can recall and sing every stanza from memory? There are many from which to select, most based on scripture and classically timeless. But every once in a while, we hear something fresh that comes along to become our latest favorite. This is one of six Psalms which talks about singing a "new song" to the Lord. We serve a God who is Creator of all and loves to make things anew. He proclaims new things to us, hidden things previously unknown. He will one day make all things new including a new heaven and new earth. Once we come to Christ, He makes us into a new person, a new creation, where our old self passes away and we are transformed. This new life instills in us a new song. Let the Word of Christ richly indwell us so we can sing Psalms and hymns and spiritual songs anew to our God with thankfulness in our hearts!

O God, let me join in union with all Your saints to sing unto You a new song of praise. Old things may pass away but You make everything new! Let all Your children dance in praise and make music unto You. For You love Your people and have demonstrated it by providing us with a sustaining salvation. It is all the more reason for me to sincerely sing for joy! I can rest assured in Your love and sing my song of praise at all times – whether simply slumbering in bed or standing strong to do Your will. Let my hand hold fast to Your sword of truth – Your Word. For by it, Your justice will prevail, putting in the proper place the princes of this world. For any judgment I render is not mine – but it is the honor You have given to those who are faithful to You. May I worthily walk in the way You desire. All praise be unto You, O LORD. Amen.

Psalm 150

1 Praise the LORD! Praise God in His sanctuary; Praise Him in His mighty expanse. 2 Praise Him for His mighty deeds; Praise Him according to His excellent greatness. 3 Praise Him with trumpet sound; Praise Him with harp and lyre. 4 Praise Him with timbrel and dancing; Praise Him with stringed instruments and pipe. 5 Praise Him with loud cymbals; Praise Him with resounding cymbals. 6 Let everything that has breath praise the LORD. Praise the LORD! (NASB)

We come now to the final leg of our journey down the Psalter trail. Previous Psalms propelled us forward, reminding us how temporary our time is here on earth. In life's rearview mirror we see just how fleeting our tenure on this terrestrial ball is. We stand on life's stage, look around and ask ourselves, "what happened?" As humans, we tend to think in terms of the most-likely scenario. As an FBI Agent, I was trained to look at all possibilities and follow the facts. But as Christians, we must also consider the impossibilities. We must not let the box of our finite mind try to contain an infinite God. As A. W. Tozer said... "What comes into our minds when we think about God is the most important thing about us." Our performance on life's stage is to not have lived under the spotlight as a soloist. Rather, we want to be a member of creation's choir, joining in the everlasting Hallelujah chorus praising Him who is worthy of all praise. This Psalm answers the five most important questions any investigator must ask when attempting to determine the facts: Who, what, when, where and why? Who should we praise? God and God alone. What should we do about it? Praise Him with everything in our being. When should we praise Him? At all times and in all places. Why should we praise Him? Because of His abundant greatness, mercy, and love. Let us each join together and forever praise the Lord!

O God, where should You be praised? Your glory is everywhere so let me pause to mingle my passionate praise from here to the vaulted vastness amidst the heavenly host. Let me approach Your sanctuary singing praises. There is no doubt why You should be praised – Your mighty deeds demonstrate Your greatness and glory. Let me praise You with all my being and with everything I have. May all the instruments of earth merge in a merry song of praise to You. You have given every living thing the breath of life – as we inhale Your love let us unite to exhale Your praise. How I long for that day when all Your people, all Your creation, join in one voice to sing the eternal song of praise. Praise You, O LORD, forever and ever. Hallelujah! Amen.

TOPICAL INDEX

(listed by Psalm)

Crying out to God:
3, 6, 29, 38, 39, 56, 57, 61, 77, 86, 88, 102, 106, 107, 119-Tav, 120, 141

Demise of the wicked:
1. 7. 11, 26, 27, 28, 36, 37, 50, 55, 58, 73, 75, 92, 94, 112, 119 (Zayin, Heth, Teth, Lamedh, Nun, Samekh), 129, 141

Desire for a humble heart:
10, 12, 25, 66, 69, 73, 86, 113, 123, 138, 140

God's Creation:
8, 19, 29, 50, 95, 103, 104, 114, 139, 145, 146, 147, 148, 150

God's Majesty:
2, 8, 29, 45, 47, 48, 68, 82, 90, 93, 96, 104, 145

God's Presence:
4, 17, 21, 24, 26, 27, 31, 37, 39, 41, 42, 43, 44, 46, 48, 51, 52, 56, 57, 65, 68, 73, 74, 76, 84, 88, 89, 95, 96, 97, 100, 119 (Samekh, Tav), 132, 137

God, our helper:
In General: 22, 28, 30, 46, 54, 63, 70, 121, 124, 140, 141
To not waste time: 4
To remain a Godly person: 4
To exhibit joy: 9
To see the upright path: 12
To demonstrate His mercy: 18

To not worry: 37

To help guard my tongue: 39

To realize this world is not home: 39, 139

To wait patiently: 40, 138

To conduct my life honorably: 50

To give what He desires: 51

To love good: 52

To see Him as our refuge: 52

To not act self-righteous: 58

To remember purpose of trials: 66

To listen only to Him: 78

To remember His miracles: 78

To walk with Him: 86

To behold His majesty: 90

To remain focused on Him: 94

To be bold: 96

His timeliness in giving it: 118

To always follow Him: 119-Gimel

To obey His commandments: 119-Tav

To let loose of self: 127

To remember I am His heir: 132

Meditation:

1, 4, 5, 48, 55, 63, 64, 77, 105, 119 (Beth, Gimel, Daleth, Zayin, Yod, Mem, Qoph), 143, 145

Salvation:

3, 13, 14, 18, 20, 21, 25, 27, 35, 37, 38, 40, 43, 51, 53, 61, 62, 65, 67, 68, 69, 70, 71, 74, 79, 85, 88, 89, 91, 95, 96, 98, 102, 105, 106, 109, 115, 118, 119 (Kaph, Ayin, Resh, Shin, Tav), 140, 143, 144, 149

Names of God:

El Kabowd
(the God of Glory): 138

El Roi
(the God Who Sees): 139

Jehovah Bara
(the LORD Creator): 127

Jehovah Elohe Yeshuathi
(the LORD God of my Salvation): 88

Jehovah Elyown
(the LORD Most High): 90

Jehovah Gibbor Milchamah
(the LORD Mighty in Battle): 24

Jehovah Helech 'Olam
(the LORD King Forever): 145

Jehovah Jireh
(the LORD Who Provides) 127

Jehovah Keren Yish'i
(the LORD the Horn of Salvation): 18

Jehovah Machsi
(the LORD my Refuge): 2

Jehovah Magen
(the LORD my Shield): 3, 28

Jehovah Maginnenu
(the LORD our Defense): 59

Jehovah Ma'oz
(the LORD my Fortress): 144

Jehovah Misqabbi
(the LORD my High Tower): 141

Jehovah M'Kaddesh
(the LORD Who Sanctifies): 143

Jehovah Naheh
(the LORD Who Smites): 135

Jehovah Nissi
(the LORD our Banner): 60
Jehovah Rophe
(the LORD my Healer): 126
Jehovah Sabaoth
(the LORD of Hosts): 127
Jehovah Sel'i
(the LORD my Rock): 42, 144
Jehovah Shalom
(the LORD my Peace): 120
Jehovah Shamar
(the LORD my Keeper/Guardian): 121
Jehovah Shammah
(the LORD Ever Present): 124
Jehovah Yowm Amas
(the LORD Who Bears our Burdens): 68

Poems included in various Psalms:

23 – O Let Us Now Come to His Table
42 – A Peace That is Deeper Still
46 – Run to the Refuge
59 – Morning Prayer
85 – The Pathway to Do
90 – Walk in a Manner So Worthy
96 – Adam's Curse Upon the Brow
128 – A Wife, Precious in the Sight of God
141 – Choices: From Eden to the Eve of Destruction
144 – Daily Armor